CONTENTS

TIME MANAGEMENT FOR TEENS AND COLLEGE STUDENTS

PERSONAL FINANCE FOR TEENS AND COLLEGE STUDENTS

COLLEGE STUDENT SIDE HUSTLE

TIME
MANAGEMENT
FOR TEENS AND
COLLEGE STUDENTS

THE ULTIMATE GUIDE FOR BALANCING SCHOOL AND LIFE FOR TEENS AND YOUNG ADULTS

KARA ROSS

INTRODUCTION

Being good at managing your time can be beneficial, and it doesn't matter if you are a parent, student, just working a job, or managing a small business. When it comes to our daily lives, we all have 24 hours or less to get all we need done, and many times the thought of so little time and so much to do can be very overwhelming. Many of us strive to do as much as we can as best we can before this time runs out. It sometimes feels like no matter how hard we try, we just can never catch up. It frightens us too because we often realize that if we don't manage our time well enough to get certain things done, it can have severe repercussions on our lives regarding family, friends, school, and work.

We sometimes don't have time to do what's good for our bodies, spend time with our family and friends, or get everything done at work. In the long run, when we fail at these parts of our lives, we feel dissatisfied and as though life is a fast-track hustle, just enough time to do the bare minimum. Sounds familiar, right? But what if I told you that there is a way to do all that you need and want to, a way to make your days a lot more fulfilling and effective?. I will show you ways to manage your time better and get more of what you want out of every day in just a few simple steps.

I will show you what you can do to get the most out of your time. I will reveal things that you may never notice and some that you never really thought were linked to helping you better manage and take control of your time. All that I have written has been tested and proven through my experiences. That being said, feel free to take what helps you and also feel free to leave behind what doesn't.

Let's get started, shall we?

1

GOAL SETTING MADE SIMPLE

To acquire what you want out of life, you must first understand what you desire. After all, how can you reach your full potential if you have no idea where you want to go, who you are, or what brings you joy?

MOST OF YOU are undoubtedly thinking to yourselves, "I have no idea what I want to accomplish with my life!" That is perfectly acceptable and expected. It takes time to figure out life's big questions, and goal setting is such an important part of that process. Learning how to use objectives effectively to get the most out of your life is an important skill to master. If you don't know what you want to achieve in life, it's like embarking on a journey with no clear endpoint. Even if you enjoy the ride, you're still going to risk winding up somewhere you don't want to be, and you're not going to choose the most efficient way!

ISN'T IT STRAIGHTFORWARD? You must first ask yourself what you truly desire in life and then go out and acquire it. Right?

. . .

UNFORTUNATELY, this is not the case. Goal formulation is far from simple and requires much skill. The difficulty is that few individuals are aware of this, never considering evaluating the goals themselves. They place the blame on their motivation, circumstances, or even other individuals. However, they rarely think about whether the problem is with their own objectives.

WHAT ARE YOUR OBJECTIVES? What exactly are your objectives? Do you want to make the Dean's List, find your calling, get a job, or get by with a mediocre degree? Everyone needs goals, and identifying them ahead of time will help you stay focused along the road.

WHAT ARE the benefits of setting goals? Life is chaotic and tends to slip away from you. There are thousands of possibilities at any given time, including new bright, flashy products, a new viral cat video, a few hundred social media updates from friends, and a slew of other activities. You took driver's education, practiced for hours on end, and learned the rules of the road as you prepared to receive your driver's license. You didn't just get in the car and decide to drive to Alaska to see some Kodiak bears and demonstrate your wonderful driving skills along the way when you went for your driver's exam, and the tester told you where to go, where to turn left, right, speed up, turn around, and so on. But what's keeping you from settling in Alaska? The explanation is that you got into your automobile with a specific aim in mind: to obtain the driver's license you'd wished for years! You knew exactly what you wanted to do from the start, and you had a clear plan that you stuck to.

. . .

IT's the same way in life. If you know where you want to go from the start, you'll most likely get there. You'll get there eventually, even if there are some delays. However, if you don't know where you're heading, you're unlikely to arrive at a pleasant place.

An Example of Bad Goal Setting

To understand how to write a good goal, it can help first to look at what makes a bad goal. Why is it that some goals don't work out the way they should? What should we do differently to avoid this happening the next time?

LET's imagine for a moment that you want to get into shape. You're planning on losing weight and building muscle – which is a pretty common goal that an awful lot of people are interested in accomplishing.

IN THIS EXAMPLE, a typical goal might involve writing down the ideal body weight and measurements you are trying to reach and then setting yourself a target – three months, six months, or one year. And then you get to it! But, this is a goal that is destined to fail. Why? Because this goal is far too vague, far too distant, and far too out of your control.

LET's fast forward two weeks, at which point you have hopefully been training hard for a while and changing your diet. Suddenly, life starts to get in the way. You find yourself bogged down with other things you have to do like that upcoming exam, paper, or party on Friday night, and you don't have the time or energy to make it to the gym today. Or tomorrow. And the day after that is looking shaky as well.

BUT YOU TELL yourself it is okay because you don't need to work out. Not working out on those days is not breaking your goal. You have plenty of time to reach your goal, and it is up to you how you will go about making it happen. So, if you take time off today, you'll just put some more time in tomorrow. Or the next day. If this week is a write-off, then you can always make up for it next week.

AND SO, it continues, week after week, until you get to the end of your allotted period and you realize you've blown any chance of accomplishing that goal.

OR HOW ABOUT this alternative scenario? Imagine that you put in the time and worked very hard every day to get into shape. But the pounds just didn't come off. Maybe this is due to slow metabolism; perhaps it boils down to those late-night snacks or just too much partying.

EITHER WAY, you get to a certain point, and you realize once again that you aren't going to make it even though you tried your best. So, what do you do? You give up, disheartened, and you quit trying.

A Better Goal

Now let's imagine that same scenario, but this time, we approach our goal differently. What would a good goal look like if you wanted to lose weight or build muscle?

FOR STARTERS, you should remove the time element. Instead of aiming to accomplish something in X number of days, how about you aim to do something toward your goal every day. Look at the goal that you want to accomplish and then break that down into much smaller steps. To lose weight, let's say you need to eat 1,800 calories or less a day. And you need to work out three times a week for an hour each day. If you can stick to this plan, you will eventually notice changes – be they big or small.

INSTEAD OF FOCUSING on the end goal, set yourself a daily plan. A daily goal is something that is entirely within your control – meaning that you cannot "fail" for reasons outside of your control. It is also completely resistant to being put off or delayed. You can't "work out today" tomorrow! Likewise, slow metabolism isn't going to prevent you from eating only 1,800 calories.

I LEARNED this concept from actor/comedian Jerry Seinfeld. Jerry developed a technique that he uses to make sure he sticks to these kinds of goals, and he calls it "The Chain." The idea is that he builds a chain each day as he completes his daily goal, each day represents a new link in his chain, and this process creates immense pressure not to break the chain. For Jerry, the process of writing one new joke each day allowed him to craft his skills and provided the foundation for his tremendous long-term success.

AN EASY WAY TO implement this strategy is with a calendar and a pen. Every day that you successfully achieve 1,800 calories or less, you put a tick on the calendar for that day. Your daily tick marks will start to build up gradually, and over time, you will come to feel proud of that row of ticks and not want to ruin it by missing one. You won't want to "break the chain."

WHETHER YOU USE this approach or not, the point is that you should write goals that are immediate and simple. Meanwhile, you can let the overarching objective "take care of itself."

Is Your Goal Too Ambitious?

There's nothing wrong with an ambitious goal. Many people say that "dreaming big" can make you more likely to accomplish your aim because it attracts attention, gravitates people toward you, and helps get people on board. If you tell people you want to fly to space, you will get a lot more positive attention than if you tell people you want to climb Stone Mountain (a quartz monzonite dome formation just outside Atlanta, Georgia).

THEREFORE, another piece of advice that often gets thrown around is for you to "have visions, not goals." Visions are abstract, and they are grand. These are things you visualize and dream about, rather than things you write down and tick off. If you want to get into shape, your goal can be to train three times a week, but your vision would be to become the best physical specimen you can – attractive to everyone and full of confidence and energy.

BUT WHILE A VISION can be as grand and extreme as you like, those smaller steps should still be small, and they should be easy. At least at the very start, your plan should be easy, and this will then allow you to build towards your higher overarching objective. Think of this as a pyramid. At the top, you have your grand vision for the future – something so exciting that it helps you to launch yourself out of bed in the morning. Beneath that, you might have your 'realistic' version of what you can achieve with your current resources. Beneath that, you might have the steps you are taking every day to achieve it.

MANY PEOPLE MAKE a mistake to lump all these things together and not consider the necessary sequencing required to move from one level to the next. Lumping is why someone who has never been to the gym before might well write themselves a new training program that requires them to train for an hour a day, seven days a week, and to do this on a diet of 1,000 calories. Is it any wonder that they don't tend to stick to their plan and fail to reach their goals?

IMPATIENCE IS your enemy when it comes to writing good goals. People want to accomplish their goals now. They don't want to put in the time or the repetitious work that it takes to reach their goals. And they certainly don't want the fear that comes from the uncertainty that they might not achieve their goals after all their work.

. . .

BUT IT WOULD HELP if you changed that thinking. Everything worth having comes with work and diligence, and this is often highly repetitive and boring. If you want to get into shape, you need to train regularly, and it takes years to get to a point where your new physique is impressive and permanent. If you want to start your own business after college, well, then there is a ton you need to learn before you even get going. Procrastinating on a goal is just as bad, by the way – which is another reason it is so important you have a clear plan of action!

A GOOD WAY TO understand this process is to look at the world of video gaming. Video games begin with a few incredibly easy levels to prevent you from getting discouraged quickly and quitting. Craft your goals the same way – if your "level one" is a massive, difficult battle, then you won't be successful.

LET'S LOOK AT RUNNING. Lots of people get it wrong when they are taking up running for the first time. Here, they aim to start running long distances right away and losing weight. It's grueling, painful, and unrewarding, and it leaves them gasping and achy for days after.

WHAT THEY SHOULD DO IS to first focus on getting good at running and on learning to like running. That means running short distances, not running too fast, not running too far, and generally not pushing themselves beyond a sensible point. This way, they can gradually start to like running, and they can gradually find themselves running further and further without even trying.

. . .

OFTEN, it only takes small changes to get to the place you want to be. The Japanese notion of "Kaizen" best exemplifies the impact of small changes. Kaizen essentially means lots of small changes that build up to significant results.

FOR INSTANCE, if you want to graduate with a 3.7 or higher GPA, then it might be easier to look at small changes you can make to get there rather than massive ones.

- Go to class every day.
- Create note cards after each lecture.
- Make sure you get 7 hours of sleep every night.
- Commit to the use of your daily planner.
- Visit your professors during their office hours.

THESE ARE ONLY a few minor adjustments that should be simple enough for most students to make. Still, they can have a significant impact on your overall GPA, eventually leading to a cumulative GPA of 3.7 or higher!

ONCE YOU'VE ESTABLISHED your objectives, it's a good idea to split them down into smaller steps or sub-objectives. It allows you to take modest steps forward while reducing procrastination.

OBTAINING A COLLEGE DIPLOMA, for example, can be divided into four sub-goals. The successful completion of one year of your program is the sub-goal for each of the sub-goals. Individual courses within each year can be broken down further into these sub-goals. Within the 16 weeks of lessons in each semester, the courses can be split down into tests, exams, and term papers, among other things. Each week is divided into days, with each day divided into the hours and minutes you'll spend in class and on assignments.

WHILE THINKING about all of the activities that will earn that college degree may seem overwhelming at first. Breaking down your goals into smaller chunks helps to reinforce the idea that there is a connected path connecting what you do today and the successful completion of your degree. Seeing these links can aid in tracking your development and determining whether or not you are on track. Now is a good time to think about your objectives and break them down into smaller portions.

PRO TIP – Many students struggle with goal-setting, which is understandable given that they have their entire lives ahead of them and that their objectives will shift over time. The objective is to choose goals that will provide you with the most possibilities and open up the most doors in the future.

A MARKETING DEGREE, for example, will provide you with more alternatives than a degree in Ancient Animal Bite Marks if all other factors are equal. When in doubt, select the course that will give you the most possibilities in the future.

PLEASE VISUALIZE the steps you'll take to achieve your goals now that you've established a list of them. Visualizing the measures you'll take to achieve your objectives boosts your chances of succeeding. Successful athletes practice how they will perform in a game repeatedly in their heads so that when game day arrives, they will be at their best. You can directly apply the strategy to any goal you want to achieve using the athletes' prior expertise.

MANY STUDENTS MAKE the mistake of focusing so intently on achieving their objective or the end state reward that they overlook the importance of enjoying their college experience. Many students rush to graduate and begin their professions that they do not make the most of their time in school. We appreciate life more when we are satisfied with our current efforts rather than fantasizing about how wonderful it will be when we reach our long-term goal.

FOR EXAMPLE, rather than just surviving the ride till we reach our goal, we will enjoy a road trip more if we opt to take an interest in the sights along the way. Similarly, rather than accomplishing the bare minimum to pass a class, we enjoy it more when we investigate the topic beyond what is required.

DON'T CREATE unreasonable goals or have too many ambitions to achieve. This is something that many students undertake early in the semester. When they discover they don't have enough time or energy to achieve their objectives, they quickly feel disappointed. Recognizing our physical, mental, and emotional limitations is vital for creating realistic goals, and school life is about more than just receiving that diploma or certificate.

Change your Mindset

While some individuals will almost surely be envious when you begin to achieve your objectives, you will most likely face your greatest challenge from within. Young adults are typically their own worst enemies, and as we start to achieve success, some primal defense mechanism kicks in. Our mind starts telling us all these insane things – which we usually believe because, hey, we're scared and afraid.

THE TRUTH IS that we have reservations about almost everything we encounter on our way to achievement. Successful people have trained their thoughts to be helpful rather than critical, and while it takes some time, you can truly train your mind to get out of your own way. Here are some techniques to ensure that you are approaching your goals with the appropriate mindset.

1. **Believe in Success:** We all have moments when we tell ourselves that we don't deserve to be happy for whatever reason. Perhaps it stems from shame or a lack of belief in our own worthiness to be happy and achieve our objectives. If your mind is telling you that you don't deserve the kind of success you want, remind yourself that it is a lie. Believe in yourself and your ability to succeed and be happy. We all deserve it, but few are ready to put up the effort required to obtain it.

2. **Develop Confidence in Yourself:** Confidence is a tremendous tool; when you have it, you are practically unstoppable; nevertheless, when you don't have it, it might be difficult to achieve anything. You can accomplish your objectives. You have

the intelligence, the drive, the attitude, and the capacity to succeed. You have everything you need to achieve your goals. You must first put forth the effort; belief will come as a result.

3. Don't Think in Extremes: Thinking in extremes - both positively and negatively – can be one of life's biggest roadblocks. We tend to think in extremes: up/down, on/off, success/failure, happy/sad, and so on. Of course, none of these extremes are absolute, but standing on the verge of anything makes it difficult to be objective about the complete spectrum of possibilities. Don't get caught up in thinking about your successes and failures in terms of extremes.

4. Don't Overgeneralize: Sometimes,, we all can be drama queens when something terrible happens. We say things like,, "Oh, I'll never be able to achieve this goal." Negative thought processes are one of the worst mistakes you can make. Saying things like: "I must be the worst person ever to try this, I am not smart like other students." is a recipe for long and difficult life. Setbacks are going to happen, and sometimes you are going to fail. It's not the end of the world, and you're probably doing better than a lot of people. Don't overgeneralize; try to look at things objectively, and most importantly, keep going.

5. Celebrate Your Success: When you reach one of your daily, weekly, monthly, or yearly goals, don't minimize it. Achieving any goal is a big deal. Every single time you reach a goal – even if it's nothing more than your daily progress update – you are building momentum. Keep going and keep meeting those goals because you'll be achieving your dreams before you know it.

Goals - A Final Thought

As you can see, learning to structure your goals correctly and having the right mindset can make a big difference in your likelihood of accomplishing your goals. The key is to set your sights high but to have concrete, small steps that you can take along the way to get there. Don't focus on how long it will take, deal with it being "boring," and focus on repeating the same few actions every day until you eventually achieve the thing you want to achieve or become the person you want to become.

IF YOU ASSESS the situation in the future after you have gained more experience and knowledge, you can rethink your approach again. Like anything else, this approach takes time, practice, and effort. In time, you will find things that work for you and things that don't work. You should make adjustments to your process as you gain more knowledge and experience!

NOW THAT YOU have your goals in mind, the next step is walking the road toward achieving them. Achievement begins with understanding our time. Let's explore how to become aware of the time you have available to you.

2
___

SMALL CHANGES...BIG IMPACT

Where Did My Day Go?

Have you ever looked at the time and thought, wow, it's 3:00 pm already, where did my day go? We have all been there at one point or another, but the first key to managing your time is to understand where your time gets spent. One very helpful way of determining where your time goes is to start tracking your time. The process here is similar to making a schedule, but it works in reverse. Instead of writing things down that you are planning to do, time logging is a process of writing down the things that you have already done. Doing this is sort of a get-to-know yourself exercise because this practice will highlight many of the habits that you might not even realize are eating big chunks of your time.

FOR INSTANCE, some people find that they watch a YouTube video or two before starting on their work every time they plan to do some classwork. That five or ten minutes a day can add up to days of lost study time over just one semester. Instead of studying for that English test, they check their social networks and update their friends that they will be offline for a few hours, which of course, leads to a few quick interactions from well-wishing friends. Other people can't seem to find the motivation to get started, to find their focus, and they find ways to procrastinate endlessly until the very last minute when anxiety finally fuels action.

WHATEVER YOUR CURRENT time management habits, time tracking will help you adjust and fine-tune your time management practices. Having accurate information about your time usage patterns is the foundation for forming good time management habits. The following are a few of my favorite recommendations to help you track your time. Please don't skip this exercise. Take the time to do this – it will truly open your eyes and help you take control of your time.

1. Time tracking is not as complex as it might first seem. At the end of every hour, make a note about how you spent your time for that hour. The note needn't be long - one sentence or less should suffice. If how you spent your time doesn't match an already planned activity, enter a comment as to what you did during that time. This way, you will be able to review patterns that emerge in your time use and make adjustments to improve your productivity.

2. Many people find it helpful to modify their planning page to facilitate tracking time. The modifications are easy enough: make two columns on your paper for each day of the week. In one column, write down the activity you are trying to achieve; in the second column, make notes on what you did with your

time. The side-by-side comparison is very revealing and an excellent way to figure out where you're not using time in the way you intend.

3. Another effective way to make changes and get results from your time management strategies is to summarize your time use by a time category such as sleep, study, work, travel, etc.

BEFORE DOING THE SUMMARY, make a sheet with different columns for each category. Your log sheet might look something like this:

ACTIVITY
  Expected Time
  Actual Time
  Variance

STUDY FOR MATH Test
  3-hours
  5-hours
  -2 hours

REVIEW ENGLISH NOTES
  2-hours
  1-hours
  +1 hour

READ BOOK CHAPTER

1-hour
1-hour
0 hours

Work on Industry Paper
2-hours
3-hours
-1 hour

Group Study Session
2-hours
1-hours
+1 hour

Sleep
8-hours
5-hours
+3 hours

Night Out
4-hours
7-hours
-3 hours

Total
22 hours
23 hours
-1 hour

Estimate the amount of time you think you spend on the

various activities listed and enter these in the "expected" row of the summary sheet. Feel free to add any additional categories that might be helpful. Then log your time for one week on an hour-by-hour basis. When the week is over, summarize your time by category for each day, add up the values for all seven days of the week, and write the totals in the "actual" row of the summary sheet.

SUMMARIZING your time use allows you to understand how much time you spend in the various areas of your life. It is almost certain that you will see a notable difference between the number of hours you expected to use in certain categories and the actual number of hours you spend.

IF YOU FIND that you spend more time in one area than you wanted and less in another, the weekly summary of time used indicates which activities to reduce to find the extra time you want for that neglected area of your life.

THE DIFFERENCES between your expected use of time and your actual use of time represent your opportunities for improvement. These differences are where your focus should be. You need to identify and adjust the patterns in your behavior that are creating these variances. Small changes can make an enormous impact over time and greatly aid you in reaching your goals. These small changes, when taken together, drive a compound effect allowing you to achieve huge rewards from a series of small but intelligent choices.

. . .

THE REASON this approach goes relatively unnoticed by the masses is that these small changes seem to make no immediate impact, no obvious impact, they don't seem to matter. Most people can't understand the cumulative effect that these small positive changes can create in their lives. They miss that these seemingly minor adjustments taken consistently over time will create significant differences. Let me give you a few examples of the power of small actions compounding over time featured in Darren Hardy's Bestselling book, The Compound Effect.

The Magic Penny

If you had a choice between taking $3 million in cash today or a single magic penny that would double in value every day for the next 31 days, which choice would you pick? If you've heard this parable before, you know the magic penny is your most profitable choice. But why is it so difficult to believe choosing the magic penny is the best choice in the long run? The basic reason is that we are programmed to believe that it takes large significant actions to make any difference in our lives. Also, our brains believe anything that takes long periods to deliver a result is painful and pushes us in the direction of immediate fun and gratification. Fun always seems to trump long-term commitment. Let's look at our magic penny example.

FOR THE SAKE OF DISCUSSION, let's say you took the $3 million in cash, and your friend decides to take a flyer on that magic penny. On Day Seven, your friend has sixty-four cents. You, however, still have $3 million, less, of course, some of those fancy purchases you made. On Day Fourteen, your friend is up to a whopping $81.92. Not looking too good for your friend at this point! You have been enjoying your millions and watching your friend struggle with only pennies to show for it.

.   .   .

AFTER 21 DAYS, with only ten days left in our story, the magic penny has only generated $10,486. For all your friend's sacrifice, she has barely more than $10,000. You, however, have been enjoying a $3 million windfall. On Day Twenty-Seven the magic penny has only generated a paltry $671,088. You are thrilled with your decision to take the $3 million. But then the seemingly poor-performing magic penny starts to gain steam, and the compound effect's power starts to take hold. That same power of that seemingly ill-advised doubling magic penny, that small doubling each day, takes hold and makes that magic penny worth $10,737,418.24 on Day Thirty-one, more than three times your $3 million.

WHAT DO you think about your choice now? This parable is meant to demonstrate the power of small actions taken consistently over time is surprisingly powerful. On day Twenty-nine, you've got your $3 million; the magic penny has about $2.7 million. It isn't until that 30th day that your friend pulls ahead with $5.3 million. And it isn't until the 31st day that your friend blows your doors off; she ends up with a whopping $10,737,418.24 compared to your now seemly small $3 million.

VERY FEW THINGS are as powerful as the "magic" of compounding actions taken consistently over time. Not surprisingly, this "magic force" is equally powerful in all areas of your life.

BETTER CHOICES, reinforced with positive habits, applied consistently over time, is the key to happiness and success in life. The sooner you realize that the habits that drive your actions are compounding your life into either success or failure, the better off you will be. The good news is that tiny, small adjustments applied to your daily routines can dramatically change your trajectory and lead to the success you desire in your life. Once more, I'm not talking about massive quantum leaps of change or a complete renovation of your life. Just like the magic penny, seemingly minor changes can and will transform everything.

The Lost Plane

Another illustration of how a seemingly minor unnoticeable change can impact your goals is the story of an airplane traveling from Los Angeles to New York City. If the plane is a mere one percent off course leaving Los Angeles, with no course corrections in route, the plane will ultimately end up about 150 miles off target, arriving either in Dover Delaware or Upstate in Albany, New York. Just like a small one percent error leads to the plane missing its intended goal, so it is with your habits. One single poor habit, which doesn't look like much on the surface, can ultimately lead to you finding yourself miles from your goals and dreams.

FOR THOSE OF you now freaked out by the thought of not knowing exactly where you spend your time, here's something to consider. We all have 168 hours available in a week. Studies report that fully half of those 168 hours – 84 hours - are used up for the "basics" like sleeping, eating, showering, etc. How do your numbers compare to these estimates? How will you spend those critical remaining 84 hours per week?

3

MANAGE YOUR TIME, MANAGE YOUR LIFE

You have no prior experience arranging for your out-of-class coursework as a student. A decent rule of thumb is to plan two to three hours of schoolwork outside of class for every hour spent in class. Yes, this means that a full-time student with five classes and a regular fifteen-hour class load per week should set aside between thirty and forty-five hours per week for study/homework.

SURE, this is a significant amount of time, especially if you breezed through high school on much less. This estimate is based on the amount of time it takes to learn well at the college level. You can alter your anticipated times up or down depending on the complexity of each of your lessons. As I previously indicated, you spent around 80% of your time learning in school in high school and only 20% of your time learning outside of school. The ratio has now been reversed in college, posing a new challenge for you as a college student. Only approximately a quarter of your learning occurs in class, and the other eighty percent takes place outside of it.

. . .

THE TRANSITION from a highly regimented high school to a largely unstructured college setting necessitates a whole new approach to your academic career. The goal is to dedicate this time solely to learning and then adapt as needed based on your experience and outcomes.

IF YOU HAVE a job and it isn't necessarily preventing you from succeeding in school, you'll need to think about your work schedule and arrange some time for yourself each week. A good beginning point would be 10 percent of your week or seventeen hours. More important than particular goals is spending enough time on education to succeed and enough time outside of school to maintain a healthy balance.

MAKE sure you leave room in your daily agenda for unplanned disruptions. Allowing some vacant spaces in your day allows you to be flexible enough to deal with disruptions or unexpected demands on your time. If the unexpected does not occur, there will be enough time to accomplish something else.

MANY STUDENTS DISCOVER that scheduling schoolwork earlier in the day reduces the likelihood of being interrupted by unforeseen circumstances. Every day's schedule should include homework. In a comprehensive study on stress, students claimed that doing homework was the most common strategy for alleviating stress in their lives.

. . .

THAT MAY SEEM strange to you, but getting ahead of the curve and finishing your homework will reduce your stress levels because you won't have that activity hanging over your head all of the time.

REMEMBER that rather than a big list of "have-to-dos," your daily calendar should contain at least some time for doing what you want to accomplish. Looking forward to something every day is beneficial to our mental health and can help us avoid burnout.

WHEN WE LOOK at our schedule on some days, it can feel daunting. If this is the case, focusing on one activity at a time and avoiding looking at the entire day can be beneficial. You'll be surprised at how swiftly you complete the day's activities.

YOU'LL HAVE to make changes to your plans and time management habits sooner or later. Keep in mind that certain time problems are predictable, while others are not; some are controlled, while others are not. Keep your cool and get back on track as soon as possible if you can't control it. Deal with time problems that you can control, especially those that occur regularly, immediately and quickly, so they don't get in the way of your goals.

SELF-CONTROL IS REQUIRED for time management. It takes time, but time management becomes an everyday habit after a short period of self-management.

- Be conscious of how you spend your time.

- Don't put off doing tasks and don't wait until the last minute to do assignments and projects.
- Allow enough time in your day to do things you enjoy, as well as eat and sleep. Sleep deprivation is a widespread issue on most college campuses.
- Make the most of your time. If you're on the bus or shuttle, make time to read while you're on the road.

STAYING one day ahead is one of the most effective time management tactics. I'm sure this remark will elicit some collective moans, but trust me when I say that keeping exactly one day ahead of your classes will make your life a lot simpler, especially when that sickness circulating campus takes the wind out of your sails.

YOUR LECTURERS WILL MOST likely offer you one of the most crucial pieces of information you will ever get — the syllabus — at the start of most of your classes. You probably never received a syllabus in high school. You had no idea what the reading or homework assignment for the next two weeks would entail. You do it in college. What is the significance of this? It's the secret to mastering your time management.

LET'S assume it's the first day of school. You receive your biology course syllabus. In most circumstances, the first day of class is a no-brainer; often, the lecturer skips the material lecture because they know that many students will quit or add classes that first week. You take a look at your handy syllabus and notice that the next class time will consist of a lecture on the first chapter of your $199.99 textbook. "Wait a minute," you might think at this vital moment "Oh, I've already decided what I'm going to do next class period. I'm not sure if this is genuinely useful information. Is it possible for me to take advantage of this?"

MANY STUDENTS TOSS the golden ticket of the syllabus into their backpack, fold it into a paper aircraft, or come up with another creative use for these sheets of paper, and then do nothing until the next class hour.

WHEN THE NEXT class period arrives two days later, you haven't read chapter one, but who cares, because your professor will talk about it. You figure that you will use the time-honored tradition of taking notes in class. After all, everyone's doing it.

BUT SUPPOSE you're spending all of your time trying to copy PowerPoint slides or copy written words on the board (your professor will most likely have handwriting that resembles some ancient language). In that case, you simply aren't going to absorb the material in most cases.

LET'S say you take some great notes - good for you! Then you take the notes, which have all of the information you will ever need, and you put them in your folder, binder, backpack, or saddle-pack, and leave them there until the next lecture. Then you take more notes, add them to the pile, and soon have lots of notes. Whoopee.

. . .

BEFORE YOU KNOW IT, you have a test or quiz approaching, so you assemble your nifty notes and start restudying them like mad. You have to set apart a large chunk of time out of your schedule to review this old information so that it will be fresh in your mind for the test.

THERE IS A BETTER WAY. Now, let's pretend that you decided to get one day ahead. After your first-class period (and I know this is hard to do because there's so much fun to be found during the first week and so little work to do), you have a heart-to-heart with yourself and decide that you will get one day ahead.

IF TODAY'S MONDAY, and the next class is Wednesday, you set aside some time on Monday afternoon or anytime on Tuesday and read the first chapter. You may even decide to take some notes, highlight, or even make notecards for definitions (more on notecards later).

WHEN YOU WALK into class on Wednesday, and your teacher starts talking, you have at least some idea and understanding around the lecture. You don't have to copy down definitions you've already read because you know they are in the book -- you remember reading them. Instead of frantically copying notes like your poor confused classmates, you can relax and make a small tick mark to denote what the professor discussed and listen to what the professor is saying.

THE LECTURE BECOMES your review session, and then you are in a much better position when test time comes. If the professor starts talking about something you don't remember reading in the textbook, take good notes. The topic is either not covered in the book (so you can guarantee the professor will put it on a test), or it's something that you didn't quite absorb the first time you read it.

IF YOU CAN DO this for each of your classes at the beginning of school, you will be in great shape. Once you get one day ahead, you can work at the same pace as everyone else, but always be a day ahead. Lectures will not be "note cramming sessions"; they'll be pseudo-reviews.

THE TOUGHEST PART is not getting lazy and letting that one-day buffer disappear. You can't let yourself slip behind because you know you're ahead. Once you lose that day, it's much harder to get it back in the middle of the semester because the pace of your classes will be picking up. If you can get ahead in that first week, the load will be much lighter.

OF COURSE, there are exceptions to every rule. Not every class is equal in difficulty, and it may be extremely hard to get that one-day edge in certain complex classes or in classes that depend almost 100% on lecture material that doesn't come from a textbook.

SOME CLASSES MAY BE JUST PLAIN hard, and if you can't get a day ahead in one or two classes, that's fine. The time that you save by being ahead in your other classes will help you enormously in that tough calculus class you're taking.

.   .   .

IF YOU FIND that reading your book is not helping you grasp the material, then talk to your professor. If they learn that you are trying to stay a day ahead, besides the inevitable brownie points that will follow, they will be willing to help you out. Professors are generally willing to bend over backward for any student putting out a serious effort to succeed in their class.

LET me mention that you may have some classes in which the professor has put together a "notes packet" containing copies of all the presentations and notes for that class. Be very careful not to depend solely on these notes, as this could be a trap. Don't let those notes become an excuse to get lazy. Don't think that the class lecture doesn't matter because you have all the material, get one day ahead in the class notes, and again, all of the lectures will be your review sessions.

Putting the System into Action

Keeping a calendar is pretty straightforward, but surprisingly I have discovered most students don't keep one their first semester or two. If they do keep one, it is usually just a class schedule with locations, so they know when and where to go until they get their routine committed to memory.

I WILL OFFER you some advice that seems counter-intuitive and conflicts with what most experts will tell you. First, let me say I am a fan of technology and using your Outlook, iPhone, or Google Calendar as a way to track your activities as most experts recommend. Still, I want this to be your secondary source of scheduling, not your primary.

.   .   .

I RECOMMEND USING AN EXCEL SPREADSHEET, a DayMinder GC520 or similar planner, and your automated calendar during your first two semesters. I know this might sound like overkill, but the idea here is not to enter events and assignments into a calendar but to develop a system that keeps you organized and on track.

AFTER A COUPLE OF SEMESTERS, you will find the system, and the process will have become a habit and will be natural for you.

LET'S look at how all these approaches work together, and everything will become clear.

FIRST DAY/WEEK of the Semester

THE FIRST THING I want you to do is to take your syllabi from each class and markdown (in pencil) all your assignments for the semester in your DayMinder, don't forget mid-term and final exams).

NOW USE different color highlighters for each class (Math, English, Communications, etc.) and highlight your assignments in your planner.

NEXT, identify areas where you have multiple assignments, test, exams, etc. all clustered together in a particular week or day. These clusters allow you to see clearly up front where you will be stressed and have little time. Like most students, you will see a convergence around spring and fall breaks and the last month of the semester. Take a deep breath, and don't panic!

NOW WE WANT to pay attention to the weights of our assignments. Review your syllabi for each class and underline in red in your planner all your significant assignments. Significant is a subjective term, and each class will vary, but in general, anything weighted 10% of your grade or higher will qualify.

ONCE WE HAVE our core class schedule, we have to make some study estimates. Use two hours of study time for each hour of class time as a baseline requirement for scheduling your week. Adjust this baseline up or down based on your comfort and the difficulty of your class material. If you struggle with Math, you should bump up your baseline to 3 hours. If you are an English expert, you can adjust the baseline down to 1 hour or maybe 1.5 hours. We now want to schedule our study time right into your planner. Planning a specific study schedule is key to avoiding procrastination. If you work or play sports and have that weekly commitment, schedule it now. Keep track of your study and assignment hours so that you can make adjustments throughout the semester.

THINGS ARE PROBABLY STARTING to look pretty crowded at this point, and you are beginning to wonder where all that free time you heard about will show up. Don't worry; by planning, you will maximize your free time.

. . .

Now we want to identify the areas on your calendar where you have little or no assignments due. Highlight these areas in Green in your DayMinder.   We will utilize these areas to pull forward work you previously underlined in red and the areas where you have lots of things converging.   Look for those large significant assignments and break them down into smaller chunks with new due dates you create for yourself. These are called milestones.   By utilizing these green areas, you will balance your workload to reduce future stress and have the time available to do your best work.

If you know you are going to go out with your friends on Friday and Saturday nights, make sure you schedule that time as well. If you will be out to the early morning hours and then sleep in until 2 pm, plan for that. Be realistic and don't set yourself up to fail by scheduling 4 hours of study time every Saturday morning when you already know you will be sleeping until early afternoon.

Now that we have everything organized and scheduled, we can enter everything into our online or smartphone calendars and set up our alert notifications.   The electronic calendar now keeps us on schedule, but our pre-planning ensures we effectively utilize our time.

I recommend that students get one day ahead in their classes as soon as possible, things happen, schedules change, etc., but by building in a day buffer, you are preparing for that unplanned event that will inevitably occur at some point during the semester.

. . .

ALSO, class syllabi are guidelines, and the due dates and assignments will change in many instances. You will want to make sure you prepare for that new last-minute paper the professor decided to throw at you in the last month of classes. Yes, it happens more often than you would like. A professor will feel that the class isn't picking up on something as a whole or that something new has happened in the field, and the professor will decide to add an assignment to strengthen your academic foundation. He or She may feel like the class has not engaged or participated as well as they should have, or they may want to allow everyone to improve their grades. Regardless, you want to be prepared.

ALSO, schedule a time to Skype or call your family or someone else important to you back home. You will be surprised at how fast the days can run together, and although you are probably texting frequently, your loved ones love to hear your voice and see your face.

THIS TEMPLATE IS straightforward to use and will summarize all your activities for you in one place (see table 1). In the tab, you merely enter your activities on the Class List and Activities Tab (see table 2) classes, study time, practices, clubs, events, etc., in the tab, and the spreadsheet will organize everything for you.

TABLE 1: Time Management Schedule

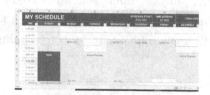

TABLE 2: Time Management Activities

EACH WEEK – Review and Plan

PICK a day each week to review the week and month ahead. Most students find Sundays work best for this review. Remember to schedule calendar review time and treat this time like you would any other required commitment. Log into your universities course management system and review your upcoming assignment lists for any changes or assignments you may have missed. As a side note, make sure you confirm all assignments you turned in are showing as turned in. Every semester students think they turned in an assignment, but the system will say otherwise. It is your responsibility to make sure your assignment was submitted and received. Use this time to clean up your email inbox and check and see if any of your professors have made schedule changes for the week ahead. The critical activity in this weekly review is to establish the specific activities and work you will perform during your allotted time slots. Initially, we just blocked off the time we knew we would need. Once we have the specifics, we can now schedule the activities and tasks we need to complete during the week. As an example, we can take the 3 hours we have scheduled to study for a particular class and break down how we will use those three hours. Are we going to review note cards, read a chapter in the text, work on a paper, etc.?

DAILY

EACH DAY BEFORE NOON, review your next day's schedule and school email account. If something new has popped up, you forgot about something, etc.. By checking the next day's activities and your email early enough, you leave yourself time to course-correct if needed. Many students check their next day's calendar just before going to bed. If they have made a mistake or missed something, they have no time to correct their error, stress levels rise, they don't sleep, and the next day's performance suffers. Students often don't get emails sent to their university accounts regularly, so they can get out of the habit of periodically checking their school email and miss valuable information such as assignments or cancellations of classes.

THE BIG PICTURE

MOST STUDENTS STRUGGLE WITH STRUCTURE, and that is natural. By creating a schedule, you are not somehow magically sucking all the fun out of your life. You are reducing your stress and improving your performance, allowing you to enjoy yourself a whole lot more. You will miss study sessions and other events on your calendar... that's ok. It is very valuable to know you missed an event and not go around fooling yourself into thinking you are on track. If you miss something, ask if you can make it up. You would be surprised how many students just assume the professor will not cut them a break. Make sure you identify what caused you to veer off course, make adjustments, and learn from the experience.

Creating Balance in Your Life

With everything that is going on in life, you need a simple system to make sure you have time for school, work, and fun. Yes, you're in college to get an education and gain the skill you need for a successful career, but you are also here to have fun, create new experiences, and hopefully, a few lifelong friends.

THERE IS A VERY simple technique you can use to make sure you keep your life in balance, a technique called *The Eisenhower Matrix or Eisenhower Box.* By utilizing this prioritization approach, you will be able to balance your hectic college life.

THIS TECHNIQUE IS NAMED after former President Dwight D. Eisenhower, the top general in World War II. He is credited with many accomplishments in his life, including leading the allied forces to victory, developing the Interstate Highway System, and spearheading the creation of NASA. As a General and a President, he was widely regarded as extremely effective and organized. We all can learn a lot from President Eisenhower, so let's take a look at how he could accomplish so much.

PRESIDENT EISENHOWER WAS famous for saying, "What is important is seldom urgent, and what is urgent is seldom important."

. . .

THE MATRIX CONSISTS of a square divided into four sections or quadrants. Here's how the four quadrants are laid out:

WE START by placing all our activities into the four quadrants, with the labels of Important and Urgent on each side. Each quadrant has a value of 1 through 4 based on their current priority.

1. "IMPORTANT" and "Urgent" tasks. These are all your level 1 priorities. If you have an exam the next day, studying is probably a top priority. Paper due tomorrow, again, a level 1 activity, connect assignment due tomorrow, another level 1 priority. Level 1 priorities are those things with immediate deadlines, things that will make the most impact on your goals and vision, and these activities should grab your immediate attention.

2. "IMPORTANT," but "Not Urgent" tasks. These are things still aligned with your goals and vision, but there is no immediate deadline staring you in the face. Maybe it is doing some extra reading on a topic in your major, attending a seminar before graduation, or reviewing your 4-year plan. You will work on these tasks whenever you have a lull in your schedule.

3. "NOT IMPORTANT," but "Urgent" tasks. These are things that you will complete after your level 1 priorities are complete or delegate altogether. Can your roommate check out that journal from the library for you? Could a friend pick up your toothpaste from the store for you? Maybe your parents need some information from you, or a friend needs a little help?

. . .

4. "Nᴏᴛ Iᴍᴘᴏʀᴛᴀɴᴛ" **and** "Not Urgent" **tasks.** These are the activities you put in quadrant 4 or activities you should eliminate. Do you really need to binge-watch Season 3 of "Orange is the New Black," or should you work on your quadrant 2 activities?

Tʜᴇ ᴜɴᴅᴇʀʟʏɪɴɢ ᴠᴀʟᴜᴇ in this matrix is its simple ability to compare activities, which are really urgent and really important. Urgent activities require your immediate attention; important activities help you with your long-term goals.

THE EISENHOWER MATRIX

Organization Matters

Usually, college students aren't quite prepared to organize all the "stuff" in their lives as they transition to college. Dorm rooms can quickly get overrun with stuff like clothes, books, computers, mini-fridges, microwaves, television sets, and the other possessions of the college student's life.

. . .

EVEN IF YOU'RE going to college locally and still living at home in the same room you've been in since you were a child, you still need to make room for the new trappings of college life. Try a few of these organizational tips.

YOU WILL NEED a few supplies to get you started. First, you will need colored file folders, a portable plastic file holder, some colored binders, a 3-hole punch, and a few small bins that will get you started.

DESIGNATE ONE COLOR for each class and store pending assignments in them as you work on them. Place these folders inside the plastic holder. Be sure to write on the tab which class each folder is for to ease identification. You can also use the file folder approach to store important papers and receipts.

THE COLORED BINDERS are used for each class to store all the papers you receive in that class. As we talked about earlier, you will get a syllabus – put this in the front. Then, whenever you get a handout from your professor, place it in the binder. Use section dividers to label what information corresponds with which section. You should also keep completed assignments in this binder for easy referral, and in case your instructor "loses" one of your grades – then you can prove you did the work! It does happen, especially when your professor is handling hundreds of student assignments at any given time. Also, a professor may easily overwrite or enter a grade in the system wrong. Having an organized method to keep your assignments will make your life much easier when you sit down with your professor to review the mistake. You would be shocked to learn the number of times a student reaches out to me the last few weeks of the semester and asks for a copy of their initial assignment outlines, so they can get back to work on the project they were supposed to be working on all semester. Don't do this; it won't end well.

KEEP an ample supply of pens and #2 pencils on hand, and use the bins for small items you accumulate like paper clips, push pins for a bulletin board, stapler, etc. It's a good idea to keep extra supplies like printer paper and printer cartridges – just in case!

NOW THAT YOU have the tools let's make sure you stay organized. Assignments can disappear in a pile of paper. Textbooks can get lost within a mound of laundry. A cluttered dorm room creates stress! Disorganization is all around us and happens practically everywhere, even in the most scholarly of places, like a college campus. But, there is an easy solution.

THE RULE with paper is very simple. There are only three things you can do with paper:

1. Act on it
2. File it
3. Toss it

FOR EXAMPLE, if you get a piece of mail, open it. Don't create a huge clutter problem by letting unopened mail pile up. You must decide what to do with your opened mail. If it is a catalog or a piece of junk mail and you know that you will not use it, toss it. Pay it, mail it, or file it in a "bills due" folder if it is a bill. If you receive a memo or note after reading it, toss it or file it away. If you get a paper returned, file it away. If you don't, the clutter and stress will build.

ANOTHER IMPORTANT PLACE TO de-clutter is your computer. If you can keep your files under control, you won't be looking in 20 different folders in "My Documents" for that English paper you wrote last week. Here are some suggestions to get rid of computer clutter.

- Deleting or archiving any e-mail you read will keep your inbox clean.
- Create a filing system- if you cannot reply right away or need to save an e-mail, place it in a folder made for that category. (Needs Reply, or Archives)
- Watch your "sent mail" folder. Delete or archive things from that as well.
- Add to your address book often. Many times, people will keep an e-mail in their inbox so that they have the address for the future. Instead of that, save the address. You'll know where to find it later.
- Utilize spam filters on your e-mail account to limit inbox distractions. Just don't forget to check your junk and spam mail folder for things that slipped through.
- Setting up folders by semester will keep your "My Documents" folder easier to navigate, as well as allow for quick reference.
- Move files to Dropbox or another backup device as a standard course of business. You don't want to lose any work, and routinely backing up your work

in case of failure can save you untold time and stress.

LIKE ANY OTHER SKILL, organization is a skill that can be learned. The most difficult part is breaking your lifelong bad habits. The key to getting better organized is to start with one small step and then take additional small steps one after the other. You may find that what you've put off for days takes only a few minutes to do. And once you see the benefits in one part of your life, you'll be motivated to expand this practice.

ALL THE TIME management and organization tips in the world can only help if you put them to use. Putting things off can be the biggest mistake most students make.

I'll Stop Procrastinating Today, Well Maybe Not Today!

Procrastination is a goal buster; wait it's more than that; it's a life buster. You might be thinking, isn't that a bit dramatic? I have always procrastinated, and I have gotten along just fine! I am here to tell you, what got you here, won't get you where you want to go. You must raise your game! And if you only change one bad habit, make it to STOP procrastinating!

IT'S easy to put things off until later, especially when you dread a task such as writing a term paper. But as a student, this is a real problem. If you put off your assignments or study for tests, you are only hurting yourself. Procrastinating leads to stress and anxiety, not to mention poor performance. You CAN stop procrastination from affecting your schoolwork.

. . .

OFTEN STUDENTS SUFFER from procrastination and find it difficult to get started working on their assignments. Most of the time, not starting seems to be related to stress, fear, or simply feeling overwhelmed with the whole process. Aim to subdivide tasks into small steps and convince yourself that all you need is five minutes working on the task to get started. Often, five minutes is all you'll need to get into the swing of things, and you can continue productively. I call this trick "The Five-Minute Hack."

SOMETIMES I HEAR students say they don't feel motivated to start their assignments; they are waiting for inspiration or a changing mood. I got news for you... people who wait on the mood to strike or motivation to hit them will find themselves doing everything last minute. Mood and Motivation aren't prerequisites to action...**it is a result of it!**

TRY WORKING for a short time and see if you can "get into it." If your motivation problem seems more substantial, it might help to realize that when you aren't motivated to do school work, you aren't out of motivation... **you are just motivated to do something else.**

MAKE every effort to develop the discipline you need to follow your plan. Your planner should always be handy, and you should refer to it often. Once you make your schedule, follow it. If you need help staying on task, work with a roommate or friend to motivate each other and hold each other accountable. Remind yourself you are focused on your long-term goals, and once you complete your work, you are one step closer to achieving those goals. And remember, by sticking to your plan, you will have more time for yourself.

IF YOU ARE STRUGGLING to stick to your plan, try this tip. Make two activity lists: "Things I Like to Do" and "Things I Have to Do." Mix up activities from both lists and work on each activity for a short period. Alternating between fun and work helps to maintain motivation and interest. All work and no fun is another schedule buster. You don't have to be working ALL the time, but you do have to complete what is required to stay on plan.

SOMETIMES, you're going to feel overwhelmed with large projects or assignments. Remind yourself that this is a normal reaction. When you feel like this, it's easier to put things off because you don't know exactly where to start and have difficulty envisioning the completed task. Divide these major assignments into smaller parts and work on one part at a time. Then put them together into the whole project and feel the satisfaction of a job well done!

YOU MIGHT HAVE every intention of doing things promptly, but time can move swiftly. There are only 24 hours in a day, and some people are just over aggressive with their planning. Make sure your schedule is realistic, and you aren't involved in too many activities scheduled close together. If you spread yourself too thinly, none of your projects will get the attention they deserve.

. . .

REWARD yourself when you complete tasks on time. Make the reward appropriate for the difficulty and boredom of the task. Utilizing rewards will help you stay on task and provide fuel for action.

REMEMBER that you're not alone. Some studies report that up to 95% of students experience procrastination as a real problem. Many students do most of the work in marathon sessions near academic deadlines and fail to use time management skills, tools, and study aids I recommend. Doing this leads to more stress in your already stressful life. Why add to your stress?

AT THIS POINT, you are probably wondering why people procrastinate on tasks related to goals they want to achieve? Procrastination often emerges as a means of distancing oneself from stressful activities. People allocate more time to tasks they judge as easy or fun than tasks they judge as difficult or boring. Dealing with the underlying stressful aspects of the activities can assist in reducing the extent of procrastination. We'll address the problem of stress management a little later.

PRO TIP - If the volume of work on your to-do list overwhelms you, you might benefit from making a "one-item list." Re-write the top item from your list at the top of a blank page and work the task to completion, then take the next item on your list and place that on a blank sheet, repeat the process until you complete everything on your original list.

SOME PEOPLE MUST OVERCOME procrastination gradually. Almost no one has trouble studying the night before a big exam. But without the pressure of an exam, many students find it easy to avoid studying. If you need the motivation for the looming deadline, remember to implement the five-minute hack.

THE KEY IS to learn the habit of getting started on a task early, i.e., the procrastinator needs to learn to initiate studying and preparing for papers and exams well in advance. Practice starting to study several times every day. As with exercising, getting started and making it a routine are the secrets to success. Other valuable suggestions include:

- Recognize self-defeating problems such as; fear and anxiety, difficulty concentrating, poor time management, indecisiveness, and perfectionism.
- Keep your goals in mind and identify your strengths and weaknesses, values and priorities.
- Compare your actions with the values you feel you have. Are your values consistent with your actions?
- Discipline yourself to use time wisely.
- A study session that utilizes small blocks of time with frequent breaks is more effective than studying in long uninterrupted marathon sessions. For example, you will accomplish more if you study/work in sixty-minute blocks and take frequent ten-minute breaks in between than if you study/work for two to three hours straight, with no breaks.
- Reward yourself after you complete a successful week.
- Motivate yourself to study. Focus on success, not on failure. Try to study in small groups. Break large

assignments into smaller tasks. Keep a reminder
schedule and checklist.

- Set realistic goals.
- Modify your environment: Eliminate or minimize
  noise/ distraction. Ensure adequate lighting. Have
  the necessary equipment at hand. Don't waste time
  going back and forth to get things. Don't get too
  comfortable when studying. A desk and a straight-
  backed chair are usually best (a bed is no place to
  study). Be neat! Take a few minutes to straighten
  your desk.
- Decide when you have had enough, and it's time for
  a change.
- Think about the activities that you use to
  procrastinate (email, TV, etc.) and set clear time
  limits on them.
- Set clear goals for each day (e.g., start CHEM
  problem set, do ENGL reading, finish MRKT
  chapter reading) and stick to them. Once complete,
  you are free to do whatever you like.
- Remember that serious academic stress usually
  follows procrastination.
- Recall the stress and loss of energy you felt the last
  time you had to stay up all night to write a paper or
  study for an exam. Remembering your feelings of
  anxiety can serve as an effective motivator to help
  you get started on time now.
- Know that overcoming procrastination is sometimes
  easier if you talk out strategies for change with
  someone else.

THE POMODORO TECHNIQUE

. . .

GETTING STARTED IS OFTEN the hardest part of any assignment, task, or project. The thought of sitting down in front of your computer for a few hours straight can cause you enough anxiety to want to head to the dentist instead. If that sounds like you have no fear, I have a solution for you. Enter the Pomodoro technique. A *Pomodoro* is simply the interval of time spent working.

THE POMODORO TECHNIQUE was originally designed as a time management technique, but it has been slightly modified to become an effective way to overcome procrastination in recent years.

THE KEY to the success of this technique is that it only requires you to focus for 20-minutes at a time. After 20-minutes you get to take a 5-minute break. When your brain knows you will reconnect to your social media, text a friend, or catch up on your email, it makes it much easier for you to engage and get started. And once started, you will build momentum, and you will be quite surprised just how much you will achieve.

TO MAKE THIS TECHNIQUE EFFECTIVE, you must be highly focused. You need to shut off your smartphone, shut off alerts on your other devices, and remove any other distractions. You need quiet, so if you have distractions that cannot be turned off, consider wearing noise reduction headphones or heading to the school library.

. . .

USING THE POMODORO TECHNIQUE, you start by deciding what the first important task is for the day (utilize the Eisenhower Matrix). Then you set a timer for 20 minutes and focus 100% on that task.

WHEN THE TIMER CHIMES, reset it for 5-minutes, get up and do some deep breathing, stretch out your body, jump on social media, whatever you want to do for 5 minutes.

NEXT, set the timer, jump back in for another 20-minutes and then repeat the 5- minute break. These 20- minute sprints are called a Pomodoro.

AFTER DOING FOUR POMODORO, you have a completed set. Now take a 20-minute break. Make sure you put a checkmark on a piece of paper or notecard after each 20-minute Pomodoro, as it is quite easy to lose track of how many Pomodoro's you have completed.

AS YOU GET into the swing of things, feel free to adjust your Pomodoro's to 25-minutes, 30-minutes, or even 2-hours.   I personally find a 2-hour Pomodoro with a 30-minutes break highly effective when I am writing books.   When grading papers, I use the 20/5 approach outlined here.   The point I want to make is that this technique is easily modified; play with the Pomodoro's to find what works best for you.

WHY PROCRASTINATION Is A Nightmare

. . .

GOOD IDEAS TAKE TIME. Whether you are working on a small assignment or a large paper, good ideas take time to develop and come together in a well-thought-out cohesive fashion. Most written assignments in college will require you to select a topic, then spend time developing your thoughts around your ideas, revising your thoughts, and finally fine-tuning and polishing things up. If you procrastinate and wait until the last minute, you won't have time to properly go through an intellectual process required to ensure a fully reflective and developed piece of work. This approach also applies to essay questions on tests and exams. You will want to allow time to reflect on the question rather than throwing out the first idea that pops into your head.

YOU WILL LIKELY RUN **out of time.** When it comes to strict deadlines-which is just about always in your college classes-you run the risk of missing the due date if you keep putting off your work until tomorrow. And the reality is that most professors will not give you an extension except in very special circumstances. It is not that they are trying to be mean, but once they make one exception, they will have to make hundreds. If your professor accepts late assignments, a grade penalty-often as much as one-third to one-half a grade a day will apply. Just don't take the risk.

YOU MIGHT BE BEING OVERLY **dramatic.** One of the key reasons we all procrastinate is to avoid the pain associated with actually doing the task at hand. In my experience, students overestimate the pain they'll feel while completing their assignments. It's quite understandable when faced with a 15-page paper, a 25-question problem set, or 50 pages of reading, you naturally feel the task is enormous and overwhelming, and the simple thought of starting makes your stomach sick. The reality is, if you just get started on a small piece and then another small piece, then another manageable piece, etc., you will see the assignment coming together. Your fear will disappear as you build on the positive momentum you have created.

THE TASK IS PROBABLY NOT AS HARD **as you think.** The reality is that thousands of students, just like you, have completed the task at hand. It's often hard to determine at the start of an assignment just how much time it'll take you to complete the assignment-especially if the topic is unfamiliar or covers a diverse area of topics. Just get started, and you will likely find that things are not as bad as you have built them up to be.

YOU LOSE **your chance for help.** Many students will want to enlist the help of a professor or a TA. But their time is limited, and many professors only maintain office hours a few hours a week on specific days only, and not every TA is timely when it comes to getting back to students. With most students waiting to the last minute, a classic supply vs. demand problem is created, especially if the assignment is challenging, and 75% of the students have figured out they are stuck three days before the assignment is due. By starting your assignments early, you won't lose the chance to consult with the professor or TA if you have questions. Even if you get answers to your questions at the last minute, you will not have time to implement your professor or TA suggestions, which will destroy your grade. Your Professor or TA will hate taking their time and providing feed-back and suggestions to see you completely ignore their advice.

. . .

CONTRARY TO WHAT **you might believe.** You won't work better under time constraints. If you put off your work until the last minute, your work will be hurried and demonstrate the shortcuts you took due to the time pressure. This experience will likely create stress, anxiety, and even guilt for putting off the work once again. This behavior will take its toll on your sleep, energy, and mental well-being. It simply is not the best combination for your health or GPA.

YOUR WORK WILL LOOK INCOMPLETE. One of the main differences between fair, good, and excellent work is that excellent work has gone through a natural cycle of thoughts, drafts, and revisions. The paper will flow naturally and follow a well-thought-out logical sequence. When the clock is ticking and your deadline is rapidly approaching, you will skip steps in the cycle and hand in an assignment that doesn't flow properly or hit on all the key ideas or concepts. Like a bad movie, the professor will easily notice the lack of effort into your work.

YOU PLACE **yourself at a relative disadvantage.** While you're busy being busy, putting off your work for another time, some of your fellow students are getting down to business and getting started on their assignments. These students will likely raise the bar for everyone and increase the gap between excellent work, good work, and average work. Many professors will fit their grade curves to a somewhat normal distribution or even limit the percentage of students receiving an A. Most universities expect the grades in a class section to follow a somewhat normal distribution or average grade target, ensuring a class is neither difficult nor easy. The university won't talk about this in their orientations or course program guides, but rest assured, behind those pillars of knowledge and

opportunity, proper course curve fitting is being discussed and
expected.

THE TASK IS THE TASK. Some students think that somehow the
task is going to get easier if they wait a little longer. If they give
it a little more time, some miracle or inspiration will strike that
will change the course of the assignment forever. Of course,
this isn't going to happen; the assignment is the assignment
once your professor assigns it. Get over it, and in the words of
Nike, Just Do It!

LIFE HAPPENS. Anytime you have an assignment that covers
some period or involves some research or builds upon lessons,
there is an increased likelihood that something distracting and
unexpected will arise, thus stopping or greatly slowing down
your ability to complete your work. You could catch the bug
spreading around campus at the speed of a viral YouTube
video. You could get food poisoning from the campus cafeteria.
Another professor could spring an assignment on you that
requires unscheduled time, or some work or family emergency
could pop up. Whatever the event, you can count on life
getting in the way, and if you have properly planned and
allowed some room in your schedule for these unplanned
events, you will be able to deal with things and not tank
your GPA.

BALANCING CLASS LOADS, assignments, work, and fun can lead
to a great deal of stress for the average student. It's important to
realize that this feeling is normal, and you will feel stressed
with so much going on in your life. You can easily start to feel
like your life is spiraling out of control, but you're not alone,

and your fellow students are feeling somewhat the same way. Consider the following:

- 85% of college students reported they had felt overwhelmed by everything they had to do at some point in the past year.
- 42% of college students stated anxiety as the top concern.
- 30% of college students reported that stress had negatively affected their academic performance.
- 25% of college students reported they were taking psychotropic medication.

IN THE NEXT CHAPTER, we'll explore how to hone your ability to concentrate.

4

HONE YOUR ABILITY TO CONCENTRATE

S uccess is heavily dependent on how you focus on what you do. Whether you are doing business, studying, working, or playing sports, focusing will help you achieve your goals. Unfortunately, we have to deal with numerous distractions in the digital environment that we live in today. Today, your friend doesn't have to pay you a visit to interfere with your schedule. A simple Facebook or Twitter message can heavily affect your to-do list.

OUR LEVELS of concentration have been heavily affected by the digital space that we float in. Most of the time, we find ourselves engulfed in social networks. What we forget is that communicating through these social platforms is not on our to-do list. How many times have you found yourself checking your emails and responding to them without any awareness of how much time has passed? This is a common thing that happens to most people. Besides going through your emails, there is a high likelihood that you will open a different tab to visit social media pages. Shortly after, you wake up to realize that you have wasted more than an hour of your prime time.

IF YOU FOUND yourself nodding about the time-wasting experience mentioned above, you should not lose hope. There are recommended strategies that you can adopt to improve your concentration skills. Before looking into this matter, let's take a closer look into some of the things that sway you from concentrating on what's important.

What's Killing Your Ability to Concentrate?

Mobile Phone

THERE ARE plenty of reasons that having a mobile phone helps in effective communication. With only the touch of a button, you can send your message to millions of people out there. However, we cannot overlook the fact that these smartphones have also affected the way we work. That's not all. They have also affected the face-to-face connections that we once had before they were introduced.

MOST PEOPLE CARRY their handsets anywhere they go. A cell phone is no longer a device for communication, but it has transformed into our best friend. Frankly, there are instances where you find yourself smiling aimlessly at the messages you read from different social pages. We no longer need the physical presence of our friends. Smartphones have occupied this space.

. . .

UNFORTUNATELY, THESE SMARTPHONES' constant vibrating and ringing derails our attention from what we should be focusing on. Instead of working or paying attention to meaningful conversations, our phones wreck our attention.

SUCH DISTRACTIONS CAN BE ELIMINATED by admitting that you should mute your phone when at work or when attending lectures. This gives your brain the ability to focus, which could eventually lead to enhanced productivity. You can find some free time to engage with your smartphone and catch up on what you missed.

NEGATIVE MENTALITY

A NEGATIVE MINDSET will also hinder your concentration. You should realize that you will be channeling your energy to worrying about things that you have no control of. We all have good and bad times. That's a fact. The last thing you should be doing is wasting your time and energy thinking about the hurdles before you.

NEGATIVITY THWARTS YOUR CREATIVITY. In the presence of negativity, you will not be as productive as you thought. Don't allow your emotions to get the best of you. Find someone you trust and talk to him or her about what you are experiencing. This will be beneficial because it creates vents to allow such negative vibes to flow away.

LACK OF SLEEP

. . .

WE ALL HAVE a story to tell when it comes to feeling sleepy during lectures. It's early in the morning, and you are struggling to keep your eyes open. This has happened to all of us at some time in our lives. Usually, this becomes a problem throughout the day. You will not study effectively since your mind is not alert.

LACK OF SLEEP has a detrimental effect on our concentration. It slows down our thought processes, making it daunting for us to focus (Schwartzbard, 2019). The effect is that you will find it challenging to complete a given task in time. There are various reasons that you might be tempted to stay up all night. For instance, if you are watching a film series, it could lure you into watching it all night. Nonetheless, it is important to stop and consider the benefit on your productivity the following day if you choose to sleep early.

MULTITASKING

ANOTHER REASON you will struggle to concentrate on what you are doing is your habit of multitasking. An interesting revelation that will strike your attention is that intelligent students don't multitask. Instead, they focus on doing one thing at a time. What's more, you ought to understand that multitasking is just a myth. The human brain cannot multitask. A perception of multitasking only does more harm than good to your brain.

. . .

RESEARCH SHOWS that when people think they are multitasking, the reality is that they are switching from one task to the other. The switch is done super quickly to the point that one thinks they are attending to multiple tasks simultaneously. Quickly switching from one activity to the other hinders optimal performance (Glowatz, 2019).

So, if you thought that you were saving time by responding to your emails while doing your homework, you need to think twice. Refrain from the urge to multitask and do one thing at a time. If there are smaller tasks that you should complete, schedule them for a later period when you are through with high-priority assignments.

Boredom

BOREDOM ALSO HAS a role to play in your lack of concentration. Unfortunately, this is something that you have no control over. There are particular occasions when you are assigned boring tasks to do. Honestly, this is unavoidable. Unfortunately, there are times when you just want to avoid what you are doing so that you don't feel bored with the task at hand. When this happens, the obvious thing is that you will try to engage in other unimportant activities just to kill time.

HOWEVER, this doesn't have to be the case, as there is a way to save yourself from the situation. If you are handling strenuous tasks, break them down into smaller tasks. This will help you realize that it is possible to complete the tasks without feeling bored. To ensure that you are excited about the entire process, reward your small efforts. Promise yourself to eat your favorite meal once you are through with the minor tasks. Eventually, you will boost your concentration levels and improve your productivity.

SOCIAL MEDIA

BEARING in mind that you know how addictive social media can be, you should make an effort to avoid the temptation to post your status and reply to your friends' messages. It takes a lot of time to browse through social networks such as Facebook, Twitter, and Instagram. You can bear witness to the fact that once you start responding to texts, your mind will be distracted. You will want to know what your friends are saying about a particular matter at hand. Therefore, it is in your best interest that you postpone your urge to post and reply to messages to a later time when you are free.

STRESS

STRESS WILL DEFINITELY AFFECT your performance at work. Your mind will not be present at whatever you are doing. Rather, your thoughts will easily sink into the difficult moments that you are going through. In extreme cases, you might risk failing to graduate due to a constant decline in your grades.

So, how do you deal with stress? Normally, your stress can be mitigated by engaging in regular exercise. It is a well-known fact that working out can make you feel good about yourself.

Additionally, you should practice meditation. Through meditation, you will boost your level of self-awareness, which will lead to improved levels of stress management.

Now that you understand the factors that prevent you from focusing, let's pay close attention to the specific ways you can sharpen your concentration.

Practicing Pre-Commitment

You can easily boost your concentration by practicing pre-commitment. Before taking any steps, you should commit yourself ahead of time to whatever you will be doing. In other words, you should embrace the idea of having a plan for every task that you will work on throughout the day. Your plan should detail the amount of time you will spend on each task. Therefore, whenever you sit down to work on a specific assignment, make sure that nothing diverts your attention until you complete that specific task.

Enhance Your Focus Muscles

When you hit the gym for the first time, your instructor will insist on the importance of building your muscles gradually. You can't wake up one day and decide to lift heavy weights because this will only harm you. The same thing applies to your focus muscles. All along, you have been struggling to concentrate. Therefore, you should start slow and work your way up gradually.

Challenge yourself with small concentration tasks. This can be spending 5-10 minutes working on one task without losing concentration. With time you can challenge yourself to work 30 minutes without being distracted. Remember, after working for about 20-30 minutes, you should take small breaks of about 5 minutes.

Identify Time-Wasters Early Enough

Another effective strategy to bolster your concentration is identifying distractions even before you begin working on an assignment. Create a list of the things that usually waste your time. Afterward, devise a plan of how you will circumvent these time-wasters. For instance, this can include switching off your phone. This will help in clearing your path so that you will focus more on what's important.

Learn to Say "No"

Saying "No" is perhaps one of the most difficult things to do, especially when you are unsure whether it is a prudent decision. It might be difficult to refuse when your friend requests you to go out and have a little fun. However, it is important to note that there is a way of respectfully saying "No" for the right reasons. Bearing in mind that your schedule is fully packed, there is no reason why you should say "Yes" just to please your friend.

SAYING "No" in such a situation would be helpful because it will prevent you from being distracted by other activities which were not part of your to-do list. Of course, this doesn't mean that you should say no all the time. The idea here is that you should say no when you are certain that you can always o out some other time.

. . .

DON'T SACRIFICE your time to please others. The bitter truth is that they might never realize that you are giving it your all to ensure that they are pleased. So, stick to your core values and master the art of saying no politely.

Stretch Your Concentration Muscles

In the same way that you need to work gently and stretch well when you hit the gym to strengthen your muscles, you should also think about stretching your concentration muscles. The simplest way to do this is by practicing daily meditation. This doesn't have to be long. By meditating for 10 minutes every day, you can rest assured that you will be more self-aware about what is going on around you. The good news is that you will also find it easy to deal with stress because your mind can focus on what is important in your life.

SO FIND an inspiring mantra that you will use during your meditation period. You can choose to meditate either in the morning or in the evening, depending on your schedule. Find a quiet place and recite your mantra for about 10 minutes. Ensure that you focus on how you are saying these words and the thoughts and emotions brought to your mind. When practicing meditation, your focus should not be on the feelings and thoughts that you are experiencing. Rather, you should only be aware of these thoughts and emotions and do nothing about them. This aids your mind in focusing on the mantra regardless of what is going on around you. Do this more often, and your concentration muscles will stretch and become more flexible.

5

IS YOUR SMARTPHONE A TIME WASTER?

S martphones have indeed revolutionized the way we communicate. With the advent of the internet, people developed a sense that they need always to be connected. Unfortunately, this has led to dwindling productivity among those who use their smartphones every now and then. What's more interesting is that, just a while ago, using your smartphone at work was considered counterproductive. Today, it is the norm. People are no longer afraid that using their smartphones will result in being seen as lazy or distracted. Employers have made things worse by allowing smartphones to be used in places of work. So, you ought to stop and question yourself whether your phone is a time-waster.

You Are Constantly Working

Smartphones provide us with the ability to work on the go. Plenty of applications can be used to bring your work home. Email apps, for example, make it possible to respond to emails without necessarily being at work. While this might sound productive, it's not. Why should you bring work home when you have the whole day to work? Knowing that you do certain activities later at home can simply make you lazy. You can fail to report on a certain project since you will work on it at home. This sounds like procrastination. Therefore, it is imperative to understand how your phone can turn you into a 24-hour working machine.

Constant Notifications

It is quite sad that most of us have turned into slaves of distraction. We have grown to accept that it is normal to be interrupted by texts, emails, and other notifications from the digital spaces that we have signed up with. One of the main reasons it is easy to get distracted by constant notifications from your handset is curiosity. You can't help but wonder what your friends are saying on social media. Also, you might be curious to know what your client said about the project proposal that you offered them.

SUCH DISTRACTIONS HINDER us from being mentally present. You are only physically present, but your mind is somewhere else. To overcome such interruptions, it is advisable to mute these notifications.

A Habit of Multitasking

The constant use of your smartphone will also drive you to develop a habit of multitasking. You will gain the perception that you can complete assignments while at the same time going through Facebook or Twitter notifications. Well, in line with productivity, this is a bad habit.

A Diversion from Productive Communication

Besides luring your mind away from work, your attention will also be diverted away from constructive talks in school. When other students are busy discussing handling their projects and assignments effectively, you might be too busy checking your phone. This prevents you from participating productively in engaging conversations with your schoolmates. This is something that you might have experienced before because your device could make you absent-minded. Instead of contributing to conversations, you find yourself grinning at something that your digital friends have said.

Using Your Phone Productively

The good news is that there are tons of ways to make sure that you use your phone productively. Here are some recommendations about how to use your phone in a way that boosts your productivity.

SEPARATE Yourself from Your Phone

A MAJOR ISSUE that turns the phone into a distraction when studying is its physical presence next to you. Most students will often place their devices close to them when studying. Some of us even position these phones in areas where they are easily accessible. For instance, if you are a left-handed person, the chances are that you will have your phone on your left side. This only makes things worse as you will be constantly tempted to check it. What's more, each time you see a notification, it will divert your attention. Therefore, it is wise to store it in a place where you cannot see it.

. . .

Practice Good Phone Habits

An interesting revelation is that your smartphone use not only affects you but it also affects the people around you. When spending time with family and friends, using your smartphone while talking to them is not the best way of enjoying time together. This is a common habit that is evident in most gatherings with family and friends. People are merely physically present, but they are busy responding to messages on their smartphones.

It is important to practice good phone habits by putting it away each time you communicate with other people. Sure, it might be hard to stay away from your phone for more than 30 minutes. However, it could help in building better connections with people.

Bunch Your Calls

People will often give excuses for the endless use of their phones. Most of them will argue that they have to make important calls, so they deserve to be excused. The reality is that they are only allowing these devices to control them. It is high time that you take control and bunch your calls. Set a time when you can make all these calls at once. This gives you plenty of time to focus on school and less on who's trying to call you.

. . .

BE Polite and Professional

IF YOU HAVE EVER RECEIVED a phone call from top executives, you must have noticed how polite they are. The first thing they ask is whether it is a good time to communicate. This is being polite, and it shows that the person on the other end of the line values your time. Ideally, this is a habit that you ought to emulate when making calls to other people. Help them understand that time is valuable, and you don't want to waste it talking.

THE CONVENIENCE that the phone provides might blind you to the realization that it is a major distraction to meeting your daily goals. Spending time on the phone is not a bad thing. However, when you are doing it at the expense of your studies, you stand to lose. It is important that you learn how to use your phone to your advantage and not to allow it to act as a time-waster.

6

ENERGY AND TIME MANAGEMENT

Your energy level and motivation are key attributes to successful time management. Just knowing what to do is not enough. Knowledge without proper action will not drive positive results. As Mark Twain was fond of saying "The man who does not read good books has no advantage over the man who can't read them."

Your energy, just like your time, is finite. Only it exists in somewhat smaller quantities meaning that it's all too easy to run out and end up completely exhausted. And that's when we start to use our time poorly and not get much done. Many will argue that you have plenty of time. Most of us do have a lot of time; otherwise, how did you manage to stream that entire season of your favorite Netflix or Amazon series? How did you find time for that latest's live stream, or how did you spend two hours today on your social media feeds? And even the busiest of us usually find time for sleep!

. . .

THE POINT here is that time management only works with action and action and motivation are highly dependent on proper energy management. If you don't manage your energy, then you'll find that you're coming back from your daily class schedule completely wiped out.

POOR ENERGY MANAGEMENT is why you end up crashing in front of the TV or staring at your smartphone or computer for hours, and this is one of the key reasons why we don't live life to the fullest! Unfortunately, this creates a negative cycle that makes you even more tired and less energetic because our bodies adapt and become much less efficient. Energy happens at the cellular level; our cells lose mitochondria and become less adept at converting glucose into usable energy. Most people are unaware of this process. People don't routinely think about energy, they don't recognize the importance of energy management, and they certainly are not in the habit of thinking about energy as a finite quantity.

LET'S look at how an example of this plays out every day across our great nation. Somebody somewhere this very moment has bought the latest product on losing weight and getting into shape. They take a look at their current daily activities, and they realize that they're spending a couple of hours in the evening binge-watching Game of Thrones. So, they figure that adding an hour of exercise most evenings shouldn't be a problem, right? So, they come up with an aggressive training program that they think will get the results quickly. Their plan will often include joining a gym, planning on five hours of running/lifting weights a week, and probably a 20 or 30-minute commute to and from the gym for each session. At the same time, they will recognize their eating habits stink, so they will change their diet, typically reducing their carbohydrate intake. With their new plan in hand, they will be filled with enthusiasm, excitement, and expectations for a quick transformation that lays just around the corner. The approach might sound admirable on paper, but in reality, it's completely delusional!

IF YOU'RE CURRENTLY NOT GETTING as much exercise as you think you should be, then it probably means that you're too tired, too low on energy, and too stressed from the daily grind of school or work or both. If you weren't, then you would likely already be more active in the evenings. If you're currently struggling to do anything in the evenings, what makes you think that you're suddenly going to be able to add five hours of intensive activity out of the gate? And all while consuming fewer carbs which are what give us energy in the first place? Do you see the problem here?

TIME IS ONLY useful insofar as you have the energy to make use of it and unfortunately, there's no getting around the fact that you need to rest and recuperate. Your plan may be to spend less time chilling in the evening, but unfortunately, the reality is that most of us can't touch that time. Recharging when you're out of energy is sadly not negotiable!

LOW ENERGY LEVELS leave you with two real options:

- Find ways to increase your energy levels so that you can get more useful hours in the day.
- Prioritize by taking other things out of your routine

to free up both time and energy for exercise or whatever else you want to spend your time on.

Sleeping Habits and Your Energy

Sleep Is Critical

WHAT DO you want to do when you feel really tired and have no energy left to do anything? You go to sleep.

YOUR BODY WILL TELL you quite plainly how important sleep is for energy. Sleep is something of a miracle cure for all kinds of ailments – it improves your memory, focus, attention, mood, and future sleep immensely. Sleeping is far more effective than any beauty treatment, any smart drug, and any supplement. Get the right sleep, and you will be well-positioned to perform on the top of your game the next day – it's that simple.

MOST OF US don't get the quality or the quantity of sleep we need, though, and as such, we find ourselves walking around like zombies. We get cranky, we get easily distracted, we get confused, and generally, we operate like shadows of our true selves. So how do you go about upgrading your sleep and recovering from your low energy levels? Let's take a look at some ways to improve your sleep quality.

TRICKS TO IMPROVE Your Sleep Quality

. . .

TAKE A QUICK CURSORY LOOK ONLINE, and you'll find that there are thousands of different tips and "hacks" that can supposedly give us better sleep. Everyone, it seems, has some tips that can lead to amazing sleep, and indeed there are many good ones out there.

BUT AGAIN, some of them involve a lot of work and very little payoff. So instead, let's focus on the tips that will make a noticeable difference and are relatively easy to implement.

THE GOOD NEWS is that if you're following the tips in this book so far, you should already find yourself sleeping much better. That's because you'll have more energy from more efficient mitochondria – and studies show that this is crucial for sleep. It's again something of a vicious cycle: low energy leads to poor sleep, and poor sleep leads to lower energy!

LIKEWISE, if you're eating healthier, you'll be getting vitamin D, zinc and magnesium, and all kinds of other important nutrients to help your body recover through the night. Finally, if you're reducing your stress, you'll find that this massively has an impact on your ability to sleep as you'll be able to switch off from the stresses of the day much more easily.

LET'S look at some specific actions you can easily take to improve your sleep.

How to Calm Your Mind

. . .

BUT WHAT IF you're someone who can't sleep? What if your mind is constantly active and you lie in bed with it racing, unable to switch off?

AN ACTIVE MIND is a problem many students face, and it can severely rob them of their energy levels the next day. You see, when you lie in bed and try to sleep, you might find that it makes you stressed. The fear of not getting to sleep, or the frustration and the expectation, are so great that they cause you to lie awake worrying. Most of us have had that terrible feeling that occurs when we look at the clock and realize we have to be up in just a few hours, and we have not gotten a wink of sleep. An active mind isn't exactly how you sink off to sleep!

TO GET AROUND THIS PROBLEM, we will take a page out of the CBT book (cognitive behavioral therapy). The idea is to change the way you approach and think about sleep. Specifically, you're going to stop pressuring yourself to sleep and to allow instead just yourself to relax. Consider sleep to be a bonus.

TELL yourself that it's fine to relax in bed and enjoy being comfy – because it is. That's good for you too. You can't force yourself to sleep, so don't try. Just lie there and enjoy not having to do anything, enjoy not having to be anywhere, and enjoy the feeling of closing your eyes and listening to your breathing.

WHAT YOU'LL FIND, quite ironically, is that as soon as you start taking this approach, you drift right off!

. . .

Should You Power Nap?

Even if you have the best plans and intentions in the world, there will be moments when you don't get the best sleep and all of your sleeping tactics fail you. What do you do in those situations? One smart strategy is to give it another shot later.

Power napping can help you get some rest, and several studies have shown that it can improve your productivity, mood, and other aspects of your life.

So, how do you take a proper nap? The key is to time it perfectly, aiming for a minimum of twenty minutes and a maximum of ninety minutes, not more and not less. The way our bodies cycle through different stages of sleep (the body likes rhythms!) necessitates the employment of these time bands. You will go through one entire sleep cycle in 90 minutes, going from the lightest stage of sleep to SWS (slow wave sleep) to REM (rapid eye movement) (rapid eye movements). You'll start to come around as soon as you wake up. You can also sleep for twenty minutes and then wake up before entering the deeper stages of sleep to avoid sleep inertia. If we have an option, ninety minutes is a better way to improve our performance.

The power sleep works like this: A power nap takes use of the benefits of the first two stages of your sleep cycle, which recur throughout a typical night's sleep. As electrical brain activity, eye and jaw-muscle action, and respiration slow down during the first sleep stage, you drop deeper into sleep. The second stage is light but peaceful sleep in which the body prepares for the deep and dreamless "slow-wave sleep," or SWS, that happens in stages three and four by reducing temperature and relaxing muscles even more. REM is the fifth stage, which occurs when dreaming gets more intense.

EVERY NINETY TO one hundred and twenty minutes, the five sleep stages resume their cycle. The first stage can last up to ten minutes, and the second stage can take up to twenty minutes. In stage two, we experience unique electrical signals in the nervous system that establish the connection between neurons involved in muscle memory, making the twenty-minute nap essential for the hard-working student wanting to recoup from a few days of missing sleep.

TAKE a Hot Bath or Shower Before Bed

ONE OF THE most effective strategies to aid deeper sleep is to take a shower. Taking a hot shower right before bed will not only relax your muscles, but it will also cause your body to create growth hormones and melatonin, putting you to sleep.

ALLOW yourself a half-hour of rest before going to bed.

THIS IS the one life hack that absolutely everyone should follow these days. Whatever else is going on in your life, set aside half an hour before bedtime to unwind and read a book. Turn off your phone and read with only a dim lamp on. Treat this time as "wind-down" time by not watching TV, checking social media, or having meaningful conversations with your roommate.

AS A RESULT OF THIS PROCESS, your mind will begin to relax and shed the pressures of the day, allowing you to feel more comfortable. In addition, less screen time means your brain will be able to produce more melatonin. When you gaze at a computer or television screen, your brain interprets the light's wavelength as sunlight. As a result, your brain behaves as if it's daytime, flooding your body with cortisol and keeping you from sleeping. And this is why it's critical to ensure that your room has very little light.

THE ADVANTAGES of having a half-hour to oneself to relax go far beyond improved sleep. Your life as a student is hectic, and you rarely have free time. It's common to feel as if you've reached your limit. Beginning to take time off to unwind will make school and life seem much more manageable.

GET Into a Routine

SOMETHING important to understand about the human body is that it works to rhythms. Your body likes routine because this allows it to learn natural rhythms – highs and lows that will stay consistent, ensuring you start winding down biologically at the right moment.

ROUTINES CAN MAKE a big difference in your ability to doze off, and it will also allow you to control the amount of sleep you're getting more closely. As you likely know, eight hours is a good ball-park figure to aim for if you can. Very few people can function properly in less than six hours of sleep a night.

Perfect Your Environment

THESE ARE THE "EASY TIPS" that pretty much everyone already knows about sleeping – but they're important, and so they're still very much worth going over. Your environment is another key to optimal sleep.

- Since most dorms can be quite loud, use a sleep machine or fan to create white noise and block out as much noise as possible.
- Get your dorm room or apartment as pitch black as possible.
- Keep your room as clean as possible.
- Invest in a mattress topper to make your bed comfortable.

OBVIOUSLY, it's also very important to wear comfortable sleepwear, invest in a comfortable bed if you are off campus (one of the best purchases you will ever make), and keep your room at the right temperature. The ideal temperature is for your room to be cool, which is how we are evolutionarily designed to sleep.

· · ·

IN THE PREVIOUS SECTION, we looked at how to get off to sleep and ensure we sleep well. That's one part of the story but what comes next is waking up the next day. How do you ensure you can spring out of bed and get lots done?

Your Morning Schedule and Your Energy

How to Wake Up Full of Energy

NOW THAT YOU know how to get to sleep, the next question is how you can wake up energized. Waking up is the key piece of the puzzle that most people overlook when it comes to sleeping well – but having a good night's sleep does not necessarily mean you'll be able to wake up easily too!

TOO MANY OF us wake up feeling groggy, sluggish, and tired, and as a result, we waste the first half of the day. Some of us will even feel sick in the morning or have bad headaches.

IF YOU FALL into this latter category, then, of course, this is not normal, should not be considered "okay," and is something you should discuss with your doctor. A few common culprits for feeling sick, having headaches, or feeling "drained" in the morning include:

DEHYDRATION – Try drinking a large glass of water before bed, and you won't wake up with a dry throat or a headache.

· · ·

Low blood sugar – When you go to sleep, you are essentially fasting for 8 hours straight without food. As a result, you can feel sick when you wake up. Some theorists even believe that this is why we have grown to eat dessert as the last meal of the day! Some people recommend having a teaspoon of honey before bed to provide a steady flow of sugar (sucrose and fructose) throughout the night.

Mold – If you have mold in your room this can leave you feeling ill owing to the mycotoxins that it releases. Some signs of mold include a musky smell and damp air. If you notice these things, it can be worth having campus maintenance or a remediation company check things out – even if you can't see mold it can sometimes be building up underneath the floorboards or behind the paint in your rooms!

Allergies – If you're waking up hoarse with a headache, then allergies are a common cause. Even if you don't think you have any allergies, remember that they can come on at any point during your lifetime, and as such, you may have developed hay fever or similar allergen. Allergies are especially common if you go to school out of state as you experience a completely new set of allergens.

Sleep Apnea – Sleep apnea is a condition that causes you to wake up for brief spells during the night because you've stopped breathing. In some cases, this is due to a blocked passage (obstructive apnea), but in others, it may have no cause (primary apnea). The best way to diagnose this is to see a doctor. Bring a video of yourself sleeping, ask a friend to watch you, your doctor will potentially have you visit a sleep clinic.

Either way, you might be prescribed a CPAP (continuous positive airway pressure) device to prevent the problem. If you are snoring, this may be a sign of sleep apnea, be sure to discuss this situation with your doctor.

IF YOU ADDRESS ALL these factors, you should find you start feeling much fresher and more energetic in the morning.

SOMETHING else that can help is to look into getting a "daylight lamp." These lamps emit a light wave very similar to the sun and will gradually get brighter in the morning. Daylight lamps can help to gradually nudge you out of deep sleep rather than waking you in the deepest stages of sleep. At the same time, these lamps can help to combat mild cases of "SAD" (seasonal affective disorder), which is a condition that leaves people feeling tired, lethargic, and even potentially depressed during the darker winter months. It can also help put your biological clock more in sync with your routine. In general, it's a very useful tool for waking up more gradually and naturally – it's certainly much better than being startled out of your sleep by a blaring alarm clock.

AND ANOTHER TRICK you can use that's slightly controversial for waking up in the morning is to use your phone. Many people will tell you not to use your phone in the morning to get up, but if you're someone who struggles to wake in the morning, it can be useful. The idea here is to set yourself up to receive something you're looking forward to in the morning – subscribe to some good YouTube channels, for instance, or join a Facebook community on a subject you're interested. Interesting content will serve as a motivation to get up first thing in the morning to grab your phone. If you can motivate yourself to do just that little bit and to start reading, you'll find that you gradually come around.

THERE'S AN APP FOR THAT – You might also consider using an app that offers sleep tracking. A great example of this would be Sleep Cycle and Pillow. These apps have a great feature that will wake you up from a light sleep by watching your movement during the night. You set the alarm – say for 7 am – and it waits for a moment near then when you're in light sleep rather than deep sleep. It might go off at 6.30 am, for instance, or 6.45 am but never after 7 am. This means you're now waking up out of light sleep instead of a heavy sleep, which helps prevent "sleep inertia." In theory, you should be much more awake.

SLEEP TRACKERS – can be great for improving energy in other ways too. Some have a constant heart rate monitor, which allows you to measure your heart rate throughout the night. Sleep trackers will give you a much more accurate measure of your sleep as well as your calories burned, and that in turn will allow you to run experiments to see which sleeping strategies are the most effective for helping you get proper rest.

WHAT TO DO FIRST?

SO, now you're out of bed, what do you do first? A healthy breakfast is a great start to your day and a coffee if you're so inclined (though in the long term, caffeine does more harm than good to energy levels).

. . .

USING THE TIPS ABOVE, you should be feeling fairly awake, but even with the best routines in the world, you'll still potentially feel a little groggy in the morning sometimes and need a bit of help waking up.

ONE THING that can help you to wake up then is to take a cold shower. A cold shower will not only shock you into wakefulness; it will trigger the release of norepinephrine and dopamine thus making you more alert and even speed up your metabolism to burn more fat. As a way to wake up, this beats a cup of coffee any day!

NEXT, you'll probably have to head off to class. If you are off-campus in a big city, then your commute is one of the very worst things for many when it comes to stress and energy. Not only is it stressful sitting in traffic or on a busy train, but it's also a waste of energy. What's more, if you walk on busy streets in the morning, your body will view this as the equivalent of being repeatedly surprised by hundreds of people. Did you know that "things moving toward us" is a universal fear that we all share? Fear and stress can drastically raise your heart rate and make you feel rather exhausted when you get into the classroom.

WHAT'S THE SOLUTION? Live on or very close to campus. Of course, you should look for a less stressful commute if possible, but at the very least, keep your commute time in mind when thinking about your energy and stress levels and be mindful to stay calm and relaxed.

. . .

IF YOU ARE NOT RUNNING off to class, when starting your day, remember that you're not performing at your absolute optimum when you first get up. A good type of work, to begin with, is something that you can do relatively mindlessly.

WHEN WE FEEL low on energy, exercise can often feel like the last thing we want to do. However, exercising is one of the most powerful ways to boost energy levels in both the very short term and the much longer term.

Exercise and Your Energy

Let's take a look at how exercise improves your energy.

SHORT TERM

IN THE SHORT TERM, exercise can give you a great energy boost which is why it's a good way to start your day. One reason exercising is so good for you in the short term is that it encourages healthy circulation. Exercise gets your heart beating which sends more blood to your muscles and your brain. That means more oxygen and more nutrients which is essentially like getting an injection of rocket fuel!

EXERCISE ALSO STIMULATES the release of lots of very positive hormones and neurotransmitters. If you've heard of the "runners-high," then you should know that jogging can stimulate the release of endorphins and serotonin. The result is that you feel very positive, very happy and of course very high in energy.

. . .

As a bonus, exercise is also one of the most potent ways to boost the therapeutic nature of your sleep (we saved this one!). When you work out during the day, you will burn more energy, which means you will be more likely to doze off at night, especially if you got lots of fresh air by working out outside.

Long Term

But the long-term benefits of exercise are much more profound. For starters, exercise will help you to burn calories and lose weight. Proper weight management means you'll be carrying less weight around with you and will feel lighter, nimbler, and far more energetic as a result.

On top of this, exercise will also help to improve your fitness. Improved fitness levels result in a stronger heart and a better VO2 max. VO2 refers to your body's ability to bring in oxygen and to utilize it for energy in a short space of time. A high VO2 max means that you can run long distances without panting or feeling out of breath. Exercise also just so happens to be the perfect antidote to all that sitting in class.

And if you can run a long distance without feeling out of breath, imagine how much easier that walk to class or that hike up to the grocery store will be!

Exercise also builds muscle, and believe it or not, that can also help you feel more energetic. The main reason for this is that it makes various activities less strenuous and tiring. If you've built strong muscles, then you'll find lifting things much easier, walking much easier, and pretty much everything else much easier too!

BETTER YET, exercise can also boost your mitochondrial count. Your mitochondria are the energy centers of your cells that help you utilize ATP and power yourself through your day.

EXERCISE INCREASES the quantity and efficiency of mitochondria and especially when you use HIIT. HIIT stands for "High-Intensity Interval Training" and is a type of exercise that involves brief bursts of exertion lasting a couple of minutes, followed by longer bursts of active recovery.

SO, while some exercise programs might have you running on a treadmill for ten minutes at fifty percent of your maximum capacity, a HIIT workout would involve sprinting on a treadmill for thirty seconds to two minutes. Power walking for three or four minutes and then sprinting for another thirty seconds two minutes for usually six to eight cycles. This type of exercise is more efficient in a shorter period and is generally a great way to give yourself a boost mentally and physically.

How to Train

USING HIIT is a good idea to get the most energy benefit in the shortest time. It would be best to combine this with some weight lifting to benefit from more physical strength (and weightlifting is very good for weight loss and improving your metabolism). I recommend three days of HITT with two days of weight training.   You Might schedule HIIT on Monday, Wednesday, and Friday, with weight training on Tuesday, Thursdays. Some students prefer three days of weights and two days of HIIT; both schedules are effective.

WHAT'S ALSO important is to avoid overdoing your training. Overdoing it is the big mistake that many people make when taking on any new workout routine, and it can end up being almost as bad as not exercising at all.

IF YOU LIFT weights until you are sore, for instance, then bear in mind that this now means you're going to be sore for the rest of that day and probably for the next two days. What's the point of being at your physical best if you hurt every time you move? Likewise, if you run too far and too fast, you'll end up feeling too weak and low on energy for the following days and nights. Continue this over-exertion too long, and it can eventually lead to "overtraining," which leaves you feeling tired, listless, and upset.

SOMETHING TO PAY attention to here is your heart rate variance. Heart rate variance shows you how well recovered you are after an interval and workout. Please make sure you train to the point where it's still fun, push yourself but not too hard, and listen to what your body is telling you.

REMEMBER - It is important that you visit a doctor before starting any diet or exercise training program.

Your Diet and Your Energy

Diet is one of the most significant contributors to low energy, particularly in general and students.

WE WOULD HAVE EATEN a diet that gave us a lot of energy and allowed us to chase down prey and perform at our best in general back in the caveman days. It is not by chance that the food accessible to us provided us with so much energy and that our bodies evolved as they did due to that diet. To put it another way, we evolved over thousands of years to flourish on what was available to us.

MANY OF US are now surviving on a diet devoid of all of that goodness (or at least barely any). Consult your doctor before beginning any diet, supplement, or fitness program to ensure that you do so safely.

LOW-DENSITY, Low-Carbohydrate Diets

IF YOU'RE like most people, you'll come home after class and pop a pizza in the microwave, grab something from the university vending machines, or get a cappuccino and croissant.

LET'S have a look at what you receive as a result of this. Well, you do receive a lot of calories in terms of energy. A typical store-bought scone contains around 600 calories. Then there's the vending machine chips, which will add another 200 calo-

ries to your diet, plus your drink and dessert, which will add
even more calories.

YOU'VE MOST likely consumed over 1,000 calories by the end,
which is around half of most people's daily calorie intake. A
poor diet causes us to gain weight, and lugging that additional
weight about with you is an unavoidable source of exhaustion.

IT'S ALSO NOT a good idea to cram so much food into your body
at once. You now have a large amount of food to process,
including low-quality protein, which will slowly pass through
your digestive system, depleting your energy for other
processes.

IN ADDITION, the calories you just consumed were "simple
carbs." The scone, chips, dessert, and drink are all simple
sweets that rapidly spike the bloodstream. That's before you
factor in all of the additional sugar. Suddenly bombarding your
body with that much raw energy may appear to be beneficial to
your energy, but nothing could be farther from the truth.
Instead, you're boosting your blood sugar, which causes an
insulin spike, resulting in a high. Insulin metabolizes sugar and
eliminates it from your bloodstream, but it is merely stored as
fat because you aren't utilizing it rapidly enough (a process
called lipogenesis). And guess how you'll feel once it's finished?
Exhausted! And you're hit by a wave of exhaustion (which, by
the way, is when most of us snack on more sugar).

WORSE YET, all those calories and simple carbohydrates have
done you no good. Why? The scone is made entirely of flour

and sugar, and the chips have little nutritional value. So, every day, all you're doing is stuffing your body with low-quality, large-quantity food to process. Is it any surprise that you're exhausted?

SUPPLEMENTS THAT PROVIDE Energy

I COULD TELL you to get rid of it right now. Stop eating that crap and reintroduce a healthy diet. However, it would be ineffective.

I'M NOT sure how I can be confident of that. Because you already knew your diet wasn't particularly healthy. You already know how much better home-cooked fresh ingredients are.

WHAT IS THE ISSUE? You don't have the time, energy, or money to change your eating habits. It's worth noting that energy is an issue here: it's a bit of a vicious circle, isn't it?

So, to jumpstart your self-improvement and drive towards more energy, why don't we start with a supplement stack. The following items can be taken with your meals to boost your energy levels significantly:

VITAMIN D IS excellent for two things: improving your sleep and helping you to produce more testosterone. The vast majority of us are deficient, so take this in the morning, and you'll start feeling a lot better.

. . .

IRON AND VITAMIN B12 are required to give us our healthy red blood cells. In case you forgot, red blood cells are the oxygen-carrying portion of our blood which our body uses to burn fat and fuel all kinds of processes in our body.

OMEGA 3 FATTY Acid is an essential fatty acid that the body uses to create cell walls. Increasing your cell membrane permeability is very important. Why? Because it helps the cells communicate with one another, it allows neurotransmitters to pass more easily between brain cells.

CREATINE IS a supplement used by athletes. Its job is to take the broken-down form of ATP (adenosine triphosphate) and recombine it for extra use in the body. What does this mean? Well, ATP is the main energy currency of all life. It comes from glucose and releases energy when the bonds connecting three molecules break apart. This results in ADP (adenosine diphosphate) and AMP (adenosine monophosphate) – a two for one. Normally, that's all the use you can get out of it, but you can reuse the energy by re-bonding the ADP and AMP back together with creatine.

THE BODY PRODUCES CREATINE NATURALLY, but you can get a little more if you take it in supplement form. In real terms, this means a few extra seconds of exertion when lifting weights or running a marathon – and it means better mental energy for performing your school work and fighting the daily stresses of college life.

.   .   .

LUTEIN IS GENERALLY THOUGHT of as a supplement for the eyes to help prevent macular degeneration. Recent studies suggest it could also enhance the performance of the mitochondria – the energy factories that live inside each of our cells. When given to mice, they would voluntarily run miles further each week on their treadmills – pointing to increased energy and performance.

GARLIC EXTRACT IS A VASODILATOR. Vasodilator means that it can widen the blood vessels to allow more blood and oxygen to get around – to the brain and muscles, for instance - thus fueling you with more energy.

VITAMIN B6 IS USED to help us extract energy from carbohydrates. At the same time, B6 helps with the creations of neurotransmitters which helps it to boost cognitive performance. Low levels of B6 have been shown to result in a lack of energy and focus and even shrinking brain tissue and Alzheimer's.

COENZYME Q10 is another substance that athletes are very interested in and which can considerably increase the efficiency of the mitochondria for enhanced fat burning and energy production.

THE PERFECT DIET

NOW THAT'S a lot of different supplements to be taking. It's quite a long shopping list, and it would get pretty expensive.

Here's the thing, though: you needn't be taking any of these supplements. Not if your diet is correct.

ALL OF THESE things can be found in your diet if you know where to look. CoQ10 and creatine are in red meats, vitamins and minerals are in all our fruits and vegetables, omega three fatty acids is in fish, lutein is in eggs.

IF YOU MAKE sure that everything you're eating is fresh and nutritious, then you'll be providing your body with all the energy it needs. You'll be able to absorb it better, and you'll be getting it in the right ratios and quantities. Meanwhile, other substances found in your diet can help to boost your energy levels as well: zinc, magnesium, vitamin C, PQQ, l-carnitine, l-theanine, and resveratrol are just a few. Eating a healthy diet is like having an incredibly expensive athlete's supplement stack! Only better.

MEANWHILE, you should try to avoid "simple" carbs. That's anything that tastes sweet (like cake) and anything white (like pasta or rice). Instead, start eating brown rice, and pasta, vegetables, spinach and have that in the place of your chips (as a rule, try to avoid processed, human-made carbs). Proper nutrition will allow the body to release energy much more slowly and provide you with a steady supply throughout the day. Don't be afraid of fat either – it contains more calories (9 per gram versus 4), but it's slow release too. Try to eat smaller portions, more often and don't over-stuff yourself.

. . .

How do you go about cooking these nutritious, fresh meals when you lack time and energy? A good plan is to prepare your meals at the start of the week. Cook up a few pots of food you can dip into throughout the week and keep what you don't eat in the freezer or plastic containers. If you purchased your universities meal plan, you generally could save time by cutting out the shopping and preparation time. Most universities now provide healthy and well-balanced meal options if you have the willpower to skip the dessert bar! A few students report they hate cooking because their roommates expect them to prepare food for them. If you live on campus in a dorm, a meal plan is likely your best choice. Most universities' meal plans include dollars to eat at your on-campus Chick-Fil-A, Starbucks, Panera, or national food chain of choice.

ON-GOING TOO FAR

WE EAT TOO many processed carbs. And if we ate less of those carbs, we'd feel much better. At the same time, though, we still need carbs. They're still an important food group in our diet, and if we get the right kind in the right quantities, they boost testosterone production and aid with our general levels of energy and well-being. Restrict carbs too much, and you'll feel tired. The occasional bit of brown pasta with your bolognese won't kill you. Many old-school bodybuilders eat nothing but rice and steamed chicken when training for competition.

LIKEWISE, while natural, unprocessed foods are healthier than cake, pie, and chips, you don't need to eat only the things you would find in caveman days. A lot of serious Paleo dieters will tell you not to eat bread, wheat, or cheese. And they will never break their diet to have a bowl of pasta.

BUT HERE'S THE THING: most of the top-performing athletes in the world have performed just fine on bread. Some of the smartest thinkers in the world drank lots of tea and ate lots of chocolate.

POINT BEING? You can perform just fine eating a relatively "normal" diet. And, our lifestyle places different demands on our body these days anyway; it's only natural our diet should adjust. In other words, don't waste your energy thinking you can only eat specific foods. Start with your current diet but make it a little healthier by cutting back on the simple carbs and by injecting more nutrients. As you feel the results, you will find your body will crave the junk less, and before you know it, your diet will be quite healthy. Some emerging research indicates gluten-free diets may have a significant impact on long-term positive brain function. As diet science constantly evolves, it makes sense to approach your nutrition and diet with a grain of salt and practice moderation in your approaches. Pay attention to how your body responds to your diet and adjust accordingly. Make sure to get an annual physical that includes blood work, as it is essential to consult your physician before making changes to your diet, taking supplements, or starting an exercise program.

Habits and Lifestyle Impact Your Energy

Once you've upgraded your diet, you'll find that you immediately start feeling more energetic. Diet is a critical part of the battle. But to improve your energy, you need to look at the bigger picture. No part of our health exists in a vacuum, and even the best diet in the world can't stand up to the wrong lifestyle or the wrong routine.

YOU'RE PROBABLY DOING a bunch of things right now that are completely ruining your energy levels. If you can find these energy black holes, then you'll be able to save yourself large packets of energy to use in other, more constructive ways throughout the day.

ALCOHOL and Your Energy

HERE COMES the bad news alcohol is very bad for your energy levels. As in, it's down-right awful.

IN THE SHORT TERM, alcohol is terrible for your energy and can leave you completely exhausted. Alcohol is a depressant, which means that it works to inhibit the firing of neurons in your brain, slowing down your thinking and making you sleepy. Alcohol, like a sleeping pill or anxiolytic, works the opposite of a stimulant. And because it causes whole areas of the brain to stop working, it can rob you of your higher-order brain function too.

IF YOU PLAN to be productive, think twice about picking up that beer or glass of wine. Drinking alcohol also has longer-term effects on your energy levels and general health. Of course, alcohol also contributes to weight gain at seven calories per gram. It can cause headaches the next day, and it significantly impairs the quality of your sleep. Try wearing a heart rate monitor when you drink alcohol, and you'll see it sends it sky-high, which isn't exactly conducive to a restful night! Although alcohol is a depressant, it amps up the body as it tries to purge what is essentially a toxin from your system.

IF YOU'RE DRINKING ALCOHOL, try to have your last glass a few hours before bed. And try eating a banana and honey sandwich as a hangover cure. It can work wonders as the banana and honey will line the stomach, replenish your energy stores, fix your electrolytes and break down acetaldehyde – a toxic substance responsible for a lot of the negative effects associated with a hangover.

WATER

SO, if you shouldn't be drinking alcohol, what you should be drinking is water.

WATER IS crucial to your energy levels as it's what the body uses for pretty much every crucial function. You've probably read stats telling you that your body is seventy percent water or thereabout, and it's true – you are mostly water.

TOO BAD THEN THAT the majority of the US population are chronically dehydrated! Dehydration leads to headaches, cramps, dry throats, and of course – tiredness.

.   .   .

How MUCH WATER should you be drinking? A good guide is to try and consume at least seven to ten glasses a day. Try this, and you should find that you start feeling energized. And remember, dehydration kills your cognitive function by up to 30%.

SITTING Too Much

As A STUDENT, the simple fact of the matter is that you probably sit far too much. You are sitting in class, sitting in the library, sitting in your dorm, etc.

SITTING IS bad for us for all kinds of reasons. The main one, though, is that it's terrible for our hearts – the longer you spend sitting during the day, the more health issues you are likely to develop over the longer term.

STRESS MANAGEMENT

SITTING for long durations is bad, but stress is potentially more destructive, which many of us experience on campus and on the job. If you are very stressed at school, you should not underestimate just what a severe impact this can have on your health, mood, and energy levels.

THE IDEA of stress is to increase our awareness, physical strength, and ability to think quickly. Thus, when we are stressed, our bodies respond by releasing dopamine, norepinephrine, and other "fight or flight" hormones. The chemical releases in your body increase your heart rate, direct more blood flow to the muscles and the brain, and heighten our awareness. At the same time, we might start trembling, our immune and digestive systems become suppressed, and we'll feel anxious and jittery.

ALL THESE EFFECTS are designed to help us in a fight or flight situation. In other words, they are meant to come on fast and be over quickly. If we saw a predator or prey, if we fought with someone, or if we saw a fire – then this would be exactly how the fight or flight system would work and, it would probably help us stay alive.

TODAY THOUGH, stress is not acute – it is chronic. Our modern sources of stress include exams, projects, papers, angry bosses, poor finances, strained relationships, and looming deadlines; all these things have no finite end or no imminent end at least. In other words, our body is constantly in this state of arousal, and as such, our immune system is constantly suppressed, leaving us susceptible to illness. Likewise, our digestion is also robbing us of the nutrients we should be getting from our food.

AND EVENTUALLY, the brain will run low on those fight or flight hormones. At this point, your sympathetic nervous system burns out, and you reach a point known as adrenal fatigue. You will then find yourself robbed of the neurotransmitters that normally help you get up in the morning and focus on the task at hand. And without these neurotransmitters, you will feel demotivated, low on energy, and listless – low levels of neurotransmitters lead to depression.

·   ·   ·

So, if you're getting to that point where you have no energy in the morning and where it's all just starting to feel a little bit too hard to carry on – you're probably experiencing adrenal fatigue as a result of stress.

IF YOU ARE in that situation, you should change some aspect of your lifestyle or routine. While it might not be easy to change your major or transfer schools, take time out of a relationship, or speak to a counselor – you must take positive actions. Ultimately, your health and your quality of life are what you should be putting first - above all else.

USING ALL the advice we've covered so far in this book, you should now be reaching the point where you are well prepared to manage your time, schedule, and energy. Even with this knowledge, though, it's important to realize that you still aren't completely in charge of everything, and you're still in some ways restricted by higher forces.

SPECIFICALLY, your energy will rise and fall with your body's natural rhythms. Your energy levels ebb and flow like waves, and at some points, you will be high in energy, and at other points, you will be low in energy. Energy levels are set partly by your internal body clock (internal pacemaker) and partly by external cues (external zeitgebers) such as social cues, eating habits, and light.

WHEN YOU WAKE UP, your body is flooded with cortisol, which helps you start shifting into first gear. Your energy then remains fairly steady until lunch, when you replenish your glucose stores and then again at 4 pm at which point you will reach a low point in your natural energy cycle. 4 pm is when many of us start feeling sleepy and wanting to curl up on the couch. We also feel tired after eating food while we're digesting, so if you eat a meal at 3.30pm, you may as well write 4 pm off completely.

YOUR ENERGY WILL IMPROVE after 4 pm but will slowly tail off until bedtime. There will be another slump, peak, and slump following dinner.

STRUCTURING Your Day for Optimum Productivity

SIMPLY KNOWING that these ebbs and flows exist and knowing when you're going to perform your best can help a great deal with your ability to stay productive and get the most out of yourself.

ANOTHER TIP IS to avoid having big plans after dinner. If you have anything productive to do, then do it before you eat. The minute you eat dinner and sit on the couch, your energy will be in decline, and your ability to be productive will decline significantly.

EBBS AND FLOWS APPLY on a larger scale as well. Specifically, you will find that you also have months where energy is high and months where you struggle. This ebb and flow can impact your exercise – you can have months of being highly disciplined and training well and then have months of low energy or a feeling you have plateaued. Don't punish yourself when this happens. Go with your body's natural inclination and try to plan tasks for the points in time when you are most likely to focus on and complete them.

INDIVIDUAL DIFFERENCES and How to Control Your Cycles

WE'VE LOOKED at the times you're most likely to be productive or sleepy during the day, and for most people, this will ring true. However, keep in mind that everyone is different. Some people are night owls and are more productive later at night, while other people are early birds and will tend to get their best work done first thing in the morning when the rest of us are still groggy and experiencing sleep inertia. Pay attention to your energy levels throughout the day, learn your cycles, and work to optimize your schedule continually within those natural rhythms.

AT THE SAME TIME, remember that you can control your rhythms to help your energy cycles sync up with what you're doing at any given time. The daylight lamp we mentioned earlier is one, and another is to time when you eat carefully. Not only can changing your eating schedule help you move that after-dinner slump, but it also actually affects your body clock. Eat dinner later, and you'll find it a little easier to sleep later. Daytime naps can also help with this.

THROUGHOUT THIS BOOK, we've covered a lot of different points, and right now your mind might be swimming with ideas for how to get more energy and how to change your routine for the better.

To HELP you cement all these ideas then, let's quickly recap on some of the tools and strategies you can now be using to get more energy:

START EATING MORE HEALTHILY
- Avoid processed foods
- Avoid simple carbohydrates
- Eat nutrient-dense foods
- Eat smaller meals, more regularly
- Eat complex carbs that release energy more slowly
- Don't get too carried away with fad diets
- Prepare meals in advance
- Supplement if necessary

EXERCISE more
- Use HIIT training to increase mitochondria
- Don't overtrain

MANAGE your sleep
- Have half an hour to relax in the evenings
- Take a hot shower before bed

WAKE up slowly
- Use a sleep tracker
- Tempt yourself out of bed with something interesting
- Take a cold shower!

. . .

PLAN YOUR DAY TO coincide with your natural energy highs and lows
- Do productive things first
- Time meals to adjust your body clock

Learn what works for you!

All of this might sound like quite a lot and especially if you're feeling low on energy. If you're exhausted right now, then can you be bothered to take up a new exercise program? Can you find the energy to bike to class? How will you ever find the time to change your whole routine? Find time to cook these fresh, healthy meals?

ALL THESE STRATEGIES might sound like a lot, and it might sound daunting, but that's why it can pay to keep in mind the Japanese principle of Kaizen. Kaizen means making small, incremental changes that all add up to something big and profound. It is like the Magic Penny doubling each day to create millions.

A SMALL STEP, like swapping your morning donut and coffee for a smoothie and experiencing how much more energy you get from this small change, will build momentum. It's a very small change, but it will make a huge difference, and you will find it very motivating.

IF YOU CAN'T COMMIT to half an hour of winding down in the evening, try making it ten minutes. If you can't commit to twenty minutes of meditation, do five minutes.

AND IF WORKING out five days a week is too daunting, commit to half an hour twice a week to begin. You get the idea.

THIS STRATEGY of small incremental changes is the exact game plan coach Pat Riley used with the Los Angeles Lakers to win the NBA Championship in the 1987-1988 season. During the previous season, the team had self-destructed during the Western Conference Finals, losing to Houston. Coach Riley spent the summer uncovering what went wrong, where they would need to improve their game to win the championship. Coach Riley and his staff identified five areas that each player on the team needed to improve.

DURING TRAINING CAMP for the next season, the coach challenged each player to improve one percent above the career-best in each of five areas. One percent doesn't seem like much, but if you take a dozen players on the team and each improves one percent in five areas, the team gains a whopping 60% improvement in overall performance.

BECAUSE THE PLAYERS saw one percent as very achievable, they could focus their efforts on small, realistic actions to improve. The results were amazing, with most players improving double digits, and one player improved an amazing 50 percent. The individual improvements translated to 67 team wins and an NBA Championship. The following season the team would repeat as champions, becoming the first team in nineteen years to win back-to-back titles.

. . .

SMALL, focused changes can go a long way on your road to success. And whether your goal is to win an NBA Championship, land that perfect job, or launch your own business, ultimately applying small changes and watching them compound over time will lead to massive success. And it all starts with just one small change!

7

CREATING BALANCE IN YOUR LIFE

S ocial life, hobbies, sports, friends, personal growth, learning independence, and other aspects of school life are all vital, and you must make use of all of them. However, there must be a balance struck. Too much of anything might detract from the broader strategic purpose of time management.

USE the tips and strategies outlined in this chapter to help improve and re-balance your life.

Working While in School

One of the hardest realities of the present educational system for many students is working part-time or even full-time. Every student's financial situation is unique, and only a small percentage of students have parents who have an infinite amount of income. Many young adults need to work to make ends meet, while others prefer to work to lessen their reliance on financial help or scholarships. So, how can you strike a balance between your career and your other obligations?

THE MOST IMPORTANT thing to remember is to communicate your daily class schedule. Make sure your boss is aware of your class schedule and speak with him or her about your time requirements. Many employers understand the struggles of working students. To have a successful coexistence with your career and your schooling, you must communicate.

MANY FAMILY-OWNED businesses are more accepting of students and are eager to work with full-time students as employees.

LOOK into getting a job on campus. Look for employment that fits into your schedule on bulletin boards, websites, the career office, and so on, or contact the human resources department and inquire about open positions. The majority of colleges will give you work in your subject of study. Working on campus eliminates commute time to off-campus employment and reduces the burden of juggling classes and work.

IN ANY PARTICULAR SEMESTER, don't try to take on too many hours. According to studies, students who work more than 15 hours at a part-time job while taking a full course load experience higher stress and are more likely to drop out of school due to that stress. While it's critical to have enough money to cover bills, it's also critical to focus on your academics.

.   .   .

MAKE the most of your free time. Review your notecards when you take a break, and read a chapter while eating a sandwich at your lunch or supper break. Discuss with your boss the possibility of studying on the job during lulls. If you work in a retail business, for example, see if your manager will let you study in between customers. When you make the most of your time, your chances of balancing work and academics improve dramatically.

WORKING while in college provides the student with more benefits than just the opportunity to earn money. Students can collaborate with teachers and administrators on campus, who can often function as mentors. Additionally, students can frequently find occupations related to their academic studies (lab work, research, etc.). Moreover, campus employment frequently allows students to explore a variety of career alternatives. At the very least, prospective employers value the fact that students worked during their undergraduate years.

IF YOU HAVE A JOB, don't be scared to tell your teachers. Most teachers have learned to ignore students who make bad reasons for not completing their tasks on time, but that doesn't mean they won't make an exception when necessary.

WORKING while in college is beneficial, but it is not for everyone. Working, like the rest of one's college life, should be viewed in context. Working should be a supplement to a student's academic endeavors rather than a detriment. Try it out; if it doesn't work or you run into academic issues, speak with your academic dean. Immediately!

.   .   .

IF WORKING GETS TOO MUCH, consider other routes for earning cash or modify your budget. You should NEVER let work hold you back from achieving your dream of a college education. There are many resources available. Take advantage of them! Use them! Go to the financial aid office and discuss your situation with a counselor there. You might be surprised by the options available.

CONSIDER some of these other tips:

- Get a work-study job if you are eligible. The Federal Work-Study Program offers jobs to eligible Federal financial aid recipients. If you receive Federal financial aid, your award letters will identify whether you are eligible for work-study and the number of hours you will be allowed to work.
- If you are eligible, you can go to your financial aid office and apply for available work-study jobs. These jobs can either be on campus or off-campus and are usually at a non-profit organization or public agency. These organizations generally let students work very flexible hours.
- Get a job that includes tips. Jobs with wages plus tips often pay the best. So, if you are looking to earn more money while in college, consider being a waiter, waitress or bartender at a local restaurant. Just keep in mind that these job hours may not be as flexible as a job on campus or a work-study job.
- Advertise your services. If you like to type or edit papers or tutor other students, why not get paid for it? Put up posters around campus that show students what you are offering and how much you charge.

Post on university social media accounts and local
online resources.

No matter what route you take to make more money, try to
find one that doesn't interfere too much with your schoolwork.
If you are having trouble finding the time to go to class or to do
your homework, try cutting back on your hours at work.

Another component of reducing stress and maximizing your
time is effectively managing your money. Whether it comes
from mom and dad or your hard-earned paycheck, money
management for college students is essential to learn.

Money Tips

Money certainly makes the world go round, and we all need to
be mindful of how much money we have and where all of it is
going. Money management is especially necessary for college
students. College expenses are ridiculously high with tuition,
books, fees, parking, room and board, rent, gas, date money,
movie rentals, etc. Effective money management is made easier
with these tips.

First, track your spending for two to four weeks to find out
where your money is going. Ask yourself if seven or eight trips
to Starbucks a week is really necessary? You probably don't
realize how much money you spend on little things like snacks
and drinks. Often, just by tracking expenses, you'll start to curb
your expenses and spend your money more effectively.

THE BEST WAY TO manage your money for a semester is to sit down and map out a budget. List sources of income such as scholarships, loans, money from summer jobs, and cash from your parents. Then list your expenses, such as tuition, books, and groceries. If your income is larger than your spending, you're on the right track!

GOING TO BUY NEW CLOTHES, going to a concert, or movie... make room for that in your budget. After all, you do need some fun and entertainment in your life. You'll get burned out if you don't have any fun. But be mindful of your entertainment expenses so that they don't get out of hand.

IF YOU SPEND, spend, spend at the beginning of the semester, you will be broke later in the term. Give yourself a spending limit for each week. Stick to it, and you won't have to eat macaroni-and-cheese every day in December.

BE careful with credit card use. Having a credit card is a good idea in case of emergencies, but having that little piece of plastic can make your spending get way out of control, very, very quick. One quick way to spend beyond your means is to charge it. Use credit cards sparingly. Once you get into the habit of reaching for plastic, it can be hard to stop.

KEEP ONLY ONE CREDIT CARD. You'll receive countless offers from credit card companies wanting to give you credit at recklessly high-interest rates to celebrate your arrival into the "real world." Find a card with a low-interest rate and use it as little as possible. And don't charge small purchases! You don't want to be paying interest on a cup of coffee!

IF YOU'RE AFRAID, you'll keep spending as long as there's room on the card, call your credit card company and request your credit limit be lowered. Keep at it. Card companies will try to boost up your credit lines, so you spend more. Just say "no" each time they try.

BE realistic about your spending habits. You can do what you want, but you can't do everything you want. You're going to have to make some choices. Whatever you choose it is going to cost some money. You need to understand you can't have everything and you have to understand there are consequences.

MAKE up for it next week if you blow your budget on something you want to do this week. If you go out to dinner and a movie one week, spend the money, be happy with your decision, then commit to staying at home the next week, eating at home, and not making any extra expenditures.

MAKE A BUDGET FOR LARGE PURCHASES. If you know a significant purchase is coming up, whether it's a road trip with friends or a car insurance premium, start putting money aside to cover it. It's far easier to save $50 each month than to come up with $600 when the payment is due.

BEFORE THE SEMESTER BEGINS, talk to your roommate about dorm or apartment expenses and divide them up. Decide who is bringing a refrigerator and who is bringing a microwave, and so on. This way, you may avoid making duplicate purchases and overspending while still having all the comforts that make college life easy.

THE MAJORITY of the large expenses occur at the start of the school year. Remember to compare pricing at online bookstores. They might be able to offer you a better rate than the bookstore on campus. Whenever possible, buy used books. Use the ISBN of the textbooks you need to search Amazon, Ebay, or Half.com. This number may usually be obtained through your college bookstore, and the prices are usually significantly lower than those charged by the bookstore.

REMEMBER that if you have a book you don't believe you'll use again once the semester is done - Thermonuclear Dynamics, The History of the Hobbit, etc. – you can sell it back to the school or advertise it online. Selling your books at the end of the semester can be a simple way to make some extra cash.

IT IS preferable to get assistance sooner rather than later. "I'm in difficulties and need $2,000," or "I spent my student loan money on an amazing spring break trip" are difficult to convey. The longer you wait, the worse it will become. While your parents may be upset that you've been so irresponsible with your money, I'm willing to bet that they'll be happy to assist you — after a lecture and tongue lashing, of course!

KEEP in mind that managing money is essentially about managing resources. Also, keep in mind that money normally functions on at least two levels within us. There's the practical side of things, where we buy things. There's also the metaphorical level to consider. Money may provide us with pleasure, friendships, and a sense of power. We must be careful not to let money take the place of emotional demands that must be met in other ways.

IF MONEY IS TIGHT, you can do several simple things every day to save money and avoid a financial crisis.

- Avoid eating fast food every day. Take a look at the school's cafeteria's meal plans. Purchase items that are quick and easy to prepare in your room.
- Clip coupons for items you buy frequently and keep them in your car so you may use them at the supermarket, fast food, or restaurants.
- Rather than going to the movies, watch a movie online.
- Consolidate errands to save money on gasoline. When you do need to get petrol, go to a station with a lot of competition nearby to enhance your chances of receiving the best deal.
- Stock up on items you know you'll need later at holiday and back-to-school bargains.
- If you can save money by switching carriers or getting a new cell phone plan, do so.
- When shopping, use a shopping list and stick to it as much as possible. • Keep an eye on the register when checking out at stores; purchases can easily scan wrongly.

FINALLY, as absurd as it may sound, considering college is a time of financial constraints, consider putting a little money aside weekly. A hundred and four dollars is still two dollars a week at the end of the year. Then, either for yourself or with someone else, do something exceptionally pleasant.

SAVING IS ALSO a form of spending. Check out these quick money-management ideas to see if they can't help you attain your college goals and ambitions. It is frequently stated, "You can manage your life by managing your time. You ruin your life by wasting your time." "Manage it, don't let it manage you," we should say when it comes to money. Now let's get down to business — having fun, making time for fun, and making the most of your college experience!

Party Responsibly

Parties and socializing are a big part of student life. And contrary to some people's thoughts, you should not deny yourself the right to enjoy the non-academic side of the university. However, some students are placed on probation or kicked out of school every semester due to poor decisions and actions taken while under the influence.   It would be best to keep in mind that partying is only a small part of the college experience. It has its pitfalls, and you need to be careful not to overdo it to affect your goals and future negatively.

WHEN YOU HAVE AN EARLY CLASS, avoid the bars the night before. You're just setting yourself up for trouble if you don't. Even if you do get up the next morning after a late night out, you won't be able to focus on your classes. The lack of focus will result in missing important information that you will need later on. Also, you won't be performing to your full potential if you're tired or hungover.

BE mindful of the downfalls of excessive alcohol use. I am not saying you have to avoid alcohol completely. If you're of legal age and you want to enjoy a drink or two, by all means, go ahead. But, it's easy for a few drinks to turn into a few more, and before you know it, you've developed a problem.

WARNING signs that alcohol may be a problem include:

- Missing classes or appointments
- Declining grades
- Aggressive behavior while drunk
- Erratic behavior while drinking
- Blacking out or poor recollection of events
- Drinking when under stress

IF YOU THINK you might have a problem, don't hesitate to seek help. Most college campuses have counselors on staff to help with problems affecting college students. Talk to your family doctor or attend an Alcoholics Anonymous meeting.

NEVER, ever drink and drive. Take an Uber, Lyft, or cab, take turns with your friends being designated driver, or walk (but be careful – you CAN get a ticket for public intoxication if you're too smashed!) Safety should be first and foremost in your mind – at all costs! Bad things do happen both on and off-campus. Always be safe and stay with a group.

. . .

THERE'S MUCH MORE to college life than partying, though. Enjoy the other aspects of the university. Join an organization that seems interesting and where you will find like-minded students. Were you student body president in high school? Look into the student council or get involved in campus politics. If you're interested in acting, consider student theater productions interested in business, technology, marketing, there is a club for that. Most colleges have hundreds of clubs ranging from soccer to science, spend some time on your universities website and check out clubs on display during orientation and other times of the year on campus.

SORORITIES AND FRATERNITIES are present on most four-year campuses. These are great places to make new friendships that can last for a lifetime. There's often a "rush" week during which time you can visit the houses and learn more about which groups you might want to join.

OFTEN, there is a voting process during which you will be accepted or rejected. Don't be discouraged if things don't work out on your first try. It is not a personal statement on your worth. Just don't give up. Being part of a fraternity or sorority can be great fun and a huge learning experience.

DON'T DISCOUNT LAID-BACK activities as well. Simply watching a movie or playing video games with your dorm-mates can be great relaxation and just as fun as going to a bar – but without the hangover!

. . .

HAVING fun is a big part of college life. You deserve to enjoy the whole experience, so be sure to make time for yourself and develop friendships and new interests.

So, what if you're a non-traditional student? Think this advice doesn't apply to you? Let's address that in our next section.

Tips for Non-traditional Students

Many older adults are going back to college to complete degrees they started years ago, fulfill a lifelong ambition, or train for a new career path. Time management for non-traditional students is especially crucial as the issue of children and family contributes to the already hectic life of a full-time college student. Some non-traditional students also juggle full-time jobs along with their studies. Finding time to study, take care of a home, work an outside job, and have a personal life seems out of reach. However, time management skills make it not only possible but also realistic.

REFER to the section in this book regarding using your planner. Having a planner and referring to it often is more crucial than ever with other activities going on in your lives. You will also want to invest in a dry erase board for your home in a calendar format to keep track of events, appointments, and homework assignments. Calendaring can be especially helpful so that your family always knows where you are. Keep the board in a convenient, well-referred place such as the refrigerator or by the front door.

. . .

USE a different color marker for each family member so you know who is where and when. List your class schedule on the dry erase board and have your family members record their activities along with times to keep track of everyone's schedule. It's a good idea to copy this same schedule down in your planner since your planner should always be with you, and you will always know how to schedule your hectic life.

REMEMBER why you are in college in the first place and make this a priority in your life. It would help if you talked with family and friends to understand that even though they matter tremendously to you, your schoolwork is a priority, and their support is needed.

ALLOT a specific time each day for studying. You need a quiet place with minimal distractions. You may want to physically write your study schedule on the dry erase board as well. Let your family know that when you're studying, you must be left alone. Then do nothing else during that time. Shut off the phone, stay put, and concentrate on your studies.

ORGANIZATION SKILLS ARE another key component to effective time management. While we have a whole section in this book on organization, some special attention needs to be taken to address your circumstances. You need to identify one specific place to keep all your books and reference materials. Keep a separate bag or backpack to hold that day's books and anything you need for class.

. . .

WHEN YOU STUDY, designate a separate study space where you can be away from your family. The key is to eliminate all distractions and focus on your schoolwork. Make sure you keep a supply of paper and pencils nearby this space as well.

TAKE ADVANTAGE OF "DOWN" time. You can study on your lunch break at work, while watching your child's soccer game, sitting in the doctor's office, or anywhere you have waiting time. Of course, in your car, commuting to class is probably a bad idea!

YOU MIGHT BE apprehensive and even nervous about returning to school, but realize that this is a normal reaction. You're returning to a setting you haven't seen in a while, and when you get there, you'll be with much younger people, which can seem overwhelming. Don't feel alone. Look around the campus. I'd bet you're not the only one there.

CHANCES ARE, the traditional college student won't care that you're older than they are. Once the class is in full swing, and you are part of the class environment, you may be surprised when some younger students come to you for help and advice.

TAKE advantage of all the resources your college has to offer, such as computer labs, library resources, help centers, and tutors. Don't be afraid to ask for help – especially from your professors. If you do not understand something in the class, arrange a meeting when your professor has office hours. Most instructors are more than willing to help out their students – especially the non-traditional ones!

. . .

ALMOST EVERY COLLEGE has a program for the non-traditional student that helps with adjusting to college life, honing your study skills, and dealing with the pressures of juggling studies, family, and work. Use these services as they are designed to help YOU!

8

TIME MANAGEMENT TOOLS

Technology has blessed us with many opportunities to enhance our time management skills. There are many tools available to us on the Internet that we can use every day to save time and make the most of our day. Let's look at twelve of the most important apps and tools you can use to help your time management.

Google Drive

Google Drive is a tool that backs up all your files. It comes with 15 GB of free space that can store anything that you have in the cloud. It is an excellent organizational tool that allows you to file many different items and put them in the right place. You can also create documents, Excel spreadsheets, and PowerPoint presentations. These items can be downloaded and saved to your computer or USB and sent to people via email. If you want to consolidate all of your items, you can do it using Google Drive. Then, you will be able to access the files anywhere you go. It is practical, efficient, and safe to use.

Evernote

Evernote is an effective tool for storing notes from lectures and to-do lists, among other things. All the items are effectively stored in the cloud, which allows you easy access. You can also organize your notes, so you don't have to sort through every file one by one. Also, you can pull it up on your mobile device or computer (O'Donovan, 2020).

MindNode

Have you ever heard of mind-mapping? This tool helps you map out your day, activities, and goals. It allows you to put everything in one place to do your work efficiently.

My Life Organized (MLO)

Looking for a way to sort through your ever-increasing to-do list? Look no further than the app, My Life Organized, which will help you effectively create to-do lists that are all consolidated in one place, so you won't be aimlessly going through life (O'Donovan, 2020).

1Password

Do you find yourself frequently forgetting your password to different apps and websites? Forget no more with this app, which uses one password to store all your passwords in one secure place, so you'll never forget your passwords again. You can easily pull up the app with your 1Password app, and then you'll save time and memory.

Pocket – Keep Your Eye on the Ball

Have you ever found a website that you liked and wanted to save for future reference? Pocket consolidates the websites you want to view and makes it easier for you to access later. Then, you won't lose the websites you just looked at and have to search for them again (O'Donovan, 2020).

Focus@Will

This app boosts your attention span and enables you to focus on the tasks at hand through interactive activities that will greatly benefit your life.

Alfred

With this tool, you can intelligently interact with your computer because you use small keystrokes and commands to access your documents, perform scans, and other computer activities. It is an effective way to save time and energy. Plus, you have the feel-good experience of knowing you are "high-tech."

TimeTree

This interactive tool lets you share calendars, to-do lists, and other key information with family members. There is no more needing to give a paper to someone. Instead, you can use your phone or computer and share everything with your friends and family. It is highly effective.

Todoist

Todoist is a great tool to capture and order all your activities to be consolidated into one big to-do list that will keep you organized. This tool works wonders for you, as you need to write down your to-do list on a piece of paper or in your notepad (O'Donovan, 2020).

Trello

Trello is an app that helps you chart your progress on various projects and tasks on your to-do list. You can create cards that represent what you need to do and then watch as you put status symbols like To Do, In Progress, or Completed. It's a motivating way to stay organized.

Forest

In this app, you will build a digital forest, representing the tasks on your to-do list and your success in completing them. You plant a digital tree and watch it grow. If you stay focused and complete your assignments, then the tree will grow. If you lose your focus, the tree will too. Using this digital tool, you will feel that you are creating something that needs nutrition and sustenance. It is a great metaphor for your life (O'Donovan, 2020).

TECHNOLOGY TOOLS ARE useful in our everyday lives. They make simple tasks much easier to accomplish. We might find ourselves unable to manage our time well, but it is possible to make a meaningful life and do tasks much more efficiently and quickly with the preceding twelve tools. Because of today's fast-paced world, time is of the essence, and we must find ways to cut down on useless time spent doing tasks that bear no meaning or significance. Therefore, it is crucial to find ways to save time that will benefit us in the long run. Use technology to save you a lot of time and trouble, so you have more time for yourself to enjoy life.

CONCLUSION

Thank you for purchasing this book!

I hope you have enjoyed reading it and that it has been helpful and valuable in teaching you how to be more efficient with your time.

The next step is to continue practicing what you have learned, and in doing so, you will continue to increase your productivity and live a happier life.

Finally, if you enjoyed this book, giving a review online would be greatly appreciated!

Thank you and good luck!

PERSONAL FINANCE

FOR TEENS AND COLLEGE STUDENTS

THE COMPLETE GUIDE TO FINANCIAL LITERACY FOR TEENS AND YOUNG ADULTS

KARA ROSS

INTRODUCTION

One of the reasons poor people are sometimes considered happier than the rich is that they do not have to deal with the guilt and self-blame that comes from the poor handling of funds. Many times, money "passes" through our coffers than stays. The art of saving and planning the use of money is essential and is key to finding peace in life. This should be instilled in our lives at a very young age so that even when we are old, we will look back and smile at our financial journey. It is good to never worry about money because you will have amassed enough to cover your needs. It is everyone's dream to achieve financial freedom earlier rather than later.

It is often said that money—whatever the amount—can never be enough, but there sure should be a ceiling to that statement. Some simple things can be done today to better your financial situation tomorrow. Unfortunately, most people only realize this late, when many years have been wasted, and there isn't much that can be done to better the situation. This book is meant to teach young people to manage their finances and build sizable financial knowledge from a very young age.

Sources of income differ from individual to individual. Some people get into jobs at very young ages and have paychecks coming in. Some may be earning dividends, getting royalties, and other varying sources of income. As young adults, the urge is usually to spend the money and live "the life." While that may be the 'in thing", being wise with your money helps you in the long run. The future depends on today.

Your personal finances are crucial to you, especially in our current economic times. It is important to know as much as you can about managing your money. You want to be armed with as much information to help you stay on track with your finances. It may be difficult, but perseverance, determination, consistency, and educating yourself will assist you in making it through.

Maybe you want to avoid drowning in debt after seeing people falling into the trap, but you don't know how to go about it. The more you try to avoid debt, the more challenging it becomes.

You probably aren't managing your money well because you don't have any prior money-management experience. Sadly, after several attempts to get vital money-management tips online, you end up with nothing, and you feel help isn't ever coming your way. Maybe you've started applying some financial strategies but don't know if they can help you attain your financial goals. Again, you probably have some bucks but don't know what to do with them. Perhaps you hope to save some money to reach a particular goal, but you don't know how much to save, weekly or monthly, to achieve your objective.

Just imagine how you'd feel knowing that you could avoid debt by saving more money. You wouldn't struggle to become a self-made millionaire if you knew the right strategies to manage your money. Maybe you wouldn't struggle to save sufficient money to attain your financial goal if someone had shown you investment accounts to grow your money.

My passion for helping teens and college students secure their future and finances birthed this book. The lessons I've learnt about money are massive, and they're presented in this book. I am about to tell you the tricks I used to regulate my finances and avert the headaches of living paycheck to paycheck. I hope you practice the tips within and reap the benefits; I'm sure they will help you manage your money and prepare for future financial obligations. With the help of this book, you can attain your money goal.

This guide is not only a mirror through which you see yourself in the future but a handy informant on how to get there. Dreaming alone is not enough. One has to act to bring the dream to fruition. This book's guidelines will help you start acting today for the life you want to live tomorrow. You do not want to look back at your young life and say, "If only I had known."

Your journey to being successful with money starts with planning, which is our focus in Chapter One. I hope you enjoy it.

1

PLAN AHEAD

It's been a long time since I finished high school, but the experiences of those days still linger in my mind. I remember how indecision almost cost me an entire academic session. My father would credit my account twice in the space of two weeks: the first credit was to settle all my educational needs, including my school fees, while the second would address my personal needs.

I DIDN'T HAVE any problem with my academic needs. The school usually addressed that as soon as each student paid their fees. So, I quickly listed my personal needs; I knew I would purchase some clothes and a pair of boots.

THE FIRST BATCH of credit came in as expected a few days before resumption. And, since payment of school fees could be made within the first four weeks of resumption, I went for my personal needs first. A week later, my father lost his job, and I was on the verge of losing an academic session.

. . .

I WASN'T my old self. Regrets were written all over me, and I felt that my whole world had crumbled. Two of my two closest friends knew that I was distraught. They asked the cause of my problem, and I told them everything. Eventually, they helped me with some money, and I was able to pay my school fees. I owe them my life.

LACK OF PLANNING can negatively impact your ability to grow your money and manage it appropriately. So, this chapter will focus on budgeting, different budgeting methods, what to include in your budgets, and a few budgeting tips to make the right money decisions. If you can't account for how you spend your money, or you're struggling to manage your finances, get your budget; the budget will pitch your income against your expenditure and expose the items you're spending money on. Again, it can help you determine the amount to save or invest.

BUDGETING IS critical to financial freedom. If you don't have a budget, you can't be successful with money. As a spending plan, the budget pays keen attention to current and future income and expenditure.

Core Reasons Why Successful People Create Budgets

Do you feel like spending all the money you earn? No problem; most teens and college students do. But that is not the best way to live. You attain financial freedom by saving and investing your money, not by spending it. Little wonder that experts say you need a budget to manage your finances efficiently (Bell, 2021).

. . .

HERE ARE the benefits of creating a budget and sticking to it:

1. Identifies your long-term goals and adheres you to them.

DO you hope to purchase a house, buy a car or take a trip to Paris, Dubai, New York, or some other beautiful cities worldwide? Fine, but you won't achieve any of these long-term goals if you aimlessly spend your money on every attractive item you encounter.

BUT YOU WON'T HAVE any problem if you have an operational budget. The budget will force you to concentrate on your goals, save money, track your progress and achieve your dreams.

IT IS painful to know that you won't be purchasing your favorite Xbox game or cashmere sweater, but when you remember that you are saving to buy a house or a car, you will gladly leave the store with nothing.

2. Helps you avoid unnecessary debts.

DON'T ALLOW anything or anyone to make you spend more than you can spare. Some people accumulate credit card debt because they can't take their eyes off certain items when they shop in stores and other marketplaces. It would make sense that, according to one study, in 2020, the average American household had credit card debts of $7,027 (Bell, 2021).

You won't have to worry about unnecessary debts if you have a budget and follow it; you will know how to balance your income and expenditure. Again, instead of wallowing in debts, you will be saving toward your short-term and long-term goals. So, this time next year, your spend-happy pals and colleagues will be visiting debt counselors while you're getting ready to move into a new house, drive a new car, or jet off to your favorite destination.

3. Prepares you for the future.

It's okay if you stick to your budget, spend wisely, and never accumulate any credit card debt, but don't forget that you will need to save more money to secure your future.

Make investment contributions an aspect of your budget, and you will have a financially secured future. How? Channel a particular percentage of your income into your 401(k), IRA, or other retirement plans. It doesn't matter if you have to cut down some expenses to secure your future.

4. Helps you deal with emergencies.

Unexpected situations like layoffs from work, sickness, injury, and divorce can be sources of your financial problem. You can't deal with these situations if you don't have an emergency fund.

YOU ARE PROTECTED from these emergencies if you have an operating budget. The budget will create room for the emergency fund. Financial experts say that an ideal emergency fund would cover three to six months of your expenses. The fund will help you avoid financial crises and unnecessary debt.

RAISING it will take some time, but don't be tempted to move a significant part of your income there. Instead, grow the fund slowly by adding a consistent amount –$10 or $20 each week.

5. Exposes negative spending habits.

I'M sure you've heard something about impulse buying. It happens when you purchase items you barely need – and that's fine; a recent study revealed that most teens and young adults spend money on items they don't need. But such habits can prevent you from reaching your financial goals.

IF YOU WANT to monitor your spending habits, budget your finances. A budget will focus your attention on your financial goals, not just your spending habits.

CREATE a budget if you want to control your money; otherwise, should it go the other way, you will have many threatening financial problems to deal with. Make sure to design your budget since you wouldn't want to lose control over your money. If you are struggling with saving and want to be free, create a budget.

Top Money-Saving Tricks For Teens And College Students

Many young people have difficulties saving money. Some would gladly spend every buck they see or earn because they often think cash will continue to flow in endlessly. They hardly recognize that unforeseen circumstances could cause them financial difficulties in the future.

DON'T BE LIKE THEM. Instead, set aside some money weekly or monthly. The little money you save will surely do your world some good. Sure, it may not now, but you will use the savings soon enough. Use these simple money-saving tricks to attain future financial success:

1. Create a budget.

IT IS SIMPLE: you can't save if you don't have a budget. Again, an allocation doesn't guarantee your success with money if you fail to stick to it.

A BUDGET SHOULDN'T STOP you from having fun or enjoying your life; it only helps you decide how to spend your money and what percentage should go toward entertainment, bills, savings, and other things you might want to achieve.

. . .

YOU CAN USE *MyMoney* or any other online mobile banking app to monitor your income and expenditure.

2. Save and invest your money.

RIGHT NOW, you may be facing some challenges in saving and investing. Don't allow the obstacles to stop you from keeping a few dollars aside every week. Soon, maybe even after a year or two, the amount you have saved will amaze you. A careful assessment of your budget will show you how much you can channel into your savings account every month.

DEAL with the investing part by asking whether your employer has a 401(k) account, then decide the percentage to contribute from your salary. You are free to increase your future contributions.

IT'S okay if your employer doesn't offer the 401(k) retirement plan: you can opt for a Roth IRA. Self-employed people can also take advantage of the IRA retirement package.

3. Save one-third of your income.

NO AMOUNT of money is too small to save. But experts say that you should strive to keep one-third of your income if you want to attain financial freedom in no distant time. For them, you will cope with future financial difficulties – like unforeseen expenses, layoffs, or home and car repairs – if you can save $1 out of each $3 you earn. Does that look difficult or even impossible? There's no obstacle you can't crush if you believe. Just cut some of the items you spend money on to increase your savings.

4. Start an emergency fund.

UNFORESEEN EXPENSES CAN EXPOSE you to financial hardship, especially if you don't have an emergency fund. Identify a high-interest money market or savings account, and put some money there. Then, should you have any future financial problems, you know where to get the money. Financial experts say that your emergency fund should be up to your three to six months' expenses.

5. Pay off your debts.

SAVING CAN BE a great way of securing the future, but don't allow your debt profile to grow just because you are trying to save some money. Pay off every penny you owe if you hope to attain financial freedom someday. Debt can cause you serious financial issues, especially when you need a loan to set up a business or make a substantial purchase. It can have negative impacts on your creditworthiness.

IF YOU FOLLOW these tricks wholeheartedly, you won't believe the amount you'll save in the next few months.

· · ·

IF YOU WANT to be successful with money, you can learn and apply a few financial skills.

Financial Skills Every Young Adult Must Have

If you are displaying any financial skills right now, I want you to know that you were not born with them. Over time, you can learn a few financial skills through mistakes, but you surely need more than your current skills to be successful with money.

EVERY TEEN and college student must have these financial skills, according to the Take Charge America Team (n.d.):

1. Basic budgeting.

GETTING to know how to plan or structure a budget is key to financial freedom. It is a skill you must have as a teenager. A budget shows your income, expenditure, and items you are spending money on. You don't have to sweat over it since tons of mobile budgeting apps you could use. Again, most of these apps are free and available for download on the *Apple* and *Play* stores.

2. Bank account basics.

YOU NEED to understand a few banking basics like overdrafts, overdraft fees, minimum balance requirements, and service fees. You will learn everything about banking in the next chapter.

3. Wants versus needs.

GET to know the differences and similarities between wants and needs as soon as possible. The concept of needs and wants is quite simple, just like budgeting, yet you can easily misinterpret them if you are not careful enough.

NEEDS COVER basic things you would use to sustain your life, such as food, clothes, shelter, and education. *Wants* are other desires, like video games and books. Wants must wait when money is tight.

4. Saving for emergencies.

TEENS AND COLLEGE students may not have a fully funded, ready-to-go emergency savings account yet. But, the earlier they know to prepare for unexpected medical bills, job loss, major car repairs, or other true emergencies, the better for them. It would be best to start saving money for potential future troubles.

5. Positive credit history.

. . .

YOU CAN EASILY ACCOMPLISH your future financial goals if you start developing or building a good credit history right now. Just know that credit card debt and other financial mistakes you make today can threaten your future financial goals. Pay all your bills in full and on time if you hope to have a clean credit history. We will discuss this more in Chapter Four.

6. Know that nothing is guaranteed.

THAT JOB you cherish so much can disappear in no time; nothing is guaranteed in this life. So, start preparing for undesirable circumstances right now, so you won't feel the impacts of misfortune when they strike. And, what's the best way you can prepare? Start saving money.

7. Understand when to get help.

TEENS AND COLLEGE students are prone to financial mistakes, just as are older generations. Some of these mistakes can be too big for you to handle, especially with the economy as it is. Still, help is just a block or two away; student loan counseling and credit counseling may be all you need to avoid an imminent financial mess.

GET familiar with these skills or face a severe monetary crisis. If you have a budget and stick to it, you will have few or no financial challenges to deal with. However, according to James (2021), the success of a budget depends on some specific issues.

Logical Things to Do Before You Create a Budget

Evaluate your financial goals and priorities before you create your budget. If you aren't doing this, you will have the wrong budget and failed dreams (James, 2021). These fundamental issues will determine the fate of your budget:

- *Purpose of the budget:* What's motivating you to create a budget? Is it because you want to purchase a house, buy a car, pay off a debt or save for retirement? If the reason isn't tangible, creating the budget and sticking to it will become very difficult. Wait a moment and reflect on what's motivating you to make that budget.
- *Significance of financial goals:* It's okay if you have many goals to reach. But, if you hope to come up with outstanding budgets, rank your financial objectives according to their importance. For example, if you want to purchase a house, buy a car, pay off debt and save for retirement, rank the goals and focus on them one after the other. If two or more goals happen to have an equal level of importance, try handling them simultaneously.
- *Budget goals' deadlines:* A deadline can make a financial goal look concrete and motivate you to attain the goal. Let's say you want to save $100,000 in your 401(k) or Roth IRA in five years; a deadline will help you figure out how much to contribute each month, to reach the goal. Again, if you set a deadline for a financial goal, you can quickly identify the expenses you need to cut to attain the goal.
- *Expenses to cut in the budget:* Identify the payments you need to cut to achieve your financial goals. For

example, instead of patronizing eateries, pack your lunch at home – that's going to save you some extra bucks. Don't wait until you develop the budget before you create a list of expenses to cut. This is a way to make each dollar count.

- *Erratic areas of the budget:* People have spending issues: some hate cooking their food at home, whereas others are addicted to shopping; some have a hard time avoiding impulse purchases in supermarkets and grocery stores. What's your harmful spending habit? Identify it and find a way to deal with it. Let's say restaurant dinners are draining your savings: start cooking at home. If you are addicted to shopping and impulse purchases, work on your mindset. Prioritize your needs, not your wants.

Reasonable Tips on How to Budget Your Money

Create a budget to regulate expenses, boost savings and attain your financial goals. Use budgeting apps or simple spreadsheets to make a budget; *Personal Capital, Count About, Digit, PocketSmith, Money Patrol,* and *Trim* are amazing budgeting apps that you can utilize to develop a budget, according to Barret (2021).

PAY attention to these tips because they will guide you through the budget creation process (Vohwinkle, 2021):

1. Compile your financial statements.

. . .

GET your financial statements before you start designing your budget. Such information may include investment accounts, credit card bills, bank statements, mortgage loan statements, and recent utility bills. The statement will show everything about your income and expenditure, especially where your money is going. So, if you're overspending on certain items, you will see it as soon as you get your financial statement.

2. Compute your income.

HOW MUCH DO you earn per month? If your income isn't fixed, pay attention to what flows in every month. Still, your baseline income could be the least that you made in the previous year. Let's say the lowest income you had in the last year was $1500. Go ahead and adopt it as your income.

3. List your monthly expenses.

STATE THE PAYMENTS you hope to make in a month. Such expenses may include insurance, savings, student loans, groceries, travel, utilities, personal care, and transportation costs. If you are struggling to identify the items you spend money on, your credit card statements, receipts, and bank statements for the last three months can be of help.

4. Differentiate between fixed and variable expenses.

. . .

MANDATORY EXPENSES LIKE CAR PAYMENTS, trash pickup, internet service, and rent or mortgage payments are fixed expenses; most of the time, the amount you pay for this basic stuff doesn't change. Should you want to save a particular percentage of your income monthly, add this amount to your fixed expenses.

IN CONTRAST, variable expenses aren't constant. They include fees on groceries, gifts, entertainment, and gasoline.

DETERMINE the amount to spend on each category each month. Survey your bank transactions for the last three months to get a rough spending estimate on your fixed and variable expenses.

5. Aggregate your income and expenses separately.

IT'S okay if your income is more than your expenses. Create a 401(k) or Roth IRA account and put the extra money there. You can also use the funds to pay off your debts (if you have any).

IF YOUR INCOME is less than your expenses, you should find a way to trim your costs.

6. Modify your expenses.

CUT some of your variable expenses when your expenses are more than your income. For example, if you eat out three or four times a week, reduce it to one. You could also terminate any memberships you don't use or take advantage of.

CONSIDER CUTTING some of your fixed expenses if you're not getting the desired results when slicing your variable costs.

7. Define your budget plan.

BIEBER (2018) RECOMMENDS that you consider your financial goal before settling for any budget plan. For example, a program that works fine for someone trying to purchase a house may not be suitable for someone who wants to save for retirement. Here are the major budget plans:

- *Zero-based budget:* Dave Ramsey made this budget approach famous; it ensures that earnings equal expenses. In other words, each dollar you earn fixes something. A zero-based budget doesn't mean that you won't be saving any money at all; it's just that all expenses are fixed and restrictive. Use this budget plan to avoid overspending, reduce or pay off debt and attain your financial goals.
- *Line-item or traditional budget:* People with spending issues or those struggling to pay off their debts can opt for this budget plan. Just write out all your expenses and categorize them into estimated, actual, and leftover expenses. Compare cumulative fees or payments with your income and use the *Tiller* app to run the process efficiently. You can then slice any expenses you consider irrelevant or unnecessary.

- *Proportional budgets:* "80/20", "50/30/20", and other budgets with loose guidelines are examples of balanced budgets. For example, anyone who adopts the 80/20 budget would spend 80 percent of their earnings and save 20 percent. Elizabeth Warren developed the 50/30/20 budget plan, in which 50 percent of revenue will be spent on your needs, 30 percent on wants, and 20 percent on savings. While needs are basic life necessities, wants aren't. Needs include rent, food, and shelter, while wants are generally entertainment-based. What happens if these budget plans do not work for you? Modify the 50/30/20 plan until you come up with a plan suitable for your financial goals.

- *Compensate yourself first:* Here's a saving model that could be used to reach a saving goal. Let's say you want to save $5,000 in the next six months, and you're using this model. At the dawn of a new month, you would remove the money you want to save before making any expenses. How much do you want to save per month? Is it 5, 10, or 20 percent of your income? What if you can't sustain the figure you come up with? You can always slice your expenses.

- *Envelope Budget:* Tends to shape how you use cash. Let's say your expense categories are transportation, groceries, and entertainment – you have to specify the amount to assign for each category. Withdraw money from the A.T.M. and address the items one after the other. Just know that you can't spend more, even if the cash isn't sufficient for the expense categories.

I recommend this budget plan for people with spending issues.

REMEMBER, no multipurpose budget plan; everything depends on the financial goals you want to accomplish.

LET'S assume you earn $4,000 each month. If you want each dollar to fix something, a zero-based budget would be applicable. The budget could look like this:

Payment	Monthly Budget
House down-payment fund	$450
Retirement savings	$600
Christmas fund	$30
Emergency fund	$80
Travel fund	$100
Car payment	$250
Insurance premiums	$200
Rent	$1,000

Utilities	$300
Entertainment	$150
Groceries	$400
Gas and vehicle maintenance	$300
Wiggle room	$40
Cellphone	$50
Clothing	$50
Total	**$4,000**

8. Select the right tool.

. . .

SIMPLY USE an Excel spreadsheet or any budgeting app to design your budget. There are several budgeting apps to download on the Play Store and Apple Store.

HOW DO you want to budget your money? The decision is all yours. Still, you need to know the right items to add to your budget.

Logical Items to Include in Your Budget

Like other people, you might be tempted to focus more on mortgage payments, grocery costs, and other monthly bills when designing your budget. Still, if you don't create room for unexpected expenses, you may end up with an inefficient allocation (Caldwell, 2020).

AN OPERATING BUDGET must include the following expenses:

1. Living expenses:

WE INCUR CERTAIN EXPENSES DAILY. Such costs may include payments on transportation, rent, feeding, and other utilities.

2. Monthly debt:

IS THERE any debt to repay monthly? It could be a student loan or a credit card debt. If there's any debt to repay monthly, make sure your budget covers it.

· · ·

3. Annual payments:

CERTAIN PAYMENTS, like car, taxes, registration, and property taxes, need to be paid yearly or twice a year. You will have problems making these payments if your budget doesn't address them. Determine the aggregate amount of the previous year's payment, then divide it by twelve to know the amount to save each month.

4. Emergency fund:

THE EMERGENCY FUND can protect you from unexpected repairs, loss of jobs, and other emergencies.

5. Fun activities:

CREATE a list of the activities you enjoy doing and state their costs. Such activities may include video games, going to the gym, or a night out with friends. Still, please make sure the activities are in their order of importance.

6. Donations and gifts:

SET some money aside for gifts and donations.

· · ·

A REASONABLE BUDGET has these items. If you are working with an operational budget, you will soon reach your goal. Still, you should be ready to trial, survey, and modify your financial goals from time to time, or you likely won't reach them.

Tracking, Reviewing, and Adjusting Your Budget

Track and review your expenses to see whether you are making the right financial decisions. If it seems your budget can't accommodate your goals, adjust it. Here's how to do it:

1. Record all expenses.

I ALREADY SHOWED you six categories of expenses to include your budget. Total your monthly expenses to curb overspending and other spending issues. Again, the budgeting app or spreadsheet used to design the budget can track and review it for you.

2. Monitor your spending.

SET a spending limit for each category. As soon as you hit the limit for a class, focus on the next one. If you aren't monitoring your spending habits, you won't attain your financial goals.

3. Analyze your budget regularly.

.   .   .

EVALUATE your budget from time to time to see if it is compatible with your financial goals and current realities. Certain life situations could impact your spending priorities and income; regular budget analysis can help you spot these situations and address them before they threaten your goals.

JUST MAKE sure your budget is working for you; should it go south, change or adjust it.

IF YOU WANT to create a fantastic budget for your goal, these budgeting cues will help:

- Save aggressively if your work is based on commission. The market might slow down a bit in the coming days.
- Divide your salary by weeks if you earn monthly to prevent cash flow issues. You can save the cash for the remaining weeks in a secure account.
- Modify your budget monthly to prevent overestimated or underestimated expenses.
- Focus on your savings goals if your income is more than your expenses. Don't boost your spending yet.
- Be budget-conscious daily. If something isn't on your budget for the day, don't spend money on it.

Start planning how to be successful with money now. As you already know, a lack of planning can harm your ability to grow your money and manage it appropriately. That's why this chapter explored budgeting, different ways of budgeting, what to include in a realistic budget, and a few budgeting tips to make the right money decisions.

. . .

BUT, you won't get anywhere if you fail to understand the basics of banking, which will be our focus in the next chapter.

2

BANKING AND SAVING

The previous chapter explored budgeting, what to include in a realistic budget, and a few budgeting tips that you can exploit to make the right money decisions. Here, you will learn the basics of banking and why holding bank accounts remains crucial to personal finance.

I WAS thirteen years old when my dad started giving me an extra $10 each week, telling me: "Kara, you can have this." I gladly took the money and spent it because I knew another $10 would be up for grabs the following week. After all, that was my little paycheck, I always told myself. The paycheck continued for a year.

THEN ONE DAY, after Dad had stopped offering me the stipend, he called me to his room and asked how much I had saved of the $520 I received from him in the past year. I told him I had spent it all, though I couldn't recollect how the money was spent.

. . .

MAYBE THAT WOULDN'T HAVE HAPPENED if I'd had a bank account. A bank account can help you define your expenses, save more money and attain your financial goals.

Benefits of Having a Bank Account

If you have a bank account, you can quickly evaluate your spending habits, cut unnecessary expenses, save more money, and reach your financial goals.

A BANK ACCOUNT is so easy to open that anyone can have one, provided they have a passport, state-issued I.D. card, or driver's license. It's okay if you don't have a bank account yet; just head straight to any bank with your proof of identification.

HERE ARE the significant benefits of having a bank account:

1. Accurate financial history.

YOU WILL HAVE DETAILED information about how your money is spent if you have a bank account. Each credit app you use won't work unless you link them with your bank account.

AGAIN, if there is any negative bank account information for you, it will reflect on your credit report. You will learn more about credit reports in Chapter Four.

. . . .

2. *Safety.*

EVERYONE WANTS to keep their money where it is safe. You may be tempted to store the money you save in your house, but you will lose it if there is a fire or robbery in your home. Instead, open a bank account and save your money there. Since each bank account is insured, you won't lose a dime if the bank is robbed.

3. *Convenience of transactions.*

EACH BANK ACCOUNT comes with a debit card or checkbook, so you can issue payments via your card. You don't have to load your wallet with cash because you will have to purchase a few items. Again, you can use your bank's mobile app to make payments from the comfort of your home.

COMPARE the fees and interest rates charged by banks in your area when you finally decide to open an account. If there are any account options tagged "budget checking" or "student," opt for such accounts, because they will have low or no fees.

HOW CAN you know the correct bank account to open?

Bank Account Options for Teens and College Students

Banks offer tons of account options for their customers. However, a bank account can be a blessing or a curse. Pay attention to your financial goal before opening any bank account.

All you need to make a sound judgment might be a few bank account tips.

So, let's discuss bank accounts:

1. Savings accounts.

MULLER (2020) RECOMMENDS PUTTING your money into a savings account if you need to save to pay your college dues, purchase a car or attain other financial goals. You can grow your money when you put it in a savings account. Simply set up a conventional savings account in any local bank.

AGAIN, there are several online savings accounts you could opt for—for example, Google *"online savings accounts in Chicago"* if that's where you live.

SAVINGS ACCOUNTS USUALLY ATTRACT a certain amount of interest monthly.

2. Checking accounts.

ONE THING I forgot to say about savings accounts is that you can't access them at any time, unlike checking accounts, which can be accessed via checks, debit cards, and your bank's A.T.M.

. . .

ALTHOUGH CHECKING accounts can offer terrific cash reliefs, minimize your spending by keeping transaction invoices and records. These records can help you track your expenses and decide what to cut to balance your finances.

LINK your savings and checking accounts together to avert overdraft charges and transfer money quickly from one to another.

3. Money market accounts (M.M.A.).

MULLER (2020) STATES that money market accounts are similar to savings accounts; you put money into both types and earn interest. But, the interest earned via a money market account is higher than that of a savings account.

SINCE THE MINIMUM balance requirement of an M.M.A. is very high, it may be out of your reach. Their higher minimum balance requirement ensures that account holders earn huge annual percentage yield (A.P.Y.).

4. Certificate of deposit.

THIS IS money you deposit for a specific time, and it usually generates more interest than savings and checking accounts. Fernando and Anderson (2021) advise that banks and credit unions offer their customers certificates of deposit. Your financial goal should help you decide the appropriate account option to create.

Prominent Bank Account Terms to Know

If you are planning to open a bank account, that's fine. But, even if your parents got one for you in the past, you still need to understand how banks work and the various terms they use to communicate with their customers (Murakami-Fester, 2020). So, I will explain some banking terms, one after the other:

1. A.P.Y. (annual percentage yield).

THIS IS the interest you gain on your deposit over one year, including compound interest. Banks encourage you to save with them by paying you the A.P.Y.

2. A.P.R. (annual percentage rate).

A.P.R. IS the interest you gain on your deposits for one year. However, it doesn't include compound interest.

3. Banks vs. Credit Unions.

BOTH BANKS and credit unions can operate online or in a concrete building. They offer basic transactions such as deposits, withdrawals, buying and selling securities, and similar transactions. Although banks are profit-oriented financial institutions, credit unions aren't.

. . .

4. Minimum balance requirement.

THIS IS the minimum amount your account must have at all times. For example, if the minimum balance requirement of your bank is $100, and you have $850 in there, you can't withdraw more than $750.

5. Available balance.

THIS IS a fraction of the money in your account, which can be used, withdrawn, or transferred to other accounts. It isn't necessarily the total balance in the account minus the minimum balance requirement.

6. Insufficient funds.

THIS SIMPLY MEANS that the amount you want to withdraw or the payment you intend to make is more than the funds available in your account.

7. E.F.T. (electronic funds transfer).

E.F.T. OCCURS when you do cashless banking operations. Such transactions include automatic bill payments and money transfers via A.T.M.

.   .   .

8. Overdraft.

THIS OCCURS when you withdraw more than your available balance. Issue a check to withdraw the excess funds. This option is available for people with overdraft accounts.

9. Routing number.

THIS IS a nine-digit number that specifies your bank. A large bank with branches across several geographic locations can have many routing numbers, so the routing number you use will depend on where you opened the account.

10. F.D.I.C. (Federal Deposit Insurance Corporation).

THE F.D.I.C. ENSURES THAT CUSTOMERS' bank deposits are insured up to $250,000. So, if the bank fails, the customers won't face any financial issues.

11. Cashier's check.

A CASHIER'S check is available for purchase at your bank. It doesn't bounce when used to make payments.

12. Canceled check.

· · ·

YOU CAN'T USE A CANCELED check for any other transactions because it has been endorsed and changed to an account.

13. Debit card.

YOUR BANK WILL ISSUE you a debit card against the funds in your account. You don't have to visit the bank to make payments or withdraw money from your account. Use the card to withdraw cash at the nearest A.T.M. or purchase goods and services online.

NO BANKING TERM should sound strange to you anymore.Still, there are a few bank fees to familiarize yourself with, as well.

Common Bank Fees to Avoid

Banks charge their customers specific service fees. Compiled by Gravier (2021), these include:

1. Maintenance or service fee.

BANKS OFTEN CHARGE their customers a monthly service or maintenance fee – such fees can be between $4 and $25. However, you can avoid this fee. How? Open a checking and savings account in the same bank, and maintain the minimum balance.

. . .

IF YOU CAN'T RUN a checking and savings account concurrently in the same bank, try to get bank accounts with no or very little monthly charges.

2. Out-of-network A.T.M. fee.

IF YOU USE NON-NETWORK A.T.M.s, your bank may charge you between $2.50 and $5 per transaction. Use your bank's mobile app to discover fee-free A.T.M.s nearby if you hope to avoid the out-of-network A.T.M. fee.

SHOULD you need to make any withdrawals with no in-network A.T.M.s, opt for a more considerable amount since the out-of-network fee is a one-time payment.

3. Transaction fee.

EACH SAVINGS ACCOUNT holder can do six free transfers and withdrawals per month; excess transfers or withdrawals are charged between $3 and $25 per transaction. If you have a checking account, use it for your daily transactions to avoid transaction fees.

4. Overdraft fee.

IT IS okay to withdraw more than you have in your bank account – just be aware that you might be charged up to $35 for every overdraft. To avoid paying the overdraft fee, set up an automatic direct deposit for the account. After all, if there's sufficient money in the account, you won't need to do an overdraft.

5. Returned item or insufficient fund fee.

IF THE FUNDS in your account can't cover your transaction, your bank will charge you. A returned item or insufficient fund fee could be up to $35 per transaction.

CONSIDER the amount in your account before making any transactions. Consider opting for notifications so that you get an automatic update on your account balance.

6. Wire transfer fee.

YOUR BANK WILL PROBABLY CHARGE you when transferring funds to other bank accounts; depending on the geographical location of the receiving accounts, you may be charged between $16 and $35 per transaction, so don't use wire transfers often. Do a wire transfer when the transaction is official, and the amount is enormous.

7. Account closing fee.

.   .   .

IF YOU DECIDE to close your account, make sure it tallies with your bank's rule on a timeline or risk a $25 early account closing fee. Each bank has its own timeline, which could be between 90 and 180 days.

IT IS best to verify your bank's timeline rule at the point of opening the account. Though, on most occasions, you probably wouldn't have opened an account intentionally only for a short period.

MOST OF THESE fees might be relatively small, but if recurring and unnecessary, they can threaten the financial stability of your bank account. You may need to consider the fees charged by banks in your area before you open a bank account.

FOLLOWING ARE a few tips on how to select a bank.

Creative Advice on How to Select a Bank

There are enough options for people who want to open a bank account; you could opt for credit unions, national banks, community banks, or digital-only banks. If you have any bank in mind already, just make sure that the bank offers services that fit your needs. Lambarena (2018) is here to guide you through the process of selecting a bank:

- *Check available account types:* We've already discussed the account options in most financial institutions. Still, if you need all the account options in one bank, I suggest you opt for a big national bank.

- *Fees and rates*: Banks tend to charge their customers for A.T.M. use, monthly maintenance, paper statements, money transfer, and overdrafts, while credit unions –non-profit financial institutions – pay higher A.P.Y. than traditional banks. Additionally, their fees are considerably lower than those of conventional banks. Also, since online banks don't keep physical branches, they have better terms than most traditional banks. So, analyze the fees and rates of these financial institutions before you open your account.
- *A.T.M.s and branches*: Consider your preferences and lifestyle. Would you prefer face-to-face transactions to a phone or online service? Do you travel a lot or need to withdraw cash whenever you are on a journey? Stipulate your needs, and check whether the bank has enough A.T.M.s and branches in the places you often visit. National banks have wider-spread branches and more A.T.M.s. Allpoint, Star, and some credit unions have extensive A.T.M. coverage. Opt for a mobile-only or online bank if you always do digital transactions.
- *Must-have technology:* You don't have to step into a branch before you track or transfer money; technology has made this a reality. But does your prospective bank have its own app? If they do, is it user-friendly? The app should have basic features like security measures, automated savings plans, and budgeting tools. Online and national banks all have the latest technology.
- *Safety:* Keep your money where it will be safe. Open your accounts with banks that are certified by the Federal Deposit Insurance Corporation (F.D.I.C.). Should you decide to use a credit union, opt for

those backed by the National Credit Union Administration (N.C.U.A.). Such banks and credit unions are insured. Check the N.C.U.A. and F.D.I.C. websites to see the list of insured financial institutions.

So, what do you need to open a bank account? Most banks require you to come in with a social security number, a government-issued identity card (S.S.N.), and your first deposit fund. No problem if you don't have an S.S.N.; you can use your tax I.D. number instead. However, if that doesn't work, look for banks that approve passports or other official I.D.s.

Do you want to apply in person? Verify the I.D. type the bank accepts first. If you apply online, the bank might ask you to send them certain pieces of the information via mail, email, or fax.

THE BANK WILL PROCESS your paperwork as soon as it receives it. Processing might take a few days or weeks, but you will get a welcome package by mail if your application is successful. Usually, the package should contain a debit card, PIN, and some complimentary checks.

Reading and Reconciling Your Bank Statements

If you own a savings or checking account in any financial institution, expect a monthly or quarterly bank statement. You are getting a bank statement because your account is still very active. Banks often send the report via mail or email.

. . .

WHAT EXACTLY IS A BANK STATEMENT?

IT SHOWS YOUR DEPOSITS, transfers, withdrawals, and other transactions. A bank statement will display your starting and ending balances for the period it covers, as well as your bank's contact information. Should there be any financial discrepancies, a bank statement can reconcile the differences. You can use your bank statement to track and trim your expenses.

HOW DO you read a bank statement? Payne (2020) advises that bank statements aren't tricky or difficult to understand. Each bank may customize its reports, but this is the likely information you will see:

1. Basic information.

A BANK'S statement should have the bank's name, mailing address, phone number, and other relevant information.

2. Personal information.

THE STATEMENT SHOULD CARRY your name and contact information.

3. Statement period.

. . .

A BANK STATEMENT covers a specific period, so expect to see the dates there. While some banks use particular days of the month, others will start from the first day and end on the last.

4. Starting and ending balances.

CHECK your balances to know whether you are progressing or regressing financially over the period.

5. Transactions.

THIS SECTION MAKES up information on deposits, checks written, withdrawals, A.C.H. transfers, A.T.M. withdrawals, direct deposits, and pending transactions.

6. Fees.

CHARGED fees will reflect on your monthly bank statement.

7. Interest earned.

THE STATEMENT WILL SHOW the interest you've earned (if there is any). Assuming you have savings or checking accounts in one bank, they will show up on a single statement.

. . .

YOU HAVE JUST LEARNED how to read a bank statement. I will now teach you what to do to reconcile your bank statement.

RECONCILING a bank statement comes with several healthy financial benefits and ensures no issues with your bank transactions. It can help you trail the previous month's uncashed checks and prevent missed or double payments; it also improves money management.

HERE IS how to reconcile your bank statement:

- Compare your bank statement with your financial records to see any deposit, withdrawal, or transfer mistakes.
- Check whether the balance on your bank statement tallies with what your records display. Are there any disparities? Fix them.
- Analyze the deposits shown on your bank statement to see whether they correlate with your records.
- Compare the listed withdrawals on your bank statement with your records.
- Check if there are any discrepancies between your checkbook and bank statement. Then, compare the figures there to your records.

Are there any figure disparities? Fix the problem. Approach your bank if you think something is wrong with the statement.

FINDING an error on a bank statement can be annoying. If you must fix the problem, here are the proper steps to take:

. . .

1. Verify the error.

IF SOMETHING SEEMS wrong or implausible in your bank statement, confirm it first. If possible, identify the proof because it may be all you have to show the bank to rectify the problem.

2. Contact your bank.

REACH out to your bank as soon as you discover the error; you can call the bank's customer service unit or send them an email update. Don't forget to send the proof.

3. Contact the third party.

SHOULD the error involve another party, don't hesitate to inform them. They have to work on their records and resolve the problem as soon as possible.

4. Adjust your records.

MODIFY your records to tally with your bank's corrections. Always try to note the identities of the people you talked to while fixing the issues.

THERE ARE no bank issues that cannot be reconciled. Just take your time to identify the cause(s) of the problem and find a way to fix it. You can usually do this with a call to your bank's customer service unit to solve any issues.

HAVE you ever felt like you don't need a bank account? If so, I highly recommend reconsidering because there are such beautiful benefits to holding a bank account.

THIS CHAPTER EXPLORED every banking detail you need to know to be successful with money. Still, you need to understand mindful spending if you ever hope to reach any of your financial goals. No problem at all, because that is what we will be going over in the next chapter.

3

MINDFUL SPENDING

I n the previous chapter, we explored many things about banking, and you saw why holding a bank account could aid your financial goals. Our focus here is on mindful spending, and we will discuss a few prudent money management tricks you should adopt to meet your financial objectives.

I WAS TALKING about my reckless spending habit in the previous chapter; I told you how my Dad gave me an extra $10 per week for a year. I never considered that I had received $520 extra bucks from him until he summoned me into his room, wanting to know what I had done with the money I received from him over the year. I quickly told him how I had increased my daily expenses to accommodate the extra $10. I wasn't spending money wisely then; I always made sure I bought everything I wanted, even if I didn't need it.

YOU, too, can develop a reckless spending habit if you fail to recognize the disparity between your wants and needs.

Understanding Wants Versus Needs

Many people don't recognize a vast difference between wants and needs, so they readily spend money on their wants first. Sadly, they then end up in a terrible financial situation because they don't prioritize their needs. You can't save money or achieve your financial goals if you can't differentiate wants from needs.

NEEDS ARE NECESSITIES LIKE UTILITIES, food, healthcare, water, shelter, transportation, and medication, whereas wants are generally items that satisfy one's enjoyment or entertainment or make one's life more comfortable. Needs are crucial to one's life; wants generally... aren't. So, when it's time to spend, work on prioritizing your needs.

STILL, needs can quickly turn into wants if one isn't careful. Here are a few examples of how needs can turn to wants:

- You are purchasing coffee, bottled water, or soda instead of ordinary drinkable water.
- You are eating out instead of cooking your meals.
- You are living in an expensive home rather than a more modest apartment.

So, if there is anything you feel like purchasing, ask yourself if you can survive without it. Don't acquire something that doesn't add any value to your life.

. . .

SCHROEDER-GARDNER (2021) CAN ADVISE you how to lower your spending simply by recognizing the disparity between needs and wants:

1. Be content with what you have.

IF SOMETHING DOESN'T ADD value to your life, eliminate it. Happiness isn't measured by the things you can purchase but by the value they add to your life.

STILL, you deserve to enjoy your life and have quality time with friends and family members. So, craft a realistic budget and stick to it.

2. Don't turn needs into wants.

PAY close attention to how much you spend on your needs or risk turning them into wants. For example, you need water to stay hydrated, so don't opt for a soda, coffee, or bottled water when you can quickly get safe, drinkable water free of charge or at a cheaper rate.

3. Think before you purchase anything.

IS THERE anything you would like to purchase? Take a break and think about whether you need that item or not. Provide honest answers to these questions:

- Will this item add any value to my life? ✔
- Why should I purchase it? ✔
- Do I have something similar to it? ✔
  Qué pasa si no lo compro?

Base your purchasing decision on your answers. These questions will help you make intelligent money decisions, and you won't have to waste money on unnecessary items.

4. Evaluate your expenses.

WANTS – like the latest cellphone or a brand-new car – can drain your money. So, check where your money is going; make sure you aren't spending money on items you barely need. Trim your expenses and save more money to attain your goals.

HOW DO you prioritize wants and needs? Categorize them into high-priority needs, high-priority wants, low-priority needs, and low-priority wants. It's pretty easy to make informed purchase decisions when your needs and wants have been categorized.

SPENDING ON WANTS isn't so bad if you can be modest; just make sure you don't prioritize wants over needs. Be careful not to accumulate debt because there are certain things you have to purchase. Create a budget and stick to it.

IS THERE any advice on how I could achieve mindful spending?

Valuable Tips on Attaining Mindful Spending

Mindful spending is the attention you give to your spending habit to ensure it supports your values, needs, and financial goals. Have a deep, conscious reflection about the items you want to purchase, to see whether they can add value to your life. As I always advise, don't rush to purchase; patience is crucial to intelligent shopping. For example, why pay $100 for a gorgeous skirt which will soon be devalued to accommodate fall and winter clothes? Be patient and look for a price cut. A few days' waiting will convince you whether you need to purchase the item or not.

WALLEN (N.D.) believes that mindful spending shouldn't rob your life of the fun it deserves. He suggests that you can patiently trim your expenses a little bit to enhance saving for a vacation, college education, or possible emergencies. He hopes these tips help you spend money wisely:

1. Opt for quality.

DON'T PURCHASE a pair of shoes that could get ragged or worn out in a few weeks or months, even if they aren't expensive. For example, a $50 dress in perfect shape next year is better than a cheaper $20 outfit, which you need to change in six months.

2. Go for generic-label groceries.

.   .   .

NAME-BRAND GROCERIES COST MORE than generic-label ones. Pick a brand-name cleaning product bottle and a generic-label variant, then compare the ingredients and cost. Feel free to repeat the exercise with other products, like canned vegetables, boxes of pasta, bottled peanut butter, and medicine.

3. Reduce food wastage.

THE NATURAL RESOURCES DEFENSE CENTER study found that each American family of four wastes about 50 percent of the food they purchase (Wallen, n.d.). Isn't that a deliberate way of wasting money? Should you need to buy any food item, make sure, it is all stuff you need.

4. Exercise a bit of patience.

DON'T HURRY to make any purchase; look for rare, irresistible discounts and offers. Make sure you get your needs at affordable rates.

5. List the items to shop for.

IF YOU HOPE to avoid impulse or unnecessary purchases, create a list of the things to shop for and stick to it. Just make sure that the items you are acquiring have long-term uses and benefits.

6. Don't try to impress anyone.

. . .

YOU CAN PURCHASE anything you need, but don't spend to impress anyone. Town (n.d.) believes that many people would gladly buy brand-name clothes and fancy cars to show off or impress the people around them. If something doesn't add value to your life, it's best not to purchase it.

7. Evaluate the long-term advantages and disadvantages of your purchased items.

IT'S okay if you feel like purchasing something you admire, but discard it if the item doesn't add any value to your life. Impulse buying is something you must try to avoid at all costs.

8. Be content.

THERE CAN BE no mindful spending without contentment; be happy with what you already have. We often feel or think that we can't survive without something, but when thinking more deeply, we realize that isn't true at all. Don't spend lavishly just because you have it; instead, stay on a realistic budget when hanging out or having fun with friends and loved ones.

9. ADOPT THE "ONE-IN-ONE-OUT" method.

. . .

IF YOU BRING an item into your residence, discard any identical or similar item in the home. You could sell the lookalike item or give it to someone who truly needs it.

YOU WILL BE LESS interested in purchasing unnecessary items if you already have the ones you value and enjoy.

10. Learn to cook your foods and repair your damaged or faulty items.

YOU WILL SPEND tons of cash if you consistently eat out. Instead, cook your meals at home. Learn to repair faulty items and start making things for yourself. You shouldn't have to spend money on everything you need.

11. Attach more value to savings.

THE MONEY you save or invest usually comes with some long-term benefits. For example, you can earn interest or returns on your protected or invested capital. But any funds you use to purchase a product will be gone forever, and products will surely wear out.

12. Stick to your budget.

YOU CAN'T MODERATE your expenses if you don't work with a budget. Get rid of any spending habits which are sifting your budget. Such practices include eating out often, expensive hobbies, and overspending on clothing and other wants.

FIND a way to trim your expenses so that you can save more money. If there's a gadget you want to purchase, make sure you don't have a similar item at home; sell it if you must buy another one. Although treats might look satisfying and enjoyable, too many delicacies tend to become a lifestyle.

RECTIFY your spending habits by sticking to your budget. And, if there are any income-draining lifestyle practices in your budget, cut them. Update your financial skills if you want to cut unnecessary spending.

Vital Financial Skills Every Teen and College Student Must Have

We all have different financial goals to accomplish; while some want to purchase a house, others are eager to save up their college fees or contribute toward a retirement plan. And, since you are still in your teen years (or maybe a few years older), you have the strength to pursue, reach and attain your financial goals.

CAMPBELL (2021) SAYS that you must cultivate the following skills if you are to lose your financial objectives:

1. Access funds.

. . .

IF YOU HAVE A BANK ACCOUNT, learn how to deposit or withdraw money from it. Understand how to use your bank's mobile app to transfer funds, check account balance, retrieve bank statements, and run other desired operations.

2. Read a bank statement.

I'M sure you remember we talked about bank statements in the previous chapter; I told you that the report contains account balance, transactions (deposits, withdrawals, transfers), interest rates, and due dates. You must understand the content of your bank statement if you want to be successful with money.

3. Set a realistic budget.

YOU ALREADY KNOW that you can't attain a financial goal without a budget, so go ahead and create one. Use the tips provided in the previous chapter to design a reasonable budget. Just make sure your earnings exceed your expenses.

4. Distinguish needs from wants.

NEEDS AID SURVIVAL, whereas wants are mere desires of life. So, focus more on your needs if you don't want to experience a terrible financial situation. We have discussed it before, but I want to repeat it, as it is a fundamental skill and consciousness.

. . .

5. Read and understand loan offers, credit and debit cards.

LENDERS TEND to exploit teens and young adults, who have little to no experience of how loans, credit, and debit cards function. So, you must learn to read and comprehend the terms and conditions of every financial agreement before you show your consent or approval. Should any of the terms and conditions look ambiguous, ask for clarification.

6. Get help.

YOU MAY NOT HAVE any inkling of an idea about the next financial hurdle you will have to cross. Sometimes, you need someone to guide you to make reasonable financial choices to attain your goals. What will happen if you don't know how to ask for help?

IF YOU WANT to be successful with money, you have to improve your financial skills.

DON'T HESITATE to track your daily, weekly, and monthly expenses if you hope to stay out of debt. Again, since you have already learned a few sensible money management tricks, tracing where your funds go won't be a difficult task.

YOUR KNOWLEDGE about credit and debt – our focus in the next chapter – can take you closer to or farther from your financial objectives. I hope to see you there.

4

CREDIT AND DEBT

T he previous chapter tracked your daily, weekly, and monthly expenses to stay out of debt and maintain a mindful spending habit. You uncovered a few practical money management tricks you can exploit to trace where your funds go. We will focus on credit and debt in this chapter and the critical topics surrounding them.

I ALREADY TOLD you how my friends helped me raise some money during my troubling high school days. If they hadn't offered help, my indecision would have ended my academic pursuit. Indecision can cripple your finances, lower your credit score, and subject you to a lifetime of debt. The credit score of a bankrupt person is always abysmal. [The score – which usually runs between 300 and 850 – defines a person's creditworthiness; a borrower with a low credit score will find it hard to get the attention of any potential lenders.] ↪ U.S. Credit Score

. . .

A PERSON'S credit history often determines their credit score. If you want to know your credit history, you will need to analyze your open accounts, cumulative debt, and repayment history. Potential lenders often evaluate your credit score to see whether you can repay loans within the agreed time (Kagan, 2021). Experian, Transunion, and Equifax are the primary credit reporting agencies in the United States, and they report, update and store individuals' credit histories. Although these agencies have their own varied ways of collecting data, they usually focus on the following five factors:

1. *Payment history* makes up 35 percent of the entire credit score. It indicates whether an individual pays their financial commitments on time.
2. *Credit utilization* makes up 30 percent. It is the proportion of credit a person is currently using.
3. *Duration of credit history* is 15 percent of the cumulative score. Longer credit histories are deemed safe and less risky.
4. *Types of credit* make up a 10 percent proportion. This shows a person's car and mortgage loans, credit card debts, and other credits.
5. *Inquiries on new credit accounts* point to the number of new accounts a person has and when the accounts were opened. This counts as 10 percent of the total credit score.

Your credit score can have a massive impact on your financial life. For example, you are a subprime borrower if your credit score is less than 640, and lenders would charge you higher mortgage interest than the regular mortgage interest rate. Why? Because they believe you may not pay them back within the stipulated time. Subprime mortgages also usually come with a shorter repayment period.

. . .

YOU CAN ACCESS your credit report once or twice via *www. annualcreditreport.com* for free. You've got nothing to worry about if your credit score is 700 or above; you will be able to take loans with a lower interest rate. People with impressive scores of 800 or more can easily attract potential lenders (Kagan, 2021).

HERE'S a table of credit scores and their financial status.

Credit Score	Status
800 - 850	Excellent
740 - 799	Very Good
670 - 739	Good
580 - 669	Fair
300 - 579	Poor

I'm sure that you would like to know where you stand; your initial rent or other utility deposits and the interest to pay on loans will depend on your credit score.

TO ADD TO IT, you should also know how to increase your credit score.

Creative Efforts to Improve Your Credit Score

A low credit score can negatively impact your financial goals. You need to borrow some money to augment your savings, to purchase a house or car; potential lenders won't find you credit-worthy if your credit score is poor, and you may not reach the goal.

. . . .

KAGAN (2021) ADVISES that you can boost your credit score if you stick to these instructions:

1. Pay your bills on time.

PROMPTLY PAY your bills at due time for the next six months to see a noticeable improvement in your credit score. There's a penalty for anyone who fails to pay their bills by the due date.

2. Improve your credit line.

REQUEST A CREDIT INCREASE if you have two or more credit card accounts. You should get a boost in your credit limit if your different credit card accounts have good financial standings.

YOU HAVE to attain a lower credit utilization rate to improve your credit score. So, I advise you not to touch or spend the credit boost.

3. Don't close your credit card accounts.

Do you have two or more credit card accounts you aren't using? Best not to close the accounts; you will hurt your credit score if you do. Let's say that you have a $1,000 debt profile and $2,500 in each of your two credit card accounts; as it stands, you have a 20 percent credit utilization rate. Should you close one of the accounts, your credit utilization rate will turn to 40 percent, and that's going to lower your credit score.

4. Hire a credit repair agent.

IT's okay if you can't improve your credit score because of time constraints; you can pay credit repair companies to do it for you. If you must strike a deal with any of these credit repair companies, make sure they secure your financial information and records.

ARE there any logical things to learn about credit scores?

Practical Things to Know About Credit Scores and Credit Reports

If you understand these simple facts, you can improve, sustain and manage your credit scores effectively (DiGangi, 2019):

1. Credit reports versus credit scores.

A CREDIT REPORT is a detailed record of credit history, credit accounts, debt collection, and credit applications frequency. It also includes judgments, liens, bankruptcies, and other public records. A credit score may be attached to the credit report – still, they are technically different items. View the credit score as numerical analysis of the factors which make up the credit report.

. . .

SINCE YOUR CREDITWORTHINESS depends on your score, check your credit report and credit score regularly with Experian, Transunion, and Equifax (if you are in the United States) to ensure they are accurate.

2. Accessing credit scores and reports is free.

YOU DON'T HAVE to pay to get a copy of your credit report from any credit bureaus. Get a copy every four months to learn the health of your finances and catch up with any inaccuracies.

3. No penalty for checking your credit score.

HARD INQUIRIES often come with financial implications, but you've got nothing to worry about when checking your credit score. Neither does the inquiry show up on your credit report.

4. Different scoring models.

EACH CREDIT BUREAU has its scores and score ranges since they work with varying scoring models. So, ask for range clarification from your credit bureau to ascertain your current credit-worthy status.

HERE'S a table on the scoring bars for major credit bureaus in the United States:

Credit Bureau	Scoring Bars
Experian	360 - 840
Equifax	280 - 850
TransUnion	300 - 850
VantageScore	501 - 990

5. Spot fraud with your credit report.

IF YOU ANALYZE your credit reports quarterly, you will likely spot any theft attempt on your identity and every financial problem. For example, if a credit card you've abandoned for some months suddenly starts spending, you can identify the issue and take appropriate action.

6. Credit scores are individual.

WHEN YOU GET married and open a joint account, perhaps you are worried that your partner's poor credit score will affect yours. The answer is it won't; credit scores are individual.

HOWEVER, moving forward, you need to be aware of the responsibility and accountability whenever you share credit because, in the end, it is still your account. If your partner fails to make the payment or sum up huge balances with your new joint account, it may affect your credit score.

7. Negative history will be wiped out.

. . .

WE ALL KNOW the importance of building and maintaining positive credit history from the get-go. However, as normal human beings, we have all made mistakes. If you have a situation in the past that has hurt your credit score, there is no need to stay down. The good news is that, as long as you start keeping and maintaining a good record, moving forward, any negative credit history in the past will eventually become less of a determining factor.

So, if you hope to build your credit score, focus more on your payment history, credit utilization, duration of credit history, types of credit, and new credit accounts.

Fundamentals of Creating a Beneficial Credit History

You may need a loan to purchase a house, buy a car, or finance education. Creditors will ask for your credit history to see whether you can manage or use credit responsibly (Take Charge America Team, n.d.). Here's how to create a positive credit history:

1. Manage your bank account well.

YOU WON'T HAVE a good credit history if you don't know how to manage your account. Try to protect the minimum balance and don't make overdrawing withdrawals.

2. Become an authorized user on a parent's card.

. . .

It's okay if you don't have your credit card; by becoming a legal user of your parent's card, you can use the card without having to be 100 percent responsible for it, though there could be certain limits and guidelines. Strike an agreement on the fraction of monthly card fees you will have to pay.

3. Procure a secured credit card.

The card should be tied to your savings account, so your credit limit can't be more than your bank account's available balance. Again, linking a credit card to a savings account is great because it will help you resist the temptation of overspending since you can't spend more than your available balance.

4. Pay bills on time.

Make sure you pay your rent, cable, utilities, and other bills when they are due if you hope to build a desirable credit history. One missed or late payment could negatively impact your score for many years. Again, there's a penalty for every bill you neglect or forget to pay in due time.

5. Get and sustain a steady job.

Sometimes, your employment history can help you get a loan or lose it. No lender will lend you money if you don't have a steady job; they need assurances that you can pay it back, including the accrued interests.

WE HAVE JUST DISCUSSED the fundamentals of credit score and how it can impact your financial future. There is another thing that I believe you should be aware of at the earliest stage possible because this thing is small in size but can hugely impact your finances if you don't utilize it properly. It is called a credit card.

WHAT ARE CREDIT CARDS?

CREDIT CARDS ARE REVOLVING credits that can be used partly or in full. They have a specific credit limit and payback period. Credit cards help you obtain funds from your bank, and you will pay interest on the money.

A CREDIT CARD is simply a metal or plastic card which helps you access credit from the issuing bank; each time you use the card to purchase anything online, the card issuer shoulders the payment (Lambarena, 2021). However, it's not free money; you will have to pay it back by the month's end, including any accrued interest. Little wonder a non-specialist would say that you are spending money you don't have each time you use a credit card.

SINCE CREDIT CARDS aren't secured, no deposit or collateral is required to borrow the loan.

. . .

How Does a Credit Card Work?

YOUR BANK SETS your credit limit as soon as you are ratified for a credit card; the credit limit is the total amount the card issuer (your bank) can lend you, so use the amount at your discretion. Your income, debts, and available credit on other cards (if you have any) determine your credit limit most of the time.

CREDIT CARD TRANSACTIONS are filtered or processed by payment networks like American Express, Visa, Discover, and Mastercard (Lambarena, 2021). These payment networks ensure that funds get to the appropriate destination while the correct cardholder is equally billed. No issues if you are billed because you can pay the amount in installments or in full. Still, if you have the means, pay everything at once since partial payments accrue more interest.

I'M sure you would like to know how the credit bureaus get your payment report. Your credit card issuer mails it to them.

LET'S see the types of credit cards you can have.

Categories of Credit Cards

YOU MAY BE ISSUED any of these credit card varieties:

1. Rewards.

. . .

IF YOU ARE USING a reward credit card, you get something back each time you use it to make a purchase. Reward credit cards come in various forms:

- *Cashback cards* offer money when you make a purchase. The cash could be a bank deposit or a check.
- *Airline and hotel credit cards* provide air miles or points, which can book space in the card's partner hotel chain or airline. However, there may be particular restrictions on how to redeem rewards on these credit cards.
- *General travel cards* come with points that can be ✻ used to make travel payments. These cards are more adaptable and functional than regular airline and hotel credit cards.
- *Store credit cards* give shopping discounts, rebates, and other benefits at the card issuer's store.

Cardholders who pay their monthly bills in full love reward credit cards.

2. Low interest.

YOU DON'T GET any rewards for using a low-interest credit card; instead, you get value for your money since the card is less expensive to use. Low-interest credit cards may have a 0% A.P.R. period, so you have ample time to pay off an enormous bargain without interest. You may not be considered for such a deal if your credit score is poor.

. . .

3. Balance transfer.

USE the balance transfer credit card to push debt from another issuer when there's a lower interest rate to exploit. However, if you don't have a good or excellent credit score, you won't qualify for these cards.

4. Student cards.

BEING a college student isn't all you need to get a student credit card; under the provisions of the 2009 *Credit Card Act*, you must be 21 years or older, and have proof of income before you can be issued a student credit card. Again, the applicant must also get a guarantor willing to risk their credit for them to build theirs (Lambarena, 2021).

NOW THAT WE'VE gone over credit cards, how would you go about using one?

TEENAGERS AND COLLEGE students often get excited when they hear people talk about credit cards; some see them as free money sources. I used to think that way many years ago when I was a teenager. Sure, credit cards can provide you with funds to purchase desired goods or products, but they can also cause severe financial challenges if you don't know how to use them (Muller, 2020).

. . .

You can use credit cards to enhance your credit and improve your money decisions.

Do credit cards come with any merits and demerits?

Benefits of Using a Credit Card

Using a credit card, according to Muller (2020), can help you to:

1. Organize expenses.

Credit cards make transactions convenient and straightforward. For example, you can book flights, shop online, and make other payments with your credit cards, all from a sofa in your living room.

2. Obtain cash-related rewards.

Again, some cards offer cash back, airline miles, and similar rewards to their customers.

3. Achieve convenience.

You don't have to carry cash all the time if you have a credit card. Also, with your credit card, you can run your transactions from home.

. . .

4. Boost security.

CREDIT CARDS ARE LINKED to banks, so they are fully secured to protect you from identity theft and fraud.

5. Improve versatility.

SEVERAL COUNTRIES USE CREDIT CARDS. Thus, travelers can always rely on them any time they move from one country to another.

STILL, credit cards have their setbacks.

DANGERS OF USING a Credit Card

COMMON DANGERS of using a credit card include:

1. Overspending.

A FRIEND once told me that money is easier spent than earned. And, since credit cards often enable you to spend money you don't have, you will overspend if you aren't reasonable with your spending.

2. Debt.

. . .

IF YOU CONTINUE to overspend money, you will accumulate debt. Credit card loans come with severe interest.

3. Awful credit history.

YOU WILL HAVE a terrible credit score if you have experienced a bad credit history. Lenders won't consider you for any significant loans or purchases if the problem persists.

Understanding Your Credit Card Statement

A credit card statement shows all your transactions with the card for a particular period; the card issuer (your bank) will send the information to you every month.

THERE IS ALWAYS a payback grace period to make partial or complete payments. Strive to pay the total amount, or be prepared to pay interest, should you carry over the balance to another month.

THERE IS some financial lingo on the credit card statement, which you need to understand to manage your accounts well. Let's take a look at the standard credit card terminologies:

1. Annual fee.

. . .

A FEE you pay for using a credit card; your bank might call it a "participation" or "membership" fee. The annual fee could be between $15 and $300, depending on the issuer.

ASK if there are banks that don't impose annual fees on their customers in your area.

2. Annual percentage rate (A.P.R.).

THIS COVERS THE PAYABLE COSTS, fees, and annual interest rate for acquiring a loan. The law requires lenders to publicize their A.P.R. Calculate the A.P.R. by multiplying the total billing periods per year with the periodic rate. For example, if you are billed four times a year, while the regular rate is 5%, the APR will be 20%.

YOU MAY HAVE different A.P.R.s listed on your credit card as balance transfers, special offers, or cash advances. If these offers have expiry dates, the balance will be added to the default A.P.R.

3. Average daily balance.

CREDIT CARD ISSUERS use the average daily balance to compute your payment due. To figure out your average daily balance, the bank adds up your daily balance and divides it by the aggregate days of a billing cycle. The bank will then multiply the average daily balance with the card's monthly periodic rate (M.P.R.).

. . .

JUST DIVIDE your A.P.R. by 12 to know your M.P.R.

4. Balance transfer.

THIS OCCURS when an unpaid credit card debt is moved to another card. Card issuers often provide extra-low teaser rates to help their customers facilitate balance transfers. Such rates or offers can be tempting, but if you can't verify when the offers will expire, don't accept them.

5. Credit limit.

THE TOTAL AMOUNT you can spend with a credit card.

6. Finance charge.

THIS COVERS interest and other charges you have to pay to use a credit card. Cash advances and balance transfers have separate finance charges. Read the lines well to identify the one you are dealing with.

7. Grace period.

. . .

CREDIT CARD DEBTS paid in full within the grace period are usually interest-free. The grace period can be 20 to 30 days after the transaction takes place.

PLEASE BE aware that some card issuers don't show such a courtesy. Cardholders with balances or debts may not be considered for the grace period.

8. Late fee.

DID YOU MISS A PAYMENT DATE? Get ready to pay the late fee. Late fees are charged monthly and could be between $30 and $35.

WHO SAYS late fees can't be eliminated in the future? Activate auto-pay on your cards if you don't want to default again.

9. Minimum payment.

LENDERS OFTEN SPECIFY a minimum amount payable to prevent your account from defaulting. The amount often approximates 2 percent of your outstanding balance.

EXCEED the minimum payment each month to reduce your credit card debts rapidly. Again, do all it takes to avoid charges.

. . .

10. Over-limit fee.

THERE IS a penalty for exceeding the credit limit of a card. The penalty is termed an "over-limit" fee. Over-limit fees can be up to $35.

YOU CAN USE your credit card wisely if you are familiar with these credit card terms.

MAKE sure that all purchase receipts are kept intact and secure; should there be any inconsistencies in your credit card statement, you will need the receipts to make necessary clarifications. Don't hesitate to put a call across to the customer care unit of your bank if there are any financial issues.

SHOULD you need help managing your credit card debt effectively, get some credit experts to counsel you.

Helpful Tips on Using Credit Cards

Credit cards can boost or hurt your credit score, but it all depends on how you use them. Still, the advantages of using a credit card will surpass its costs. Here, I will give you a few valuable tips on using a credit card:

1. Pay the balance in full.

. . .

You can evade excessive interest or finance charges if you pay your credit card debt in full during the grace period. Remember that late payments usually attract financial penalties.

Sometimes, due to unforeseen errors, you may end up paying only the minimum balance. If this continues, your debt profile will keep increasing monthly until you can't cope with it anymore. It's okay if you can't pay the whole debt at once, but try to beat the minimum payment to lessen or reduce your debt profile. Credit card issuers usually penalize cardholders who go below the minimum balance. If you can't pay the debt of a particular credit card in full, don't use the card to make payments.

2. Opt-out of pre-screened offers.

Don't open two or more credit cards at a time. Instead, focus on using just one card for your transactions. Visit *www.optout-prescreen.com* to cancel all your credit card pre-screen offers.

3. Get a reward card with a low interest rate.

Opt for a credit card with a low-interest rate, credit limit, and no annual fee. Again, it is okay if the card offers cash-back; such cards won't cause you any financial distress.

4. Set up auto-pay for your credit card bills.

. . .

AUTOMATE THE PAYMENT of your credit card debts so you don't miss them. You know you will be penalized if you fail to pay back your balances within the grace period.

5. Use only one card.

PEOPLE with multiple credit cards usually overspend. You can resist the temptation if you stick to using just one credit card.

6. Don't allow anyone to use your card.

UNDER NO CIRCUMSTANCES should you permit another person to use your credit card, especially if they won't pay you back for their purchases. Remember that you will be the one to settle the bill at the end of the month.

7. Maintain your balance.

IF YOU HOPE to keep your credit card debt under control, make sure it is less than 30 percent of your available credit.

8. Moderate your credit card applications.

. . .

IF YOU MUST MAKE another credit card application, make sure it is six months after the last one.

9. Review your account regularly.

ANALYZE your credit card account weekly to trail your spending and prevent fraud. Most credit card issuers now offer mobile apps that show all of the transactions, as well as a text notification as soon as your credit card is being used. Make sure all the transaction records are accurate. Report if you find any discrepancy.

HAVE you got any annual fee credit cards? Don't keep them active or open if you don't want to harm your credit score. You can't have healthy credit if you don't know how to use your credit card wisely.

NOW LET'S talk about something that most people think is creepy and can haunt your entire life if you don't manage it correctly. It is called *debt*.

Different Categories of Debt to Know

Each debt or loan has peculiar payment strategies, tax implications, and consequences for your credit score. Let's talk about these debt categories:

1. Credit card debt.

. . .

WE'VE ALREADY SAID a few things about this. Remember to focus on paying the debt fully within the grace period, to avoid unnecessary interest and fees.

2. Mortgages.

THESE ARE INSTALLMENT LOANS, so there's an agreed term for you to pay them back, which could be between 15 and 30 years. Since mortgages are secured loans, the purchased home automatically becomes the collateral so, should you halt payments, the lender may seize the equity and sell it to recover its money.

INTEREST RATES on mortgages are usually pegged between 3 and 5 percent. However, interest on adjustable-rate mortgages (A.R.M.) can vary yearly.

PAYMENT FOR A MORTGAGE is mainly made once each month for the term. If the property is your principal residence, your tax-deductible may be in the region of $1,000,000, whereas home equity could be up to $100,000.

PROMPT PAYMENT of mortgages can boost your credit score since it shows lenders you are a credible borrower.

3. Auto loans.

. . .

AN AUTO LOAN is quite similar to a mortgage; it is secured and has an installment payback period, usually between three and six years. Since the car serves as the collateral, the lender can seize and sell it to recover its money.

LONG-TERM AUTO LOANS usually attract lower interest rates than short-term ones. Auto loans don't have any tax implications.

4. Student loans.

THESE UNSECURED INSTALLMENT debts have flexible payback terms. Still, student loans have varied interest rates. For example, if you decide to take the loan via the United States Department of Education, the federal government will fix the rate, and it won't change before you pay it off.

MOST STUDENT LOANS have a 10-year payoff time, but there could be deviations. For example, if you can't afford your student loan, you can have a chat with your loan servicer about the need to opt for an income-based repayment plan.

WITH A GROSS INCOME of $80,000 or less, your tax-deductible student loan interest could be up to $2,500.

5. Medical debts.

. . .

LIKE STUDENT LOANS, medical debts are not secured. Again, they do not have a specific payment structure or period; each hospital or healthcare provider has its billing section. It's okay if you can't pay the entire bill at once; set up a realistic payment plan with your healthcare provider.

YOUR MEDICAL EXPENSES may be deducted from your federal taxes if they are more than 10 percent of your modified gross income.

6. Personal and payday loans.

THESE ARE cash advance debts which you may decide to pay when you get your next paycheck. Kagan (2021) affirms that these short-term loans have high-interest rates, which can go as high as 780% in annual interest rate (A.P.R.), depending on which state you are taking the loan from. A payday lender in California, for example, could ask you to pay 459% (A.P.R.) interest on a 14-day, $100 loan. Again, these loans have high finance charges because each $100 loan can attract a $15 finance fee.

I ADVISE you again to focus on paying off your debts since they can negatively impact your credit score and creditworthiness.

Potent Debt Repayment Strategies

Daly (2020) advises that you can use any of the following techniques to pay off your debts:

. . .

1. Debt snowball.

YOU ARE USING "DEBT SNOWBALL" if you always focus on using extra funds, you have to pay off your smallest debt before attending to bigger ones. Let's say you have three credit cards, which have $400, $2,000, and $5,000 worth of debt on them, respectively. After you've made the minimum payments on the three cards, you realize that you still have $150 of leftover funds, so you pay the money onto the $400 card. As soon as you clear the $400 card, you focus on the card with the $2,000 debt.

WITH THIS DEBT REPAYMENT TECHNIQUE, you can eliminate debt quickly and focus on the next one. However, more enormous debts command bigger interest rates than smaller ones, so a debt snowball may cause you savings issues since you aren't concentrating on paying off your high-interest-rate debts first.

2. Debt avalanche.

THIS IS the direct opposite of the debt snowball method: extra funds are first channeled into the highest-rate debts. As soon as a debt is paid off, attention then shifts to the next highest-rate debt.

SINCE THE HIGHEST-RATE debts command more interest, the debt avalanche method can help you save more money. Also, with this debt-repayment strategy, you can pay off a massive portion of your aggregate debt more quickly. However, more time will be required to eliminate the balances on your debt profile, which could be tough on motivation.

3. Debt consolidation.

THIS IS all about integrating several debts into one. A popular way to make this happen is by using a balance transfer credit card or personal loan to pay off all the debts.

YOU ONLY HAVE one monthly payment to make if you are using the debt consolidation technique. So, apart from making the debt repayment process more manageable, you won't have to worry about missing the due debt date. Again, with this method, you will enjoy a lower interest rate.

HOWEVER, if you don't have a good credit history, you can't opt for debt consolidation; remember that you need good credit to be considered for a debt consolidation loan or balance transfer credit card. The loan, for example, has a very reasonable interest rate.

4. Debt management plan.

A CREDIT COUNSELING agency can help you manage your debt profile for a fee. They would communicate with your creditors and arrange a debt management plan for you.

. . .

ARE you wondering if you could afford the payment plan? The agency would have a thorough financial discussion with you before it can negotiate with your creditors. As soon as the program clicks, you'll pay the agency once each month, and they'll dispense the money to your creditors. Since you make one monthly payment, this method makes debt repayment more manageable. Just be aware that credit counseling agencies will negotiate your fee waivers and monthly payment amount, but not the number of your debts.

IF I WERE YOU, I would watch these strategies closely to see how they work and select a suitable one.

Good Versus Bad Debt

It's okay for your parents or guardians always to tell you to avoid debt, but some people can't afford to purchase a home or buy a car unless they borrow money. Such loans are justifiable since they can add value to your life. Good debts might include mortgages, small business loans, and student loans.

BAD DEBTS, in contrast, won't benefit you in any way. Instead, they cause terrible financial issues (Smith, 2021). Although a reasonable debt comes with long-term benefits, a bad one doesn't have any usefulness at all. If a debt can boost your net worth and earn or make more money, the debt is a favorable one. If you borrow money to finance a project which doesn't deliver R.O.I. (returns on investment) or simply obtain a loan just for consumption, the debt is a terrible one. High-interest loans and credit card debts may constitute bad debts.

. . .

WHILE GOOD DEBTS address a person's *needs*, bad ones focus on their *wants*.

ACCORDING TO SMITH (2021), your financial situation and how much you can afford to lose often determine the status of your debts.

I'M sure that you won't have as much of a problem getting out of debt now since we've discussed some powerful debt repayment strategies you could use. If something looks blurry, reread the process to clear your doubts.

WE DISCUSSED critical topics surrounding the concepts of credit and debt management. It would be best if you got started with it. And that is what you will learn in the next chapter.

5

INVESTING

I n the previous chapter, you learned every crucial topic about credit and debt management. Here, I will expose the heart of investing, why you need to be an investor, and the appropriate steps to get started. I'm sure you will be eager to start your first investment when you finish reading this chapter. But, have a bit of patience because there are plenty of tricks to learn in the remaining three chapters.

TWELVE YEARS after we left high school in Charleston, South Carolina, I again met one of my friends. He was already a very wealthy man. I asked him how he could attain such wealth since he hadn't even turned thirty by then. He told me how he had saved $200 weekly in an investment plan for ten years and made about $140,000. He later invested that money in stocks and real estate.

HOW DID he become so rich in twelve years? I asked myself. Nothing was hidden about his upbringing: no inheritances, nor could his father afford to give him the kind of life other teenagers like him had while growing up.

You, too, can be successful with money if you start saving and investing. Stocks and real estate can fetch you some cool cash, but they aren't the only investment options available. Retirement plans can be wonderful avenues to grow your money and prepare for the future.

Start saving in a retirement plan right away if you hope to attain your financial goals early in life. Just opt for a high-interest plan which could quickly grow your money. You need to start saving and investing your money because your social security benefits can't offer you a comfortable retirement.

Here are some of the retirement accounts you could set up, according to Lauren Barret (2021):

- *401(k):* This is a retirement account you can open through your employer. Pre-tax payroll deductions are used to fund the account. Make sure you contribute sufficient funds to earn the full match if your employer offers any.
- *403(b):* You get to open this account through your employer if you work in a nonprofit firm or educational institution.
- *IRA:* This is an individual retirement account. You don't need your employer to open an IRA account. If you are self-employed or your employer doesn't offer a 401(k) retirement plan, the IRA can be a lifesaver.

Have you heard about the Roth IRA? It's an account you fund with after-tax money, so when you eventually want to withdraw your money, you won't pay tax on it. Roth IRA is the best way teens, and college students can save for retirement. Conventional IRAs are tax-deductible, unlike the Roth IRA accounts.

IF YOU AREN'T ready to retire, don't withdraw your IRA, 403(b), or 401(k) savings.

HOW CAN you select the right investment option to grow your wealth?

Choosing the Right Investment Option to Grow Your Money

Getting started with investing might seem risky, but you can be successful with it. Again, no matter how much you've saved, there's always a reasonable investment option you can opt for.

JUST MAKE sure you consider your income, expenses, assets, liabilities, and financial goals before you opt for any investment options. These tips can help you select suitable money-making investment options (Lam-Balfour & Royal, 2021):

1. Define your investment goals.

YOU CAN'T MAKE a perfect investment choice if you don't understand your investment goals, risk tolerance, and tools to achieve them. You can categorize your investment goals into short-term and long-term goals;

- **Long-term goals:** Retirement seems to be the universal long-term goal. A down-payment on a car, house, or college tuition may also be considered a long-term goal.
- **Short-term goals:** A Christmas piggy bank, emergency fund, or the following year's vacation qualifies as a short-term goal.

2. Identify the help you'll need.

PICK the investment option which suits your goal and channel your money into it.

SOME PEOPLE, especially first-time investors, often look for experts who can help them invest their money. If that's what you want, I have good news for you: Robo-advisors will handle your investments perfectly, at affordable rates. Robo-advisors are online investment consultants. They use advanced tech and computer algorithms to manage and grow the investment portfolios of their clients. So, you can trust them when you need automatic rebalancing, tax optimization, and human help.

3. Get an investment account.

. . .

Do you plan to purchase stocks or bonds? There's no way you can do so if you don't have an investment account. In Chapter Two, I told you that you could have a money market, certificates of deposit, and checking and savings bank accounts; similarly, there are a few investment accounts you should know about before you start investing your money.

PLEASE BE aware that some investment accounts hold tax advantages for retirement. Again, each version has its withdrawal rules. For example, you will be penalized or taxed if you withdraw your savings from your 401(k) account when you aren't due for retirement. There are other general-purpose investment accounts you could use to purchase a home, buy a car or attain any other goals. Popular investing accounts include:

- *401(k) retirement plan:* I already said a few things about this employer-sponsored investing account. So, if your employer offers the plan, embrace it.
- *Conventional or Roth IRA:* IRAs are a 401(k) lookalike; while 401(k) is provided by a person's employer, IRAs are designed for self-employed people. I already discussed IRAs at the beginning of this chapter.
- *Taxable account:* You might call this a non-retirement or non-qualified account. It's a flexible investing account that doesn't focus on any goal or objective. Since the account doesn't have any rules or specific tax advantages, you may withdraw your money anytime you want.
- *College savings accounts:* You will enjoy tax perks when you save your money in a college savings account. Notable college savings accounts include

Coverdell and 529. Contact an online broker when you are ready to open a college savings account.

4. Open the account.

SELECT YOUR ACCOUNT provider as soon as you decide the type of investment account you want to open. You have two main options;

- *Online broker:* Choose this option if you want to self-manage your account, buy and sell funds, real estate, bonds, and stocks.
- *Robo-advisor:* Hire a Robo-advisor if you are busy or don't have the required skills to manage your investments efficiently. Robo-advisors are investment experts and will charge you an annual fee, pegged at 0.25 or 0.50 percent of your R.O.I. (return on investment), to run your investments.

5. Select investments that suit your risk tolerance.

CONSIDER the amount of risk you could tolerate before choosing any investment opportunities. If you can't cope with high-risk investment options, embrace low-risk ones. Still, most times, high-risk investments yield substantial monetary returns. If you must take any risk at all, make sure it is a calculated risk.

. . .

HERE IS a list of the most common investment opportunities:

- *Stocks:* These are individual company shares; stocks confer company ownership on those who purchase them. For example, if you buy shares in Coca-Cola, you automatically become part of the company's owners. The monetary value of stocks usually increases over time.
- *Bonds:* A company can issue bonds to raise funds to finance a project or debt. Since bonds are fixed-income investments, purchase them to gain regular interest payments. Bonds have fixed maturity terms, so you won't get the principal amount you invested until the bonds mature.
- *Funds:* Exchange-traded funds (E.T.F.s), mutual funds, and index funds are veritable investment options you could use to purchase bonds, stocks, and other investment items. With these funds, you can diversify your investments and boost your income.
- *Real estate:* Financial worth or value of properties continually improve from time to time. So, if bonds and stocks do not thrill you, why not consider purchasing a house?

Buying a home doesn't mean you should become a landlord. Grow your money by investing in real estate investment trusts (REIT) or any online real estate investing forum.

DOES INVESTMENT HAVE ANY BENEFITS?

Why Do I Need to Invest?

People used to keep all their money in a savings account or even under their beds. But, inflation can threaten the value of the money you save in those places. Invest your money in a long-term investment option like 401(k), stocks, or real estate to subdue the threat of inflation (O'Shea & Lam-Balfour, 2021).

HERE ARE the main reasons why you need to start investing your money:

1. Investing combats inflation.

THE VALUE of your money keeps improving if you invest it.

2. It improves income.

START INVESTING your money if you want to attain financial freedom.

3. It secures the future.

ONE SURE WAY TO safeguard your future is to invest in a retirement plan, like 401(k) or Roth IRA.

REINVEST your returns to make more money.

How to Invest with Little Money

Don't wait until you become super-rich before you start investing your money. Cut your expenses and invest the extra money you have left (Weliver, 2021). Here is how to get started:

1. Use the cookie jar approach.
    This approach suggests that saving and investing are closely related. So, consider saving some money before you start investing it. For example, start saving $10 in a shoebox, envelope, or cookie jar weekly – if you do that consistently for a year, you will have $520.

WORK on your spending habits if you want to save more money. If you prefer online savings accounts to traditional savings tools – like a shoebox or envelope – *Chime* or *Aspiration Plus* would be perfect. If you need additional information about these online accounts, you can check their websites.

AS SOON AS YOUR "COOKIE JAR" has saved up enough money, channel it into one of the investment options you would like to invest in. You can keep repeating this as many as you like.

2. Hire a Robo-advisor.

YOU CAN STILL BE successful in investing, even if you don't have any investing experience. A Robo-advisor can help you manage your investments. Apart from their modest fees, you can start investing $500 or less if you hire a Robo-advisor.

. . .

ARE YOU A FIRST-TIME INVESTOR? I suggest you opt for *Wealthfront*. They'll charge 0.25 percent of your R.O.I. (returns on investment), but be assured that you won't pay a dime for your first $5,000; they will do it for you for free. However, you must have $500 to start investing with *Wealthfront*.

WHAT HAPPENS if you don't have up to $500? Use *M1 Finance* instead. You are good to go if you have $100, their minimum starting balance, and they won't charge you commissions or fees.

BETTERMENT IS another option you could opt for if you need a Robo-advisor. Start investing with them with $100 or less since they don't have any minimum starting balance. However, their management fee is 0.25 percent of your R.O.I.

3. Opt for brokers with a zero-percent commission.

STOCKBROKERS USED to charge a commission each time stocks were sold or bought. At the time, you couldn't venture into investing if you didn't have several thousand dollars. The whole thing has now changed, and some brokers charge little to no commission at all now. So, with as little as $1, you can start an investment.

AGAIN, you can invest your spare bucks in businesses with partial or fractional shares. So, if you don't have the funds to purchase a full share, go for a fraction of the share. Let's say you want to invest in a huge company like Apple or Google – a share of the company could be up to hundreds or even thousands of dollars. So, you can just purchase a fraction of the share if you don't have that much.

PUBLIC AND ROBINHOOD are amazing investing apps you could use as a green investor.

4. Embrace micro-investing.

I JUST SPOKE about purchasing mere fractions of shares. Yes, even those super small investments can grow your money.

LET'S say you consistently save up $50 per month and put it in your cute piggy bank. After ten years it will become $6,000. But, by investing it consistently, you will save around $8,000 (assuming a conservative 6-7% annual interest rate) – an easy $2,000 extra with the same amount of saving!

FEEL free to check and use *Acorns* to apply micro-investing of your spare money (Rapacon, 2019).

SO, don't allow anything or anyone to stop you from investing your spare money. Start small and watch your investment grow. Just keep in mind a few investing rules you need to apply to attain your investment goals.

. . .

5. Enroll In a Retirement Plan

YOU CAN START by investing in your employer-sponsored plan that you can afford. You can invest as little as 2% of your salary, and you will not even notice it. Even if you are on a tight budget, this is something you can do. You can increase the contribution gradually as your salary increases or as your budget loosens up. It is a good way to start saving even with very little monthly income.

6. Start an Online Business

STARTING an online business is one of the easiest ways to make money for yourself. This is a business that is run on the internet. It is also called e-business. Starting an online business is an exciting venture. It, however, is not as easy as it might seem. One needs to be organized and determined to make it work. The online business world is pretty congested, and you need to put in the effort to set yourself apart from the rest. An online business can be selling goods online, coaching and consulting, digital marketing service, freelancing, and virtual assistant work. You can do this from the comfort of your home, and therefore very little capital is needed. This is an ideal business type for young people who are highly computer literate and want to start making money at a young age.

Investing Rules to Keep in Mind

Hey, you can't get rich or attain your financial goals if you don't start investing your money. You must choose the right investment option to grow your money or lose it. Bieber (2018) recommends that you apply these investing rules if you ever hope to attain wealth via investments:

1. Take advantage of compound interest.

I HAVE ALREADY SAID a few things about compound interest in this book. Compound interest is the act of reinvesting your investment returns to make more money. If you reinvest your returns, you can make huge money from your small and steady investments. Soon, you can attain your investment or financial goals, including financial freedom.

HOW? Invest in assets with reasonable return rates, though the earlier you start, the better. Such assets may include stocks, bonds, and real estate. Reinvest your investment returns into these assets and watch your money work for you.

2. Understand risks versus rewards.

EACH INVESTMENT HAS its unique risks, and high-risk investments usually have higher returns. So, evaluate the potential risks and rewards of an investment before you channel your money into it. Each person has a risk tolerance level.

YOU CAN INVEST in high-risk stocks if you want to be successful with money. Should things then go south, you should have adequate time to recover. Just make sure you don't put all of your money in a single high-risk asset, especially when you get older. Instead, identify a few low-risk investment options and diversify your investment. You will have better chances to keep your money growing positively.

3. Invest for the long-term.

YOU HAVE ALREADY LEARNED a few things about short-term and long-term investments. That's fine but concentrate on long-term investments if you hope to grow your money. And don't invest funds you'll soon need or money you can't afford to lose.

FOR EXAMPLE, you need to tie up money for several years if you invest in a retirement plan like 401(k) or Roth IRA. Early withdrawals from these accounts often come with penalties.

AGAIN, if you invest in stocks or real estate, like other assets, you may have to leave your money for many years to avoid any downturns.

4. Invest in assets you understand.

You will lose your money if you invest in assets you are unfamiliar with. So, best to take your time to research and understand the fundamentals of the investment area(s) you're yearning for. That way, you can avoid every investment disaster.

IT'S okay if you want a Robo-advisor to oversee your investments for you. Robo-advisors are investment professionals, and they charge reasonable fees.

. . .

DIVERSIFY YOUR PORTFOLIO.

I'M sure you'd do everything you can to avoid significant investment losses. So, consider diversifying or spreading your investment funds across several assets, different industries, and locations. Don't put all your money into a single investment.

YOU HAVE ALREADY SEEN the heart and soul of investing, why you need to be an investor, that you should start early, and the unique steps to take to get started. It's okay if you want to start your first investment straight away, but best to create an alternative plan, so you won't suffer any setbacks if the initial plan doesn't work. With our focus on plan Bs in the next chapter, we will discuss the benefits of having backups to deal with unforeseen investment circumstances.

6

PLAN BS

I n the previous chapter, you saw the essence of investing, why you need to become an investor, and the creative steps to start investing your money. This chapter is strictly on the benefits of having backups and how to create alternative investment plans, to prevent any unforeseen setbacks.

I CAN TELL you that nothing is guaranteed in this life. Don't relax simply because you have a paying job already. If you fold your arms now and eventually lose your job tomorrow, how would you cope? Won't that signal the end of your unique financial goals?

IF YOU CREATE MORE income streams, you can earn more than your weekly or monthly wages and salaries, so you won't put your freedom and lifestyle at risk. Let's say you have three streams of income. For example, should one stream suffer a decline, the other two streams will generate money to pay your bills.

Exposing the Wrong Way of Creating Multiple Streams of Income

There may be some misunderstandings going around about grabbing multiple streams of income, but it's much simpler than it seems. Split your investments into different business fields to create additional sources of residual income. Simply build more streams of income to avert unnecessary risks or losses (Tressider, n.d.).

I HAVE MET people who see investment as a money game; they admire the process of building wealth because it is exciting. So, since they enjoy the game, they are eager to invest their money into stocks, bonds, real estate and other investment platforms simply because they want to create more income streams. Such people are always at risk of losing their money because they don't see investment as a challenge.

ONE WRONG WAY TO get started is to venture into several investment options at the same time. Let's say a person creates a new business, invests in stocks and purchases real estate properties within two months – the person won't be able to manage these investments and may suffer terrible losses. Reckless risk isn't a wise business strategy. You will fail if you are so irrational that you invest in business fields you know little or nothing about. It would help if you had sufficient preparation or knowledge to succeed in any business or investment.

. . .

I WOULD BE LYING if I said reckless risks don't work out sometimes. But, most times, people who take reckless risks end up disappointed. You need *calculated* risks to experience success in your investments, not reckless ones.

AGAIN, you aren't the only one trying to create additional streams of income. Your success depends on how well you can compete with other professionals trying to use the business field to improve their earnings. So, anyone who tells you that it's going to be easy is not being entirely truthful. There's always a price to pay for any additional stream of income you create.

Exploring the Proven Ways to Create Multiple Streams of Income

Here is a step-by-step process for building multiple streams of income:

1. Master your first stream.

WHAT IS your current income stream? Is it stocks, bonds, real estate or a personal business? Be deeply passionate about it. Also, try to understand it thoroughly before you start to create another one.

WHY SHOULD you master your first stream of income? Because it is where you'll learn essential investment skills and how to combat and overcome success barriers.

. . .

2. Systemize the first stream.

CREATE a string of systems to maximize the first stream so that it doesn't require your attention all the time. You may need to hire some ~~Idea~~ s or use technology to manage the income stream. Do a few auto-pilot studies to perfect your systematizing skills.

3. Leverage your resources to build more streams of income.

USE your energy and free time to add extra income streams which could fit your skills, knowledge and network, or start from scratch with each stream.

FOR EXAMPLE, let's assume you are a marketer. You can make more money conveniently if you develop another income stream to use your current marketing skills, network and databases.

ROBERT KIYOSAKI, the author of *Rich Dad Poor Dad*, is a perfect example of someone who leveraged their resources to create extra income streams. He went into real estate and later added paper assets. He used his investment experience to create a very successful publishing business.

ARE there any income-building ideas or suggestions you could use to boost earnings?

Ideas for Additional Income Generation

It's always the case that there are additional specific financial goals to attain or more stuff to purchase; we all need money for lots of reasons. Many people say that it's easier to spend money than earn it.

I OFTEN TELL people that the problem isn't saving money but generating additional income. How can you save any if you aren't earning more than you need to run your home, especially if you are married? Elliott (n.d.) thinks people aren't making more money because they are bereft of money-making ideas.

USE any of these financial ideas to enhance your earnings:

1. Freelancing.

I KNOW someone who earns an extra $300 every week from a famous freelancing company, on top of the salary he gets from the tech firm he works with. Freelancing can fetch you some extra money, too, if you make it a side hustle. You could offer writing and coding services or work as a virtual assistant online. Freelancing offers flexible job options you can easily do from the comfort of your home. Set up a freelancing account on *Upwork*, *Fiverr* or *Freelancer* if you would like to earn extra money through freelancing. There are also tons of writing jobs on *ProBlogger* if you have a passion for writing.

. . .

2. Start a home-based business.

RESEARCH TO ASCERTAIN the everyday needs of people in your neighborhood, then start a home-based business that can meet those needs. Just make sure that the business excites you, or you'll soon lose enthusiasm. Again, either the business suits your existing skillset, or you learn how to do it.

FOR EXAMPLE, you can start a home-based brownie or cake business if baking thrills you. Should you crave sewing, create some gorgeous crafts during your free time – you can sell them via Etsy or Amazon.

3. Develop a course and sell it online.

CREATE an online course on any topic and sell it through *Teachable.com* – just make sure the course can add value to the lives of prospective buyers. If it does, many people will place orders, and you'll soon earn the trust of your readers or viewers (if the course is a video). *Teachable* currently sells any course which can add value to people's lives. But, based on bestseller tips, you should focus more on web-based cartoons, painting, digital scrapbooking and card magic.

THERE ARE SEVERAL ALTERNATIVE PLATFORMS, too, other than *Teachable*, which you can check out. Just use the power of *Google*, and you will instantly find out that creating and selling online courses has now become a real deal.

. . .

4. Investments.

YOU ALREADY KNOW how to run a successful investment. Bonds provide interest, while stocks yield dividends. And, if you venture into rental properties, you stand to gain rental income.

5. Peer-to-peer lending.

MANY PEOPLE ARE MAKING extra money via peer-to-peer lending outlets, like *The Lending Club*. You can also identify any of these platforms and start earning more regular bucks.

6. Social media influencer.

BEING A YOUTUBER, Blogger, or Instagrammer (not sure if that's a word), I would all put under the general category of being an influencer. If you're able to build a sizeable audience on any of these platforms, you can start to monetize your pages, whether through putting ads on your YouTube channel or blog or getting paid by brands to promote products on your Instagram feed. Being an influencer is also a great way to get tons of free stuff in exchange for promoting products/services to your audience.

SOCIAL MEDIA now can become a powerful asset, especially if you have a significant number of followers/subscribers. Any business outlets know that social media wields enormous marketing strength; you can reach out to advertisers if you can use social media to boost their sales and improve their businesses. Find a way to convince them that you can use social media to promote and enhance their business, and they will pay cool cash for you to do it.

START MARKETING your social media skills to business outfits in your local area before you start looking elsewhere.

7. Online surveys.

SURVEY JUNKIE, like other online survey platforms, can pay you when you share opinions which could help brands improve their products and services. Create a profile on their website to start taking these online surveys. You get virtual points for each survey you complete and can redeem the points via *PayPal*.

8. Affiliate marketing.

YOU ARE an affiliate marketer if you earn a commission by helping people or companies promote their products or services (Lake, 2019). Bloggers, online entrepreneurs, and anyone with a website and stable audience base can be a successful affiliate marketer.

PROSPECTIVE AFFILIATE MARKETERS should understand marketing strategies like display ads, search engine optimization (S.E.O.), content marketing, unboxing, product reviews, email marketing and paid search engine marketing (S.E.M.).

AMAZON, *ClickBank*, *Rakuten* and *ShareASale* are complex affiliate networks where you can earn lots of commissions on several products and services.

HOW CAN you become an affiliate marketer?

- Identify a company or product to promote.
- Register as an affiliate marketer to obtain a personal affiliate link.
- Add the link to your website.

If someone visits your site and clicks the link, they will be taken to the product's page to make a purchase, and you'll get a commission for each item bought via your affiliate link.

9. Vending Machines

I do have some personal experience in this business. When I was 13-years old, I bought my first Vending Machine. A used vending machine typically costs anywhere from $800-$3000, so it does require significant upfront investment; however, if you find the right location, they can be quite profitable for a minimal amount of effort required. Think about it; a vending machine is a perfect business. It's like running your own mini store with no employee or rent costs. A vending machine in a solid location can earn $50-$100 per week. Some of the locations you might want first to approach are factories/warehouses, hotels/inns, auto body shops, office buildings, and other high-traffic locations. You also don't necessarily need to buy the standard snack vending machine to get started. You can start small by buying a gumball machine for $200-$300 or simply by buying an honor box for $30-$70. An honor box is essentially a snack box where you leave snacks in a box and trust people to leave money in the slip of the box. You might want to place one of these in an area where people often wait, like a nail salon or a barbershop. Based on my assumptions, you can probably make $10 a week running one of these. Overall, vending machines are great businesses for young adults and teens to operate. You just need to make sure you find a good location before buying one!

PICK and utilize any of these money-making ideas and see your income grow.

OTHER THAN HAVING multiple income streams, there is something else that you should consider as plan B if something unexpected happens. It is insurance.

Efficient Insurance Options for Teens and College Students

If you hope to secure yourself, your family, and businesses or investments, purchase insurance. Should there be any illness, accident, or disaster, insurance could save you tons of dollars (Loudenback, 2019). Some say you should clock up forty or forty-five years before considering purchasing health and auto insurance policies, but life and disability insurance have nothing to do with age; I honestly think you should buy them now. Unfortunate events like accidents, disasters, and illness are common, remember. If you are hit with any of these lethal events and have no insurance to fall back on, your entire financial life will crumble. Across many U.S. states, for example, car insurance is inevitable, whereas life insurance depends on your decision.

AGAIN, insurance is relative; someone's policy type or proportion of coverage may not suit another person's financial need and situation. Also, should you have a baby or secure a new job, the scope of your insurance will change. An insurance program could be an alternative plan to prevent emergencies and save more money.

INSURANCE OPTIONS CAN INCLUDE:

1. Health insurance.

CHECK if there's any health insurance scheme in your workplace. Ask if your employer offers high-deductible health plans. You might need premium health plans to qualify for the H.S.A. (health savings account).

HOWEVER, if you have to purchase personal health insurance, check the available options to select an insurance plan you can afford. Analyze the plans offered and look at the quotes carefully from different insurance providers. Try to find the lowest rates and see if you are eligible for a subsidy based on your income. Consider using your parents' health insurance plan if you aren't quite twenty-six years old (Fontinelle, 2021). If your parents don't have a health insurance plan, opt for one which suits your income. Although some conditions can't be avoided, try to stay fit and healthy if you don't want to spend on medical bills all the time.

2. Renter's insurance.

IF YOU LIVE in a rented apartment, you have to obtain renter's insurance to protect your property from incidents like burglary or fire. Please go through the policy carefully to know the items your insurance will cover.

3. Disability insurance.

ILLNESS OR INJURY could prevent you from working to earn a living. Disability insurance can protect you from the financial agony of being unable to work. It will ensure that you keep receiving an income until you get well.

4. Auto insurance.

DRIVERS in 49 U.S. states are expected to purchase an auto insurance policy. Get auto insurance if you have or drive a car; the insurance will cover potential car damage and bodily harm caused by an accident.

IT'S hard to find a successful investor who doesn't have backup investment plans. I'm glad you've now seen the benefits of having backups and how to create alternative investment strategies to address any unexpected investment lapses.

Now you need to understand taxes inside out since returns on investment (R.O.I.) are taxed. That's exactly what you'll learn in the next chapter.

7

INCOME TAXES

I n the previous chapter, you saw the benefits of having backup investment plans and creating powerful alternative strategies to deal with unforeseen investment knocks. We will concentrate on taxes here, and I will tell you the fundamentals you need to know.

PAYMENT OF TAXES isn't a choice; it is obligatory for people who are earning money. You must understand how income is taxed, even if you have yet to receive your first paycheck. Let's assume a company offers you a $2,500 salary per month. Calculate the after-tax value of the salary to see if it could sustain and assist you in achieving your financial goals and obligations. PaycheckCity.com, like many other online calculators, can be used to estimate your after-tax salary.

AGAIN, remember that income taxes are due as soon as you are paid and may be deducted from your paychecks. So, if you just got your first job, congratulations. You may still be living with

Dad and Mom, but since you now have a job, you will be paying various taxes, like every other American, if you live in the U.S. (Aspiriant Fathom, 2017).

Do You Need to File Taxes?

First, you need to figure them out based on your marital status and annual gross income. Here is the latest standard deduction for the 2020-2021 tax year (*Nerdwallet*, 2021):

Filing status	2020 tax year	2021 tax year
Single	$12,400	$12,550
Married, filing jointly	$24,800	$25,100
Married, filing separately	$12,400	$12,550
Head of household	$18,650	$18,800

So, for example, if you are single and your current monthly salary is $1,000, which will bring you an annual of $12,000, it means you don't have an obligation to file your taxes because your annual gross income will be less than $12,400. But, let's say you get a raise to $1,500/month – which will bring your annual income to $18,000 – then $18,000 - $12,400 = *$5,600*, which will be taxable, and you have to file for it.

HOWEVER, even if you don't need to file taxes, you may still want to do so. If your employer withholds taxes from your paychecks, or you qualify for earned income tax credit (E.I.T.C.), you can get a refund, even if your earning is less than the filing requirement.

LEARNING How to File Your Taxes

. . .

YOU COULD USE an online program or tax software to file your taxes. But, if you don't feel like doing it yourself, hire a certified public accountant or a tax preparer. Lest you forget, you will need the *1040EZ* tax form, employer-generated *W*-2, income stubs, and *1099-MISC* to file your taxes.

LET'S say your modified total income stands at $72,000 or less; you won't pay a dime to file your federal income taxes using the *I.R.S. Free File. TurboTax*, like many online tax preparation companies, offers free tax-filing services in partnership with the I.R.S. People with a 1040 return or who aren't qualified for itemized deductions can use *TurboTax* free tax-filing services.

↳ Understand this better as an international

JUST BE aware that April 15 is the due date for taxes, though you should check the I.R.S. website to know the deadlines for different tax filing methods. File your taxes early if you hope to get your refund soon; you might lose your refund to an identity thief if you delay the process. Also, run the filing procedure electronically to have the rebate quickly deposited into your bank account.

USE a check to pay your taxes, or simply run the payment directly from your bank account, debit, or credit card. No problem if you can't pay the entire tax bill by the due date; talk to the I.R.S. to see if you can reach an installment agreement with them.

THERE ARE a few effortless tax-filing things you can learn to run the process efficiently.

Helpful Tips About Filing Taxes

Remember that your annual tax return must be filed with the I.R.S. on April 15 or earlier! And, since you may have to do it personally, I advise you to keep a thorough record of your income and expenses. Be organized and start working on your earnings and expenditures. With that, you won't have any issues creating a detailed record of your income and expenses. Essential things to deal with include:

1. Pay as you go.

HAVE YOU HEARD OF "PAYCHECK SHOCK"? If this is your first job, you probably haven't. By the time your first paycheck is issued, you will know what paycheck shock means. But I won't let you wait until then. Paycheck shock occurs when you suddenly realize that the amount paid into your account is lower than the salary you bargained with your employer.

THE LAW COMPELS your employer to deduct state and federal taxes from your salary, including Medicare and social security funds. You likely filled the W-4 form before starting your current job and stated some allowances there. The amount you pay to the I.R.S. and state tax agencies depends on what is said in the form. So, after your taxes and other funds have been removed, your take-home could be 20 or 30 per cent lower than your cumulative income.

2. Tax returns.

. . .

YOU NEED to file your annual tax return to avoid any horrible, income-shrinking tax deductions. Tax regulations could be time-consuming and complicated. Still, you won't have to struggle to file your tax if you understand the process.

ALWAYS REMEMBER that your income taxes run through January 1 and December 31 without breaking. Your employer(s) should send you *Form W-2* and the previous year's cumulative earnings, paid taxes, and other contributions. Your bank will also send you your earning and interest updates. Since you may need your annual tax records to correct possible figure disparities, I suggest keeping them secure.

GET ready to file a federal tax return if you are single and don't hang on anyone's tax return, especially if your annual income is up to $10,350. If you can find someone who would claim you as a dependent, it is best to do so. Then, if any of these situations apply to you, file the tax return:

- You earned over $6,300.
- You have over $1,050 unearned income, like interest or dividends.
- Your total income is up to $6,310 or more.

Check whether your state has a different tax requirement.

MY ADVICE IS to keep your tax receipts in a secure place.

Vital Things to Know About Taxes

Tax day pops up only once a year, yet keeping up a stunning tax profile can feel like a year-long task. You could file your tax or hire a tax professional to do it, but you might end up with a few money issues if you don't understand specific filing obligations (Erb, 2016). Here are crucial things you must know about taxes:

1. A federal income tax return isn't for everyone.

SOME PEOPLE ARE exempt from filing a federal income tax return, even if they earned income during the calendar year. For example, your filing status, age, the amount earned, and the source of the revenue determine whether you should file the tax return or not. For more information or clarification, visit the I.R.S. website.

2. Enjoy tax breaks and credits if you can't file a federal income tax return.

SINCE TAX CREDITS are dollar-for-dollar reductions in tax due, they offer more financial benefits than tax deductions, which only reduce a person's taxable income.

EVEN WHEN YOU owe no tax, the American Opportunity Credit (A.O.C.) may send you money in the form of credits. Tuition and fees fall under A.O.C. qualified expenses for students. The maximum credit for each eligible student is $2,500, and 40 per cent of this fund may be refundable.

. . .

WORKING people and those with moderate income could opt for the earned income tax credit (E.I.T.C.). Some people erroneously assume that you must have kids before being considered for the E.I.T.C., but having kids may only boost or improve the benefit. Although people without qualifying kids could access credits to the tune of $503, those with three or more kids could achieve up to $6,242.

3. Certain deductions don't require itemization.

IT WOULD BE best to itemize to enjoy most deductions, so they miss out automatically since most taxpayers don't itemize. Yet, all isn't lost since the I.R.S. has a few deductions you can enjoy without itemization. Just grab *Form 1040* and check its front page to see these deductions. Some of the deductions include moving expenses, IRA, and student loan interest.

4. Make estimated payments if you are self-employed.

WE USE A PAY-AS-YOU-GO TAX SYSTEM. That's why your employer withholds taxes from an employee's paycheck and transfers the same to the I.R.S. (Internal Revenue Service). So, the employee may owe taxes, break-even, or be owed by the I.R.S. at the close of the year.

SELF-EMPLOYED FREELANCERS, landlords, shareholders, and everyone with *Form 1099* can make estimated payments. Such people can download *Form 1040ES* from the I.R.S. website and use it to make their estimated payments.

PAY your estimated taxes quarterly if you fall under this category. Should you pay late or skip a payment, get ready to pay a penalty fee.

5. File a return when you can't pay off your tax bill.

IF YOU FAIL to pay your tax bill or file a return, you will be penalized. Still, you can avoid one of these penalties and lessen the financial mess on your wallet. Don't empty too much if you can't pay off your tax bill on tax day; there are a few payment plans or arrangements you can make with the I.R.S. if you don't want to pay with your credit card all at once.

6. Due dates matter.

MAKE sure you file your returns and pay your tax bills by due dates to avoid interest and penalties, which could pile up quickly. Ask for an extension if you believe you can't file your returns or pay your tax bills by their due dates.

7. An extension of time to pay tax bills is different from an extension of time to file returns.

. . .

I ALREADY SAID you could ask for an extension of time if you believe you can't file your tax return when it's due; use *Form 4868* to request an extension. Extension of time comes with no cost if you don't owe any tax bills. But, should it go the other way, you would have to make payment to avert penalty and interest.

Understanding the Process of Tax Computation

Tax owed depends on the income you generate.

THERE ARE two forms of income: earned and unearned. Earned income covers earnings on paid jobs and may include salaries, wages, tips, and commissions. Unearned income isn't the direct gain of your weekly or monthly efforts. Most times, it comes from your investment, technically called R.O.I. (returns on investment). Such returns usually come in the form of capital gains, interest, or dividends.

ALTHOUGH YOU MAY ONLY HAVE to pay income taxes for your unearned income, you could be subjected to income and payroll taxes for your earned income. Gifts, life insurance proceeds, child support, after-tax premiums on disabilities, and inheritance are not taxable.

THE I.R.S. USES a cycle of ranges (also called "brackets") to depict or represent your incremental income. Then, they will evaluate your modified gross income (after they've made some deductions from your cumulative income). Qualified moving expenses, alimony, and IRA contributions are some of these deductions.

. . .

TAX DEDUCTIONS WILL REDUCE your earnings a little bit. However, you can claim a standard or itemized deduction. The standard deduction is a fixed amount based on your filing status, whereas itemized cover the deductions which may apply to you. Itemized deductions include property taxes, medical and education expenses, charitable contributions, and mortgage loan interest. Opt for standard deduction if you have a straightforward financial situation. But, should you be someone who gives a lot of money to charity, pays income taxes, extensive medical bills, or runs several investments, choose the itemized option.

LEGITIMATE ITEMIZED DEDUCTIONS INCLUDE:

- Property taxes, like state income or sales taxes.
- Health-related expenses greater than 10 percent of your A.G.I. (or 7.5 percent if you are 65 years or older).
- Mortgage interest on residences to the tune of $1 million and interest on residence equity loans up to $100,000.
- Generous donations to tax-exempt institutions.
- Margin interest and other investment interest expenses.

Other things you could itemize are:

- Employer-withheld expenses, like professional dues, uniforms, and unreimbursed travel expenses.
- Investment advisor fees.
- Tax-preparation fees.

However, these additional expenses must exceed 2 percent of your A.G.I. before you can itemize them.

REMEMBER that you can't deduct credit card interest, political contributions, or loan interest on a private car.

STILL, you could claim a personal exemption for yourself, your spouse, and your qualified dependents. The exemption is the amount you could deduct from your adjusted gross income (A.G.I.). The amount was $3,950 as of 2014. There are three categories of personal exemptions that you could claim:

1. Yourself.

EACH PERSON CAN CLAIM one exemption for themselves.

2. Your spouse.

A JOINT RETURN could be filed by married couples: one for the husband and the other for the spouse.

3. Dependents.

PEOPLE with qualified dependents can file an exemption for each of them. A dependent could be one's child or relative.

. . .

WHAT MAKES ONE A QUALIFIED DEPENDENT?

A CHILD'S AGE, residency, relationship with you, and means of support can make them eligible. Again, apart from your relationship with a relative, their qualification depends on their gross income and the amount of support you can give them. Should you need further clarification on this, visit the I.R.S. website *www.IRS.gov.*

CALCULATE your tax due and taxable income as soon as you know your A.G.I., deductions, and exemptions. A comprehensive tax table and advice on taxable and non-taxable income are readily available on the I.R.S. website; again, the tax due depends on your tax rate. Should you need to estimate the amount you owe or refund you should get, subtract your payment (tax credits) from your tax due.

BE aware that your A.G.I. is a vital fraction of your tax calculation. To calculate the A.G.I., certain deductions need to be made from your cumulative income. These deductions, according to Schwab (n.d.), include:

- Deductible IRA contributions.
- Alimony.
- Contributions to a self-employed retirement plan.
- Penalty on early withdrawal of savings.
- Teacher education expenses, to the tune of $250.
- Qualified education interest.
- Qualified higher-education expenses.
- Half of self-employment taxes.
- Self-employed health insurance.

- Qualified moving expenses.

Why is the A.G.I. so important?

YOUR ELIGIBILITY for certain credits and deductions depends on your A.G.I. For example, if your A.G.I. is more than $114,000 or $191,000, you can't contribute to a Roth IRA as a single or married tax filer, respectively.

Clarifying the Truth About Tax Rate

The tax rate covers the percentage of income you pay in taxes; the amount depends on the size of your income. There are two significant types of tax rate:

1. Marginal tax rate.

THIS IS the ratio or proportion of tax paid on the last dollar of your taxable income. In other words, your marginal tax rate is the additional tax paid on each extra dollar you earn.

2. Average tax rate.

THIS IS the regular tax you often pay. Divide the total tax paid by your total earnings to calculate your average tax rate.

. . .

FOR EXAMPLE, John is single, and his taxable income stands at $40,000. His marginal income tax rate would be 25 percent, whereas his average tax rate could be a bit lower.

LET'S say you want to quit your current job because you desperately need a salary increase. Asking for a raise isn't a bad thing, but you must first consider the impact of your marginal tax on the raise. For example, if your marginal tax rate is 10 percent, 10 cents of the extra dollar you earn will be used to pay tax. So, you may not be getting the raise you so desire.

HERE'S a table on the U.S. statutory marginal tax rates:

Rate	For Unmarried Individuals	For Married Individuals Filing Joint Returns	For Heads of Households
10%	$0 to $9,950	$0 to $19,900	$0 to $14,200
12%	$9,951 to $40,525	$19,901 to $81,050	$14,201 to $54,200
22%	$40,526 to $86,375	$81,051 to $172,750	$54,201 to $86,350
24%	$86,376 to $164,925	$172,751 to $329,850	$86,351 to $164,900
32%	$164,926 to $209,425	$329,851 to $418,850	$164,901 to $209,400
35%	$209,426 to $523,600	$418,851 to $628,300	$209,401 to $523,600
37%	$523,601 or more	$628,301 or more	$523,601 or more

Source: Tax Basics

THERE'S another tax rate you must know about if you hope to be successful with money. It's called the "combined marginal tax rate," capturing federal and state income tax rates. For example, if your federal and state taxes are 25 and 5 percent, respectively, your combined tax rate will be 30 percent of your taxable income. You can't get the actual value of your R.O.I. if you aren't familiar with this tax rate.

Using Tax Credit

Use a tax credit to reduce your taxes, dollar for dollar. The tax credit doesn't just lower your taxable income like a deduction. It ensures that the reduction reflects on the amount of taxes you'll pay. For example, a $100 credit automatically lessens your taxes by $100 (Schwab, n.d.).

DEDUCTIONS, as you already know, are removed from a person's income to lower their taxes. Tax credits reduce the tax amount a person owes. You may still owe some tax amounts after you've claimed all deductions available. However, you can use tax credits to lessen your tax debt or erase it (Schreier, 2021). Tax credits come in three major types: nonrefundable, refundable, and partially refundable.

NONREFUNDABLE TAX CREDITS can only be used in the current reporting year; you can't carry them over to the coming years. Although a nonrefundable tax credit may be used to lessen or lower tax liability to zero, you can't use it to get a tax refund. Nonrefundable tax credits include mortgage interest credit, lifetime learning credit, credits for adoption, and dependent care credit.

REFUNDABLE TAX CREDITS offer taxpayers the entire amount of the credit. For example, each taxpayer will get a refund for the credit if the refundable tax credit decreases their tax liability to zero. Earned income tax credit and the premium tax credit are examples of refundable tax credits.

IT's a little different with a partially refundable tax credit. For example, if your tax liability is zero before using the total amount of a tax credit, the remainder credit may be refunded. The American education tax credit is an excellent example of a partially refundable tax credit.

TAX CREDITS COME in different forms, so opt for the one which suits your income and personal situation. Available tax credit options include:

- Qualified adoption expenses.
- A qualified child under 17.
- Child and dependent care credit.
- Residential energy.
- The American education tax credit, for the first four college years' qualified expenses (once known as the "Hope Credit").
- The lifetime learning credit, for improving job-related, skill-enhancing expenses and undergraduate, graduate or professional degree attainment.
- A premium tax credit, used when purchasing health insurance for individuals and families.
- The earned income tax credit, for low-income individuals and families.

Earned income tax credit is quite different from other tax credits already mentioned; it only offers a refund, not a credit against taxes due. Visit the I.R.S. website to learn more about it.

. . .

LEARNING Everything About Tax Refunds

THE I.R.S. PAYS a lot of tax refunds every year. Still, many teens and college students know little to nothing about these refunds.

A TAX REFUND is a repayment to a taxpayer who overpaid their taxes to a state or federal government (*Tax Refund*, 2021). Many taxpayers often see a refund as free or bonus money, but that's not the truth; it's nothing but an interest-free loan a taxpayer gives to the government.

INTEREST-FREE LOANS, like tax refunds, may negatively impact your finances, but you can avoid them. How? Get to know why you overpaid your taxes and prevent possible recurrences. Here are the likely causes of overpaid federal or state taxes:

1. The taxpayer didn't fill their I.R.S. *Form W-4* correctly.
2. The taxpayer didn't update the form to indicate they have a child and are entitled to a child tax credit.
3. The taxpayer deliberately manipulated *Form W-4* to generate an enormous tax refund.

So, the refund you get depends on what's being withheld from your paycheck. Still, if what's removed is too little, you'll be charged an underpayment penalty. U.S. savings bonds, personal checks and direct deposits may be used to issue your tax refunds.

.   .   .

REFUNDS ARE FASCINATING, but you gain more if you don't overpay your taxes. Refunds are interest-free loans, remember.

Understanding Payroll Taxes

A payroll tax is a proportion of an employee's paycheck, which is withheld by the employer and sent to the government through the I.R.S. The tax may be deducted from employees' wages, tips, and salaries (Kagan, 2021).

FOR EXAMPLE, in the United States, federal payroll taxes are mainly used to finance Medicare, workers' compensation, and social security programs. So, these taxes are often tagged as FICA or MedFICA on pay stubs.

WAGE or salaried employees should know that they won't shoulder the entire payroll tax; payroll taxes are usually split into two equal sums: the employer settles a fraction, while the other part is withheld from each employee's paycheck. Self-employed people have to pay the full amount.

CERTAIN PAYROLL TAXES have yearly limits. For example, if your income is more than the social security wage base, you won't have to pay the social security tax in the United States. As of 2021, the wage base is pegged at $142,800.

SOCIAL SECURITY HAS A SALARY LIMIT, but Medicare has none. For example, a 6.2 percent social security deduction applies for a maximum salary of $142,800. Indeed, Medicare doesn't have any salary restrictions, but you will pay 0.9 percent for

Medicare if your income is $200,000 or more (apart from 2.9 percent for Medicare).

FREELANCE WRITERS, musicians, contractors, small-scale business owners, and other self-employed people need to pay their payroll taxes, also known as self-employment taxes. The self-employment tax rate is 15.3 percent and covers social security (12.4 percent) and Medicare (2.9 percent). But, don't forget, you'll pay an extra 0.9 percent of your self-employment earnings on $200,000 or more.

PERHAPS YOU NEED to open a tax-advantaged account to lower your taxes.

Uncovering Tax-Advantaged Accounts

A tax-advantaged account means a tax-deferred or tax-exempt investment, financial, or savings plan. Such accounts come with a few tax benefits and may include partnerships, U.I.T.s, municipal bonds, and annuities, as well as IRAs, 401(k), 403(b), and similar retirement plans (Chen, 2021).

MANY INVESTORS and employees use tax-advantaged accounts to improve their financial situations. For example, employees use Roth IRA, 403(b), 401(k), and employer-sponsored retirement plans to secure their future, even as each high-income taxpayer is eager to embrace the tax-free, municipal-bond income.

. . .

Tax-exempt and tax-deferred statuses remain the standard methods people use to reduce their tax bills. Decide which methods (or both) to use to enhance your finances. after you've analyzed the timeframe to get their benefits.

- *Tax-deferred accounts:* You will get immediate tax deductions on the entire amount deposited in a tax-deferred account. However, you will be taxed for successive withdrawals. Conventional IRAs and 401(k) plans are popular tax-deferred retirement accounts in the United States; as suggested by the account's name, taxes on income are delayed or deferred. Let's say $40,000 is your taxable income this year, and you saved $3,000 in a tax-deferred account. This means you only paid tax on the remaining $37,000. Perhaps you adopted the saving strategy for the next thirty years or until you retire. Any withdrawals you make will reflect on your taxable income: for example, if you withdraw $4,000 from the tax-deferred account, your taxable income will jump from $40,000 to $44,000, which means you would start paying the taxes you've been delaying for the past thirty years.
- *Tax-exempt accounts:* A tax-exempt account offers several future tax benefits, including future tax-free withdrawals. Since contributions are after-tax dollars, tax-exempt accounts have no immediate tax advantage. Investment returns in a tax-exempt account are tax-free.

Roth 401(k) and Roth IRA are prominent tax-exempt accounts in the United States. So, if you put $1,000 in a tax-exempt account and invest the funds in a 3-percent annual-return mutual fund for thirty years, the account will make an extra $1,427 (excluding the initial $1,000 deposit); the $1,427 won't be taxed.

WHILE TAXES for a tax-exempt account are paid now, those for a tax-deferred account are paid later.

Tax Records to Keep

Don't discard any financial records, including your tax documents, because you might need them. Taxpayers should secure their tax returns for at least seven years. Should there be any disparity in your tax records, you will need your tax statements to reconcile or harmonize your tax accounts.

TAX ITEMS TO PROTECT INCLUDE:

1. Documents that clarify your income and deductions- Such documents include receipts for generous contributions, W-2, 1099s, and canceled checks.
2. Papers which highlight home improvements and ownership statements. Be aware that you will need these documents to compute your tax basis if you have to sell your property in the near future.
3. Records of your investments, especially those indicating the items you either purchased or sold.
4. Statements for your retirement accounts and after-tax contributions

Secure these documents if you hope to avoid tax-related financial problems in the future.

. . .

WE UNCOVERED everything you need to know about federal and state taxes in this chapter. Going forward, I'm sure you won't have any problems managing your taxes.

IN THE NEXT CHAPTER, you will learn vital tips to make significant decisions later in your life. Hope to see you there.

8

"ADULTING" DECISIONS

I n the previous chapter, we analyzed federal and state taxes, and you learned how to manage your taxes. Great! This chapter will lead you toward making crucial decisions to improve your finances and increase your money.

I WAS a sweet sixteen when I first nursed the idea of owning a home. I told myself I could achieve the dream before marking my 24th birthday if I started saving from now. Indeed, that was a very optimistic goal, but it was possible. That time, I already had four different, regular freelance jobs, which were fetching me a few extra bucks per week. And, if the money I saved wouldn't be enough, I would take a loan to attain the objective.

I FELT I should let Dad know what I intended to achieve in the next eight years. He said: "Son, owning a house breeds so much satisfaction and happiness, but the extra costs of maintaining a home can endanger your finances, so don't rush it." I told myself that I wouldn't rush it and finally bought a house when I turned thirty. You may hurt your finances if you rush to purchase a home.

Should You Rent or Purchase a House?

If you feel like buying a home after seeing your friends purchase theirs, that's totally normal. I will encourage you to do so if you can afford it. But, if you can't, consider renting an apartment. Buying a house when you aren't ready for it can cause you several financial problems.

How will you know when you're ready to purchase a house? Provide honest answers to these questions:

1. Have you settled your student loans and other debts?
2. Have you saved a full emergency fund?
3. Can you raise a 10 or 20 percent down-payment for a 15-year, fixed-rate mortgage?
4. Is the house payment 25 percent (or less) of your monthly salary?
5. Will you live in the location for the next five years or more?

Go ahead to purchase a house if your answer to all of these questions is *yes*. Should you say no to any of the questions, I suggest focusing on improving your earnings and growing your money first.

Pros and Cons of Purchasing a House

. . .

EVEN IF YOU said yes to all of the questions above, you must make sure that you *want* to purchase. I'm sure you'll make the right decision after you've seen the pros and cons of purchasing a home:

PROS:

1. Each payment brings you closer to being a homeowner.
2. The home's value will improve over time, and you may cash it in at any time. For example, the house you purchased for $250,000 today could sell for $330,000 in the next two or three years.
3. You tend to enjoy several tax benefits. For example, you could list your mortgage interest as a deduction on your tax return.
4. You are free to renovate the house, change the paint or do anything you like with it.
5. You can enjoy more privacy, security, and peace of mind.

Cons:

1. You can't travel or relocate quickly since selling a house at the desired price might be difficult.
2. You'll have more financial responsibilities and expenses to settle. These expenses include homeowner's insurance, homeowners' Association (H.O.A.) fees, utility bills, flood policy, and property taxes.
3. The home value may start to decline. For example,

the pipe could leak, and you would have to get it fixed.

Pros and Cons of Renting a House

HERE ARE the pros and cons of renting a house:

PROS:

1. You can travel or move from one city to another.
2. You don't need to worry about any instability of housing expenses.
3. The landlord will shoulder the cost of house maintenance.

Cons:

1. Rent could increase yearly.
2. You can't enjoy tax deductions, property value, or financial incentives.
3. You can't customize your space without the landlord's express permission.
4. The landlord may terminate your tenancy or sell the house.

Analyze the pros and cons of purchasing or renting a house before you make your housing decision.

Top Housing Tips for Teens and college students

It would be best if you only decided to rent or purchase a house after you've been through the pros and cons above. Should you have any issues arriving at a decision, these tips can bridge the gap:

1. How long do you intend to stay in the house?

PURCHASE a home if you'd like to live there for five or more years. Consider renting an apartment if you think you'll be leaving the house soon or traveling frequently.

2. Will your current life situation change soon?

YOUR HOUSING NEEDS depend on your situation; don't purchase a house if your status might change in the next three or four years.

3. What can you afford?

REMEMBER that you must create a budget and stick to it. Renting a house isn't as expensive as purchasing one; you have to pay so many upfront costs when you buy a home. So, don't buy a house you can't maintain.

YOU CAN SAVE up some money to purchase a house while you're living in a rented apartment.

.   .   .

4. Have you weighed the pros and cons of renting or buying a house?

RENT an apartment if you won't be staying in the area for more than four or five years, especially when you aren't ready to become a homeowner yet.

STILL, if you have the money and believe it's time you had your own house, you can make a purchase. Just make sure the price is reasonable.

Efficient Steps on Purchasing Your First Home

Buying a home is deemed a massive financial goal or landmark in life since it requires a considerable commitment. Preparation is crucial if you hope to attain the goal soon (Caldwell, 2020). A first-time homebuyer can enjoy many financial benefits, like tax breaks and access to state programs or federally backed loans; these benefits can lower their down-payments.

SHOULD you decide to buy a home, take these simple steps:

1. Determine your level of readiness.

OWNING a house can be very expensive. Again, it comes with extra costs like electricity, home repairs, garbage pickup, utility fees, taxes, and insurance. These costs can threaten your finances if you aren't ready for them. Consider your budget and savings to see how much you could put on a mortgage payment.

Check if you have sufficient money for the down-payment and closing costs. It's okay if you hope to get a loan, but it will interest you to know that lenders usually restrict house expenses to 30 percent of borrowers' monthly gross income. So, it would be best to check your credit to see if you've any chance of qualifying for a loan.

2. Consider the type of home.

THERE ARE many home options to choose from. While some crave a multi-family building housing two to four units, others prefer a simple, conventional, single-family home. Other alternatives include a condo, duplex, and townhouse. Just make sure the home you are purchasing has the specific features and conveniences you admire. Does the house meet your size, neighborhood, and layout specifications?

3. Reduce or pay off your debt.

FIND a way to reduce your debt or pay it off before purchasing a house. You should also improve your emergency fund if you hope to cope with the extra costs of owning a home. You will not be ready to own a cottage yet if you still have a bunch of high-interest credit card debt to service or pay off.

4. Shop for a loan.

. . .

SOMETIMES YOU NEED a loan to acquire or purchase a house. So, I would say you should get pre-approved for a mortgage before looking for a residence to purchase. The pre-approval can give you an idea of the amount you can afford.

USE a mortgage broker if you want additional options. Since the broker can show you many loan companies and programs, you can easily choose the best rates.

5. Uncover the best loan types and payment options.

OPT FOR A 15, 20, or 30-year mortgage loan since they will have a lower monthly payment.

MORTGAGES CAN HAVE adjustable or fixed payment rates. While market conditions usually fluctuate the adjustable rate, a fixed-rate mortgage isn't affected by economic or market instabilities; stability in monthly payment can be attained if you choose the fixed-rate mortgage – but, should rates fall, you'll miss out.

6. Be pre-approved.

DON'T PLACE an offer on a house if you haven't been pre-approved for a loan. Why? Because no seller will entertain an offer that doesn't come with a mortgage pre-approval. So, apply for a mortgage and complete the paperwork to get the pre-approval.

. . .

7. Prepare a down payment.

A DOWN PAYMENT can reduce your costs. For example, you can get private mortgage insurance (P.M.I.) if you make a down-payment of 20 percent of the actual price of the home. Success in homeownership doesn't depend on the 20 percent down-payment, but you must evaluate the cost of P.M.I. suppose you're purchasing a residence. Review the rates of major online mortgage lenders to get the most affordable one.

8. Get an experienced real estate agent.

FIND the agent once you are pre-approved for a mortgage and have decided the amount you can afford. After listening to your needs and wants, the real estate agent should explain the market and identify a home that suits your budget and needs. The real estate agent should help you negotiate the terms and counsel you through the paperwork until the deal is completed.

9. Inspect the home.

CAREFULLY INSPECT the home to ensure that it has all the conveniences and features you want. The home inspection isn't a home appraisal; consider hiring an independent home inspector to do the task. A home inspector will check the home to see any issues or hidden problems; from the inspection, you will know if the house has termites, mold, or foundation problems, or whether there's a roof you need to replace. The findings should guide you during negotiations.

. . .

10. Be patient during escrow.

PREPARE to go through the escrow phase once the bid and offer have been accepted. The escrow ensures that documents, money, and other vital information are prepared and processed and can offer sufficient protection to the buyer, seller, and lender.

THE ESCROW STAGE could take up to three to five weeks, depending on the factors which need to be considered.

11. Close and move in.

SIGN the decisive papers once it is the closing date. The escrow agent will make sure the funds get to the appropriate parties.

ENJOY YOUR HOME, but don't forget to visit your bank to update your address. Consider setting up your utilities and discontinuing the old ones to save money and avoid late fees.

Dealing with a Car Purchase

Each person has their own relative thoughts about cars; while some fancy the latest arrivals, others fear new cars. It's pretty easy to purchase a new car nowadays, all thanks to no-down-payment offers and low-interest auto loans (Mercadante, 2019). You have to ask yourself if you honestly need a car.

. . .

LET'S say you already have a car. For example, if the vehicle needs regular repairs and maintenance, you will struggle to cope with the repair bills. Buying a new car could then be a reasonable action. If your current vehicle no longer suits your lifestyle or family size, buy another one.

STILL, consider the financial implications of a new vehicle on your finances. A new car can be costly; it can drain your savings and subject you to hardship and debt.

ANALYZE these factors before sanctioning your decision to buy a new car:

1. Repair bills on the current car.

ANY VEHICLE, new or old, must be maintained from time to time. An ageing car may require endless and costly repairs, and this could weaken your finances.

LET'S say you need to pay $400 monthly to acquire a new car; you will have paid $4,800 in twelve months. Compare this amount to your car's annual repair expenses to make an informed decision. For example, if you have three repairs per year on your vehicle at $1,500, don't purchase a new one yet. But, should you spend $3,500 for five or six repairs a year, get a new car.

. . .

2. Too much downtime.

IF YOUR CURRENT car breaks down often and takes tons of money or time to be fixed, consider getting a new one; you might not want to go carless or depend on other drivers and rental cars all the time.

FOR EXAMPLE, you might spend only $1,500 to repair your ten-year-old vehicle. That's inexpensive, isn't it? Still, if the car had eight or nine breakdowns in a year, and you had to go carless for thirty days, you might then decide that keeping the auto makes no sense. Dependability and costs can determine if you should keep your old car or purchase a new one.

3. Revamped equipment.

TODAY'S AUTOS are so reliable that you can ride the same car for ten or fifteen years, all thanks to improvements in technology. But, you might not get the equipment you admire in an aged vehicle. For example, suppose your old car doesn't have safety features like anti-lock brakes, forward collision warning capability, and airbags. In that case, you may decide to purchase a new one, especially if you have kids to protect.

4. Doesn't fit your lifestyle.

A CHANGE in your lifestyle can affect the suitability of your old car. Let's say you've been using a fuel-efficient, subcompact car all your single life; you will need a larger car when you get married or start having kids.

YOU MAY NEED a new car if you change occupations. For example, the vehicle you were using for daily commuting may not be suitable now that you're self-employed. You may need a large storage vehicle, like a pickup truck or S.U.V.

AND, should you leave a pastoral area to an urban district, where streets are narrow, a pickup truck or S.U.V. won't fit in. You will need a small, comfortable car.

JUST MAKE sure you can afford a car (and its added expenses) before purchasing or hurting your finances. It's okay if you can't afford one; several alternative options to owning a car are available. No problem if you don't have the money to throw at a car right now; you can save money to purchase it conveniently soon.

HERE, I want to show you a few alternatives to owning a car:

1. Public transportation.

YOU COULD USE a public vehicle to get to your destination. The cost of using public transportation is very affordable, though if you live in areas where efficient public transport is not accessible, you will struggle to move around.

. . .

2. Car-sharing clubs.

IF YOU HAVE any scheduled appointments, you can hire a car via a car-sharing club.

3. Ride with Uber or Lyft.

RIDING companies like Uber and Lyft can move you from one place to another. They are suitable for suburban and night travel.

4. Bicycles and walking.

SIMPLY WALKING or using a bike to get to nearby locations are more great options. You can walk or ride a bike to improve your health.

Should I Purchase a New or Used Car?

I had to answer this question many years ago when my crazy, fourteen-year-old van broke down, and I wondered whether to buy a new or used car. After I had test-driven a few cars, I asked myself whether I should go for a new or used one. I asked myself if I could afford a new car.

SINCE I HAD THE CASH, I went for it. Because most people around my age then couldn't afford a new car, I soon became the guy everyone talked about. I liked the frenzy but dared not tell anyone that the car drained all of my savings.

MAYBE I WOULD HAVE MADE a different or better choice if I had considered the pros and cons of buying a new or used car. So, before you decide on the vehicle to purchase, Weliver (2019) advises you to carefully analyze the benefits and drawbacks of new and used vehicles:

ADVANTAGES OF A NEW CAR:

1. Manufacturer warranty.
2. No prior owners, accidents, or mechanical faults.
3. Limited maintenance costs for two to three years.
4. Low financing rates.

Disadvantages of a new car:

1. Higher tax and insurance costs.
2. Unknown dependability for the model year.
3. Sudden devaluation.
4. Highly expensive.

Advantages of a used car:

1. Slower depreciation.
2. Lower tax and insurance costs.
3. Less costly.
4. Reliability data for the model year available from consumer reports.

Disadvantages of a used car:

1. Higher financing rates.
2. Unknown accident or mechanical record.
3. Higher maintenance costs.
4. Higher dealer markup.

I'm sure you can make a wise choice once you consider the merits and demerits of used and new cars. Again, base your selection on what you can afford, your personal preferences, and what's safe for you.

SHOULD you decide to purchase a used car, the following tips can be very useful:

1. Don't shop for the car until you know the price range for financing it.
2. Determine the total payments of the loan.
3. Grab a reliable car that will serve you for a few years.
4. Take a test drive.
5. Let a mechanic check the car.
6. See the car's history report.

PURCHASING a Car with Cash

YOU'RE GETTING a loan or paying with cash to purchase a car. If you have the full amount in cash, you will probably buy the car outright. Buying a car with cash means you can avoid the interest that comes with car loans. However, using your cash reserves to purchase a vehicle probably isn't right since that money could shift into your savings account.

. . .

USE PART of your savings to make a substantial down-payment if you don't have any leftover financial cushion – that way, you can have the auto loan and accrued interest reduced. But, if you have strong credit, which qualifies you for a low-interest car loan, you could use your savings to purchase the car. Again, since you have good credit, the dealer may give you cash-back offers and unique financing options.

LOOKING at the benefits and drawbacks of purchasing a car with cash can help you reach a reasonable decision (Brozic, 2020). Here are the two crucial benefits of buying a vehicle with cash:

1. It curbs overspending.

YOU CAN EASILY STICK to your budget when buying a car in cash. Let's say you've budgeted $25,000 for a car, for example, and in the course of the interaction, the dealer starts suggesting additional extras, like a heated steering wheel, all-weather floor mats, and a few splash guards. These add-ons could cost you an extra $2,000, but you can avoid them if you stick to your budget.

2. It averts interest payments.

YOU CAN AVOID interest if you purchase a car in cash. If you make a $5,000 down-payment for a $30,000 car, for example, you need a $25,000 auto loan to complete the transaction. With a 4.5 percent interest rate and 48-month repayment term, you will pay $2,364 interest. You can avoid this sum if you buy the car in cash.

You've seen the benefits of acquiring a car for cash. We will now consider the significant drawbacks:

3. It can drain your savings.

Buying a car with cash can drain all of your savings and make you incapable of dealing with potential emergencies.

4. It could stop you from achieving other financial goals.

Let's say you are contributing to a retirement account or building your emergency fund. You simply can't attain these goals if you use all of your money to purchase a car.

Opt for car financing if you can't purchase your dream car in cash.

How to Get Car Financing

These auto-financing tips from Weliver (2021) can help you obtain an auto loan to purchase your dream car:

. . .

1. Check your credit score and report before obtaining a car loan.

BAD CREDIT CAN'T STOP you from getting a car loan; it's just that you'll pay more if your credit isn't good enough. And, should you fail to meet up with the monthly repayment plan, the bank (or lender) can repossess the car.

LIKE MANY FINANCIAL TOOLS, Credit Karma can be used to analyze and appreciate your credit score to know if you can attain the most favorable car loan rates.

2. Obtain financial quotes if you don't have perfect credit.

PEOPLE with outstanding credit can access special dealership rates, but you have nothing to worry about if your credit isn't that good. Complete a credit application with an online lender if you hope to raise a car loan; you will learn the maximum amount of the loan and the interest rate once you have done so.

3. Keep the repayment term short.

A LONG-TERM LOAN attracts more interest than a short-term one. So, consider making the repayment term quick if you can afford it.

4. Put a 20 percent payment down (minimum).

. . .

I'M sure you won't like to owe more than the vehicle's current value, so make a minimum down-payment of 20 percent. The more, the better if you have the budget since it will lower your total interest.

5. Pay car fees, taxes, and miscellaneous expenses in cash.

DON'T GET a loan to finance sales tax, documentation fees, registration charges and related expenses.

Getting Married and Starting a Family

Marriage can change your financial, legal, and tax status, including your future choices. What your would-be spouse is bringing to the union may have a significant impact on your financial picture. So, if you hope to have an eventful marriage, you and your spouse must be on the same financial page. Why? Because money troubles top the chart of likely causes of divorce today. When you are on the same money page as your spouse, you can build a financially secure and healthy marriage. How can you achieve this? Have a financial talk with your spouse before you get married.

HERE'S how to make it happen:

1. Be open about your financial situation.

TALK FREELY about each other's assets, liabilities, and financial responsibilities. Get each other's credit scores and reports, and review your balance sheets together. Discuss potential concerns and find a way to deal with them.

2. Do a prenuptial agreement if one partner has more assets or earns more money than the other.

SHOULD DIVORCE OCCUR, such a treaty can safeguard premarital assets, solidify responsibility for acquired debts before marriage, and offer spousal support.

3. Devise a plan to improve each other's poor credit.

LIFE IS BETTER if you both have outstanding credit scores.

4. Set mutual financial objectives.

IF THERE ARE any questions you would like to discuss with your partner, write them down and talk about them.

5. Talk about how to merge your finances.

DISCUSS the money-managing strategy you guys are comfortable with. Agree on whether to set up a joint account or keep separate accounts. If the joint account works, decide the amount each person will contribute to the account monthly. If you're opting for individual accounts, decide who will be responsible for which particular expenses.

DON'T FORGET to talk about how to file taxes: will you file jointly or separately?

6. Plan your wedding and decide how to raise funds for the event.

CREATE a wedding budget and try to stick to it.

HONEST MONEY DISCUSSIONS can salvage a disastrous relationship and prevent a marriage from potentially ripping apart. Are there any other ways you could begin a financially stable marriage?

Starting a Family

Starting a family is an exciting, life-changing decision, but it comes with many financial obligations. You might have heard people say that the cost of purchasing a home amounts to a fortune; still, that's far below the cost of raising a child or two. For example, you will spend up to $227,000 to raise a child in the United States, excluding the child's college tuition.

I'VE ALWAYS TOLD young couples to build a family they can maintain. If it takes $227,000 to raise a child, how would you finance two or three kids? Consider these expenses before you start having kids:

- Childcare costs.
- Increase in regular expenses.
- Baby-proofing costs.
- Insurance needs.
- Documents which need to be updated, like wills, retirement plans and insurance policies.
- Education costs.

Are you still willing to be a parent now? Linton (2021) says that you aren't ready if you haven't hit the following money milestones:

1. *Reliable career.*

YOU MUST HAVE a stable job before becoming a parent – just make sure that the job can sustain your growing family. Identify and pursue careers that your children can maintain. Strive to earn a salary that can address the needs of your family.

2. *Emergency fund.*

UNEXPECTED EXPENSES CAN POP up in the family; as a parent, you need to be prepared to deal with emergencies each time they occur. That's where the emergency fund comes in. Make sure the fund has up to three- or six-months expenses.

3. *Retirement plan.*

. . .

THE COST of raising a child increases as the child grows. So, open a 401(k) or a Roth IRA account and start saving money. The fund will help you avoid the financial burden of retirement. Don't jump into marriage if you aren't contributing to a retirement plan.

4. College savings.

YOU AREN'T ready for marriage if you haven't started saving for college. The student loan debt issue continues to rise at an alarming rate every year, and, from the look of things, the problem won't turn around soon. Still, you can protect your future children from this hassle by saving for their college education now. That way, you will give them a financial edge when they eventually hit college age.

DON'T RUSH into starting a family without adequate preparation.

Financial Points to Evaluate Before Starting a Family

Starting a family can change everything about you, including your finances. Since you're leaving the singles' club, you have to modify your wants, needs, and expenses to suit your partner and kids (if you already have or will be having children). For example, you may have to purchase another car if your current vehicle isn't suitable for your family. Also, you will have to look elsewhere if your home doesn't have adequate space for your family. You're going to hurt your finances if you don't prepare financially before starting a family (Clarfeld, 2018).

. . .

CONSIDER these financial steps if you hope to start and run a successful family:

1. Obtain wills and related documents.

I KNOW it's hard to think about the time you won't be around to attend to your children's needs, so address your estate matters now. Talk to an attorney if you don't have wills and relevant documents; you don't have to wait until you start having children. Should anything happen to you or your spouse, your children will be comfortable. I'm sure the joy of every parent is to see their children happy and safe.

APART FROM DRAFTING YOUR WILLS, the attorney should provide powers of attorney, living wills, healthcare proxies, and other vital documents.

MOST PEOPLE WON'T WANT to discuss their mortality, but that's a critical parenthood responsibility.

2. Create a new budget.

WHEN YOU START A NEW FAMILY, you have to modify your living costs, employment status, housing expenditures, childcare, and medical expenses. So, you've got to create a thoughtful budget to approximate your income to reach these daunting changes.

. . .

3. Identify the right life insurance.

MANY YOUNG PARENTS don't know the benefits of life insurance. Instead of concentrating on potential income providers, like life insurance, they focus on the amount they need to sustain their family lifestyle; they don't acquire substantial assets or get close to their maximum earning years. But, you should know that you can quickly pay down mortgages and debts, fund a child's education and maintain a family's lifestyle with life insurance.

HOWEVER, you may struggle to determine the insurance type to purchase since permanent coverage could slightly strain your family budget. Let an experienced insurance professional guide you through the available insurance policies. Then you can opt for the one which suits your family's needs.

4. Re-analyze your savings and investment plans.

START PRIORITIZING SAVING and investing your money if you haven't been doing so. You can't concentrate solely on saving and investments once you have a baby.

CONSIDER OPENING a savings account in U.G.M.A. or 529 plans to fund the education of your future children. Just make sure that you invest consistently, and remember to grow your emergency fund.

. . .

STARTING A FAMILY IS STRESSFUL, but it's a phase you will enjoy as a parent if you plan for it. You have to start planning for the future because you will probably start a family someday.

I'VE ALREADY TOLD you that the future is all about money. That's why this chapter has all the tips you need to make reasonable adulting decisions. Start saving and investing your money right now if you want to build a great future for yourself and your family.

CONCLUSION

"*Personal Finance for Teens and College Students*" is a money-management guide for teens and college students who hope to enjoy their lives and attain their financial goals. The eight-chapter book provides great tips, insights, and strategies for setting unique financial objectives and how to reach them with commitment and attention.

The key highlights of this book include:

1. Logical steps for creating budgets, sticking to them and growing your money
2. Helpful tips on creating a bank account, analyzing bank statements and avoiding unnecessary bank fees
3. Practical guides on differentiating wants from needs, exhibiting critical financial skills, and attaining mindful spending habits
4. Good techniques for credit card use, minimizing debts, and improving one's credit score

5. Sensible investment options to exploit to sustain, maximize and grow your money
6. Creative ideas for building additional sources of income, to attain financial freedom
7. Useful tips on filing taxes and using tax credit
8. Efficient strategies for making profitable adulting decisions

As you strive to stay on track to improve your personal finances, keep in mind that you can do it if you just try. If you take the first initial step forward, you will be in the position to achieve your present and future financial goals. So, stay focused, persistent, determined and consistent and you should be on your way to staying in control of your personal finances.

Rest assured that you will gain the required tools and resources to achieve your heart's goals. Don't hesitate to utilize the money-making strategies you have already learnt in the book.

Who says you can't be successful with money and life?

I would like to hear from you. If you enjoyed reading this book, kindly leave me a review through your favorite online book retailer.

Many Thanks.

COLLEGE STUDENT
SIDE
HUSTLE

100+ WAYS TO START MAKING EXTRA MONEY
FOR THE BROKE COLLEGE STUDENT

KARA ROSS

ISBN - Ebook: 978-1-954937-03-1

ISBN - Paperback: 978-1-954937-04-8

ISBN - Audiobook: 978-1-954937-05-5

INTRODUCTION

People love to boast about their side hustles. But if you don't yet have a side hustle and aren't sure where to begin – maybe you're not even certain what a side hustle really is – you might be feeling a bit out of the loop.

College isn't cheap, but sometimes working a traditional job doesn't fit into a busy student's schedule. Side hustles – short-term work you can do in your spare time – are perfect for college students. Learn how you can leverage side hustles to put a little extra cash in your pocket and ease the burden of being a starving college student.

A good side hustle is about building a business for yourself. And today, the best side hustle ideas are those that have the potential to earn unlimited income—something beyond just $1,000 a month.

A side hustler's calling card is a scrappy, experimental mentality that views resource constraints as a thrilling challenge, not as a sign to give up. Side hustlers come from diverse backgrounds and sell wide-ranging products. There is, however, one similarity they frequently share: while building their venture in the early morning or twilight hours, they do the best they can with the time they have.

Thousands join their ranks as people rediscover that saving money and having a full-time job only goes so far. With a side hustle, there's a hard floor, while the ceiling for making more money is almost limitless. But that doesn't make it easy. What goes into the emerging art of starting and sustaining a good side hustle to make money?

I've put together this introduction to side hustles to bring you up to speed. Read on for examples of side hustles, how they work, and the benefits you can gain from getting in on the side hustle craze.

1

WHAT IS A SIDE HUSTLE?

A side hustle is any type of employment undertaken in addition to one's full-time work (whether school or a job). A side hustle is generally freelance or piecework in nature, providing a supplemental income. Side hustles are often things a person is passionate about, rather than a typical day job worked to make ends meet.

A side hustle is not the same as a part-time job. While a part-time job still entails someone else (your employer) calling most of the shots (including hours worked and what you'll be paid), a side hustle gives you the freedom to decide how much you want to work and earn.

A side hustle is a means of earning income on top of your main full time pursuit such as your college classes. You may have also heard the terms moonlighting to describe a side hustle.

Depending on your goals, a side hustle may just be for fun, or you may have the intention of building this into your main source of income at some point in the future. It could be as simple as walking dogs after class or building a freelancing business in your free time.

No matter what, you work on your side hustle when you make time for it after or before school hours. With financial security being a problem for nearly half of Americans, side hustles prove to be a viable option for many people working on paying for college, getting out of debt or testing the entrepreneurial waters.

Why Should You Have a Side Hustle?

A SIDE HUSTLE can be a great way to build extra income and additional skills outside of college classes. It can be a way to escape a part time job you don't like, a shortcut to financial independence, or just a way to practice entrepreneurship in a low-risk manner.

What is the Most Popular Side Hustles?

By RAW NUMBERS, the most popular side hustles are freelancing, network marketing, real estate investing, and participating in the "gig economy" through apps like Uber and Lyft. Be sure to check out the full list of ideas in this book to see which one could be a fit for you.

The Importance of a Side Hustle

As YOU CONTINUE on the path to financial independence, you have two main ways to accelerate your progress. You can either reduce your expenses or increase your income. A side hustle is a perfect way to increase your income.

Let's explore how a side hustle can dramatically affect your future financial trajectory and how to start your own side hustle.

How a Side Hustle Works

A SIDE HUSTLE is work completed outside of one's day job, and therefore the work tends to take place during evenings, on weekends, or during vacation breaks. It provides additional income while offering the flexibility to complete work outside of the traditional 9-to-5 hours of most jobs.

You can start your own side hustle business, or you can complete work on a freelance, contract, on-call, or part-time basis for a company.

For those who aren't quite ready to quit their current job or are terrified by the prospect of becoming an entrepreneur, side hustles can provide an outlet to explore passions, test ideas, and grow a solid customer base should you ultimately decide you want to continue doing it as your full time career.

2

WHY YOU SHOULD CONSIDER A SIDE HUSTLE

"If you do what you've always done, you'll get what you've always gotten." – Tony Robbins.

You've probably heard of a side hustle before. It doesn't necessarily have to be a complete side-business or even make that much money. A side hustle is all about your personal growth, development, and entrepreneurial creativity. Think about what you would supplement your current work with if you had the chance. Maybe you want to start a podcast related to your areas of study, write a personal blog, or sell crafts on Etsy. Whatever your side hustle may be, it's all about finding your passion and following it through — Without the major commitment of leaving your current work or investing all of your time into something you're not certain of.

According to a study, about 37% of adults in the U.S. have a side hustle. And they can pay pretty well, at an average of nearly $700 a month! No wonder another study shows two-thirds of Americans would consider diving into the side hustle business in addition to their current jobs. But why are side hustles so alluring, and how can they help you reach success? **Here are three ways a side hustle can be a really great idea!**

- **You can add to your savings.**

OF COURSE, one of the fascinating aspects of a side hustle is making money in addition to your current salary (or, if you don't currently have a job, making money off something you're passionate about). Depending on your side hustle, there's potential for earnings, and that extra money is a great way to start shoring up your savings or pay off your student loans. Or, you can invest the money into your current business!

MAKING A LITTLE EXTRA cash on the side can also help alleviate some financial stress, making your day-to-day happier rather than filled with worry about making ends meet. And hey, if you want to use that money to treat yourself, go for it! Your side hustle is all about you doing you.

- **It will develop your skills and experience.**

LET'S SAY you decide to start selling your craft projects online. It's a great way to engage your creativity and make a little extra money — But you'll also probably develop new skills along the way without even realizing it. You'd learn how to communicate with customers, market your brand, determine your pricing, and much more. These are beneficial skills for the business world, which are transferable to other jobs besides your side hustle. And who knows? The more experience you gain with these skills, or whatever skills you develop from your side hustle, the more clarity you could gain on whether or not your current career path is truly what you want to pursue.

- **It's a great way to test the waters.**

AS MENTIONED EARLIER, a side hustle is a fantastic way to dip your feet in the waters of other ventures without a full commitment. If you're just not sure what you really want to do as a career, side hustles can help you get there. Maybe you're considering a career in professional writing — Create a blog, and see how it makes you feel! Or you can tutor, teach online courses, walk dogs... Your options are endless!

WHATEVER YOU DECIDE to do with your side hustle, remember that the point is your satisfaction. If you find you're not enjoying your side hustle, you can start a new one! Or decide that side hustles just aren't for you. That's what's so great about them — They're flexible ways for you to gain experience, learn what you love, and test out what you're interested in without committing all your time, energy, and finances to them. So, what are you waiting for?

3

BENEFITS OF A SIDE HUSTLE

Aside hustle can offer you the opportunity to explore
your passions or pursue your dream job without
sacrificing the steady paycheck of a day job. A side
hustle provides an injection of extra cash flow to your bank
account; it can also boost overall life satisfaction.

Another benefit of having a side hustle is that they allow
for flexibility in the workplace and working hours. Often, side
hustles are solopreneurial or entrepreneurial endeavors, and
when you're the boss, you get to call the shots – including when
and for how long you'll work. This can be appealing to those
who feel weighed down by a traditional job's rigors and
expectations.

The increased financial freedom that a side hustle provides
can help pay for college, get out of debt and help save for a
rainy day, or build a nest egg. It can also provide for a bit of
discretionary spending on your monthly budget.

A side hustle typically does not require a large financial
investment upfront. Some side hustles focus primarily on
providing a service, while others involve selling goods you
make yourself or procure from a third party and resell. Many of

these gigs don't require formal education or specialized skill to be profitable. Some people find their side hustles end up earning them more than their full-time gig.

Since there is no minimum requirement to put in a set amount of time at your side hustle, you're free to take on two or three – or even more, as time permits – at any given time. This can help open up an unlimited stream of additional income. And, in case things ever take a turn for the worse at your current job, you have the security of knowing you won't be complete without a paycheck until you land your next working opportunity.

How a Side Hustle Can Transform Your Life

A SIDE HUSTLE brings more financial freedom and flexibility into your life. When you are no longer entirely reliant on your current job's income (or your parents allowance), you may start to enjoy that power of knowing that you would still have an income without it. Even if you have no plans to leave your current job, it is always nice to know that you have options.

Imagine if you earned even just an extra few hundred dollars a month. Consider how that would impact your budget for the better. It could allow you to pay down debt ahead of schedule or build your investment portfolio more quickly. If you channel the money you are earning into your financial goals, you could reach financial independence (FI) much sooner.

Aside from the additional income, a side hustle could be an avenue to explore your passion. For example, you could start a business that has always been stuck in the back of your mind. Since it would be a side hustle, you wouldn't feel the pressure of needing to make your fledgling business fully support you and you have the opportunity to enjoy the business-building process.

Do You Have Time for a Side Hustle?

In most cases, you have time for a side hustle. Even if you only have a few spare minutes each day, you could use that time to build a side hustle.

One of the best things about a side hustle is that you can pick something that suits your schedule. You'll be able to find a hustle that works for you, even if you don't have too much time.

However, it will come down to your priorities. If you don't make time for a side hustle, you won't have the time for one. After all, most of us can easily waste hours on the couch with a good TV show. If you choose to use your time hustling instead of wasting it away, you might find that you had more space on your calendar than you realized.

4

HOW TO FIND A SIDE HUSTLE

I f you are trying to find a side hustle, then the number of options might seem overwhelming. After all, there is an unlimited number of side hustles just waiting to be uncovered.

Start your search with your interests. What do you like to do in your free time? Is there a way to monetize it? Would you still be happy doing this hobby if it turned into a side hustle? It is important to think through these questions before committing in a big way.

Also, you need to consider your reasons for starting a side hustle. Are you looking for something lucrative? Or do you want to build your passion project even if you don't earn a lot of money? Make sure that you are clear about your financial goals of a side hustle before you dive in.

Finally, consider the amount of time that you want to commit to your new side hustle. If you only want to commit 2 hours a week, then don't sign up for something that will require more time.

If you want something flexible with no time commitment, ride-shares, or food delivery might be good options. However, if you want to replace the income from your current job, then you'll have to think bigger.

Best Practices for Side Hustles

While there are plenty of pros to having a side hustle, that's not to say there aren't some things to consider before diving in with both feet first. One consideration to weigh before taking on a side hustle is a potential conflict with your current schedule. If you're taking 21 credit hours over the semester, you may just not have the time in your schedule that is required for the particular side hustle that you choose.

You should also be careful not to over-commit yourself. Taking on more work than you can realistically handle will result in disappointed clients, which can hinder your ability to secure additional work.

Keep in mind that a side hustle means giving up some of your free time, but with the benefits that can be gained, many side hustlers find the sacrifice to be well worth it. There's no reason not to start one today with so many pros of having a side hustle.

5

QUESTIONS TO ASK WHEN CONSIDERING A SIDE HUSTLE TO MAKE MONEY

S ide hustles are a great way to earn extra income, but they require a bit of legwork upfront to get traction like all new ventures. If you don't choose an idea that fits your current lifestyle, it's easy for this extra work to sink to the bottom of your to-do list and, eventually, fall by the wayside. For this reason, unique side hustles often feel less like a chore and more like a creative outlet that places craft and commerce on equal footing.

Although side hustles don't always become full-time jobs, it's common for side hustlers to gravitate toward this option once their venture becomes profitable enough. If you want a side hustle that could eventually become your career, **here are some things to consider:**

- **Does the idea fit your current schedule?**

You're going to be dedicating a meaningful amount of time to this side hustle, so it helps if that time fits into your schedule. A side hustle should be something you can do outside of your classes and school work, but that won't interfere with or keep you from excelling in those classes.

Things will come up with your school schedule. Some days, you may have to work overtime to finish up a project, or you may have obligations like counselor meetings and group projects. If you want to make sure you put time into your side hustle, it helps to pick something easy to re-schedule. Side gigs like dog walking, real estate, or babysitting might seem appealing, but they could be more difficult to arrange around your regular schedule.

- **Does the idea align with your passions and interests?**

Having a full-time class schedule is enough to zap most people's creative energy by the time the day winds down. And after time well spent with friends and personal responsibilities, it's easy to see just how hard it can be to carve out additional headspace to work on a side project. But it's these hours tucked away in life's margins that tend to be the best time to do the focused work needed to get something off the ground. The workday is done, the weekend is still a couple of days away, and since you've already watched all the true-crime documentaries on Netflix, your schedule is wide open.

But, try as you might, sometimes you just won't want to work. That's why it's ideal if your side hustle closely pairs with what you're passionate about, even if it's not the end-product itself. That might mean you enjoy some aspect of running things behind the scenes, immersing yourself in a new topic or field of interest, or a desire to do something to help people. Whatever the appeal, a good litmus test is that you're drawn to the work when you're procrastinating on something else—that little bit of enthusiasm can go a long way.

- **Is the idea financially viable?**

Although the need for profitability shouldn't burden every hobby, most of us have student loans and bills to pay. By our definition of a good side hustle, we are looking to create some kind of return on time invested. That means your side hustle needs to be financially viable and relatively stable over the long term—not just a part-time side job.

Most side hustles aren't profitable right away since your primary focus is tweaking your product or service and finding how best to reach your first clients or customers. You want to keep costs low in the early stages and work exclusively on "ringing the cash register" or proving out your idea with a sale so you can see what the numbers look like.

What does that mean exactly? Since the start of any project is completely lopsided in terms of time put in and revenue that comes back out, you don't need to be concerned with tracking your sweat equity. But as you make progress and start earning money, it's important to understand how much it costs you, in time or dollars, to get a client, customer, or sale and ultimately turn your effort into profit. If your resulting margins or hourly wages put you in the red, your side hustle may not be sustainable.

How to Develop a Successful Side Hustle

So, you have decided that a side hustle is the best way to make money, but you don't know where to start. Look no further; here's a list of steps to follow to develop a successful side hustle today:

- **Make a list of what you're interested in.**

You need to love what you are doing as a side hustle for it to be successful for you. This job will be done on your own time and outside of class hours, so it will take a lot of energy and motivation to make it stick. Only something that you are passionate about will drive you this much. Brainstorm side hustle ideas around your interests and skills to discover the best ventures to start or see if you can turn a hobby into a business.

- **Decide early if you will invest money.**

Side hustles shouldn't cost too much money, but they may require some investment upfront for things like website hosting, branding, and tools. You may decide that you want to do advertising to find your first customers. Whatever your growth and expansion plan is for your side hustle, you need to be aware of your spending before it happens. Plan your spending accordingly, and measure your success to know whether you should continue.

- **Make sure there are no conflicts of interest.**

If you have a current job or have connections that could lead to a conflict of interest with your side hustle, it is not a good idea to continue with it. Sometimes, the best advice is to try something else or shelf your idea for another time to don't end up doing something you regret. Starting a side hustle with a conflict of interest could lead to costly lessons learned.

- **Schedule time for your side hustle.**

A side hustle takes time out of your schedule daily, so ensure everything is going right. It is impossible to set up your website, schedule your content, and forget about everything until next month. Set aside time in your calendar regularly for your side hustle, and outline actionable goals for this time to ensure what you are doing is valuable. Aim to give three to four evenings a week and perhaps some hours on the weekend to your side hustle, depending on what it is.

6

10 COMMANDMENTS FOR SIDE-HUSTLE SUCCESS

S ide hustles are extremely popular. An estimated 44 million people in the U.S. have a side hustle; that's over six times the number of workers who hold multiple jobs. The process is easy; it only takes a few hours to set up your own small business. But does making a side hustle actually pay off, both professionally and personally? That's a lot harder to know in advance.

Here are the 10 commandments for side-hustle success:

- *Consistently crush your school work.*

Side hustles are fun, but side hustles are also distracting. It's tempting to think about, dwell on, and even occasionally work on your side hustle when you're focused on school.

Don't. One, it's just wrong. And two, you aren't that stealthy. People will notice -- and no matter what your side-hustle dreams, losing your scholarship or getting kicked out of college is the last thing you can afford.

When you start a side hustle, your goal is to be great at two things: Your school work and your side hustle.

So even before you start your side hustle, focus on being a superstar with your studies. Work as hard and efficiently as possible. Get more done than anyone else, if only so you can work on your side hustle without regret and without raising concerns about your performance and dedication to your class work.

- *Never take on side-hustle debt.*

Many business ventures require spending money before making money. That's why some small businesses take years to turn a profit. A huge percentage of startups fail because they never turn a profit -- much less pay back their investment.

How can you avoid that? Start a side hustle you can fund through savings -- or better yet, that you don't need to fund. Provide a service that only requires the tools you already have. Sell products you either make or can procure by consignment. Prove to yourself that there is a market -- and that you can serve that market -- before you take on any debt.

The only real business is a business that turns a profit -- and it's a lot harder to turn a profit when you're paying off a debt you didn't need to incur. If you can't find a way to start your side hustle without going into debt, find a different idea.

- *Don't use a side hustle as an excuse.*

Imagine metalworking is your hobby. You've always wanted a larger forge. So you start a side hustle. And you buy the bigger forge. But you don't need it. Not yet. You just want it.

Plenty of failed side-hustlers admit they started their business as a way to rationalize the purchase of something they had always wanted to own. A nicer car "because I will need to make a great impression on clients." A bigger workshop "because I will need room for all the woodworking equipment I'll need."

If you want something -- and there's nothing wrong with that -- don't use starting a side hustle as an excuse to buy it.

- ***Don't spend money the customer won't see.***

You might have a cool office at your part-time job. You might have cool amenities.

I don't think your side hustle should.

Before you spend money, always ask yourself one question: "Does (this) touch the customer?" If it doesn't, don't buy it.

Spend what money you have where it makes a real difference to your customers -- because without customers, you don't have a side hustle.

- ***Only spend money on actual efficiency.***

It's tempting to think ahead, to forecast needs, then spend money based on those forecasts.

You need more supplies before you actually demand or need more equipment before you actually have demand.

Or needing greater efficiency before you need to be that efficient. Sure, buying a certain tool could make you X times faster at performing a certain task, but if you currently don't have enough customers who will pay you to perform that task beyond your current capacity, don't buy it.

Allow yourself to be inefficient until you have enough work to make greater efficiency truly matter.

- ***Always follow a strict side-hustle schedule.***

When your "normal" workday ends, your side hustle workday is just beginning.

Decide how many hours you think you can spend a day on your side hustle. Then add 25 to 50 percent to that number. If you're thinking two hours, make it three or four.

Then commit to that schedule. Write it down, and if your schedule says you will work from 6 p.m. to 9 p.m. every evening, and from 9 a.m. to 3 p.m. on weekends, work those hours.

See the schedule you create for your startup the same way you see your current class schedule -- as non-negotiable.

Then work that schedule.

Otherwise, you won't see any progress, you'll quickly get discouraged, and you will never have given yourself a fighting chance to succeed.

- *Dream big, but focus small.*

Almost every side-hustler dreams of finding an enabling customer, that one big customer that will let you bypass the "hustle" and truly launch a business.

How many actually find an enabling customer? Out of over one hundred people I talked to, one. (And that was an accident; the customer approached her before she had thought about starting a side hustle.)

Instead, do what Dharmesh Shah recommends: Rather than finding a way to make a million dollars, find a way to serve a million customers. Start small—Prospect where you have a reasonable chance of success.

Along the way, you'll learn. You'll build your skills. You'll build a customer base. Later, you can leverage that customer base -- and everything you've learned -- to hunt a bigger game successfully.

- *Only do what generates revenue.*

Sure, you might need to spend a little time on admin and infrastructure. But not much. You don't need fancy spreadsheets. You don't need comprehensive reports. You don't need a catchy brand or a mission statement.

What do you need? You need work -- and you need to do the work so you can get paid. Successful side-hustlers focus on two things: Selling and working.

It may be true that when you do what you love, the money will follow, but only if what you love doing actually generates revenue. If it doesn't pay, put it away.

Successful entrepreneurs eventually spend more time working on their business than in their business. Later, that might be true for you as well, but for now, a successful side hustle requires working in the business -- because that's the only time you actually make money.

- *Always default to action.*

Making plans is great.

But stuff always happens.

Most people who start a side hustle don't make it past their first three action items before adapting to reality.

Spend a little time planning. Then spend a lot more time doing. If you're unsure, do something -- and then react appropriately.

It's easy to think and plan and evaluate yourself out of ever starting a side hustle.

Remember, it's not life and death: It's a side hustle. See starting a side business as the grand experiment that it is. Never forget that the fun is in the doing -- not the thinking.

- *See your side hustle as "me time."*

When you choose your side hustle, pick something you

want to do. Pick something you want to achieve. Pick something you want to be, and actively work toward it.

Not only will you enjoy the sense of accomplishment that comes with progressing toward a goal -- even if that goal is doing something purely for fun -- but you'll also feel better about yourself and your life.

In short, see your side hustle time as "me time." Because it is -- it's time you spend making the most of your life. See it as the time you spend that will leave you feeling fulfilled.

Sure, other people might be chilling with Netflix. And that is one form of "me time."

But so is a side hustle -- because when you choose the right side hustle, and you give it your all, that means you're making the most of every hour you have.

Which is the perfect definition of "me time."

7

100 GREAT IDEAS FOR POSSIBLE SIDE HUSTLES

You might take up a side hustle for several reasons. Firstly, it provides extra income on top of your main source of income. Secondly, it allows you to pursue a passion that you don't get to explore much in your main job.

A THIRD REASON some people take up a side hustle is to test whether a different career field might be right for them. It's a good way to explore other career opportunities without quitting your main job. It also allows you to network with people in a new career field, which is a great way to explore career options.

HERE ARE THE lists of 100 great ideas for possible side hustles you can do:

1. Garage Sale Flipping.

You can start with selling stuff around your dorm room or apartment, and then once you have a little bankroll, you can go to garage sales around the area to find cheap items to sell for a profit. There are apps where you can find garage sales such as Yard Sale Treasure Map and you can sell your findings on local websites like eBay, Craigslist, and OfferUp.

GARAGE SALES ARE ENJOYABLE. Plan yours effectively, and you'll be confident of a good time as well as a profitable sale. They are a fun way to come up with some cash. These let people free themselves of things they don't use. There could be some things available that you acquired but have never got around to using.

GARAGE SALES ORGANIZING Tips For Set-Up

THERE MAY BE cash in your clutter. You have heard the phrase, "your trash is someone else's treasure." A garage sale is one way to put theory into practice. Attentive marketing of your goods by doing an organized set up of your garage sale is the key to receiving the highest prices.

- **Sort logically.**

SORT your discards into logical groupings such as clothes, books, tools, seasonal decorations. If customers see a haphazard mix of items, they will quickly leave your garage sale. Garage sale aficionados usually have particular items in mind when they shop and do not want to spend time sifting through unrelated stuff.

- **Display well.**

SET UP tables and clothing racks to display your wares. Shoppers do not like to bend over and pick through items lying on the ground. If you do not have a clothing rack, improvise by placing a pole between two stepladders. Box your books by subject, spine up, so it is easy for customers to flip through them without making a mess of your display. Label the boxes or use large cards to divide groupings of books.

- **Highlight special collections.**

DISPLAY THE GLASS items separately from your books and craft things to make them more attractive and seem special. Perhaps cover the table with a tablecloth. Make sure glassware is clean. People will be more likely to buy and pay more for wares in pristine condition. Have a separate table for holiday items. Make the display festive and group items in calendar order Valentine Day, Easter, 4th of July, Halloween, etc.

- **Money matters and pricing.**

USE A FANNY pack to hold your money. Unfortunately, dishonest people also frequent garage sales and look for opportunities to steal unattended cash. Have plenty of small bills and quarters to make change. You do not want to lose a sale just because you can't make change. Price book categories consistently-e.g., paperbacks 50 cents, hardbacks $1. Do the same with DVDs. Sell craft items by the bagful. Label and sell the craft bags for a flat rate. Price everything clearly. Customers do not like to search for someone to ask prices.

- **Expect to be insulted.**

EXPECT PEOPLE to give insulting offers for your things. That is the nature of garage sales. Decide on your goal for your garage sale ahead of time: Do you want to make money or get rid of stuff? You usually will get less for items you sell at a garage sale than you would at an online auction. But you also do not have to go through the hassle of listing, taking photos, and shipping items.

- **Free attraction.**

THE WORD "FREE" is magic. Have a box of free stuff out front with a large FREE sign on it to attract people to your sale. Include toys to keep children occupied while the parent's shop.

- **Plan what not to do with the leftovers.**

DO NOT bring anything back into the house. The stuff is in the garage sale because it is time to move on. If you do not get reasonable offers for your more expensive items, you may get more for them as a tax write off for a charitable donation than you would if you take a low ball offer. Call for a pick up by a charitable organization.

THE KEYS to a successful garage sale are organization and a realistic attitude. If you set up your merchandise in an attractive way and greet customers with enthusiasm even when they offer you 10 cents for a $2 item, you will be counting cash instead of hauling away clutter at the end of the sale.

2. Clothing Resale.

YOU CAN start with clothes in your closet that you don't wear anymore (as well as your dorm buddies or roommates), but once you have a bankroll, you can buy secondhand clothes at thrift stores and garage sales. You can sell your finds for a profit on Poshmark and Mercari.

ONLINE CONSIGNMENT STORES

ONLINE CONSIGNMENT STORES CONNECT you with shoppers all across the world.

SECONDHAND CLOTHING STORES exploded into a $28 billion industry in 2019, according to Statista, and are expected to reach $64 billion by 2024. Some stores pay you upfront for your pre-worn outfits. Others share a percentage of the profits once your item sells.

. . .

HERE ARE some options for online consignment and second-hand stores for you to sell used clothes:

- thredUp.

IF CONVENIENCE IS IMPORTANT, then look into thredUP because it does everything for you. All you need to do is order one of its signatures, "clean out kits," and send off your clothes.

THREDUP WILL SORT your clothes and decide which ones to accept. When your items sell, thredUP will pay you on consignment.

THE COMPANY will donate unaccepted items to charity, or you can pay $10.99 to get them back. ThredUP accepts women's and children's clothes and accessories.

- Tradesy.

IF YOU SELL used clothes with Tradesy, you need to upload photos of your items to the site. Tradesy will enhance your photos, so they look market-ready.

YOU'LL SET THE PRICES, and Tradesy takes a flat commission fee of $7.50 for items sold for less than $50 and a commission rate of 19.8% for items sold at $50 or more. The company also sends you a prepaid, pre-addressed kit for shipping.

- **Poshmark.**

IF YOU HAVE any high-end labels or designer clothes, you can sell them with Poshmark. You'll set your prices, and Poshmark takes 20% of the selling price for items sold for $15 or more, or there will be a flat fee of $2.95 for items sold for less than $15. The company also helps you with shipping by sending you a prepaid, pre-addressed shipping label once an item sells.

- **Le Prix.**

LE PRIX SELLS exclusively designer labels, like Chanel, Louis Vuitton, and Gucci. To sell with Le Prix, you can reach out to one of its boutique partners near you or request a prepaid shipping label via its White Glove Consignment Service. Le Prix has boutiques in various cities, including Los Angeles, New York, Miami, and Washington, DC.

OTHER PLACES to Sell Clothes Online

IF YOU'D RATHER SELL your clothes directly to the customer, you can use one of the websites below. You'll have to do a little more grunt work, but you'll get to keep most, if not all, of the profits.

- **VarageSale.**

VARAGESALE TOOK THE concept of yard sales and moved them online. Here, you can sell clothes online to people in your area. If you get any bites, you'll set up a meeting spot to make the exchange.

- eBay.

PEOPLE HAVE BEEN selling goods on eBay for a while. You're pretty much responsible for everything when you sell used clothes on eBay. By selling high-quality items and shipping on time, you can build up a good reputation as an eBay seller.

- Your Instagram account.

FINALLY, you could advertise your clothes on your Instagram account. Thousands of people set up their own stores this way with the hashtag #shopmycloset. While you can't technically sell on Instagram, you can take bids in the comments and use Paypal to finish the transaction.

THE ONLINE CONSIGNMENT market is a popular space, meaning it can also be competitive. What can you do to make your outfits shine?

TIPS FOR SELLING Clothes Online Successfully

ON A SITE LIKE THREDUP, you don't have to worry about marketing your clothes. Professional photographers will take care of it for you. If you use a site like eBay or VarageSale, then you'll need to think about presentation. **Consider these three tips when you sell clothes online:**

- **Take lots of high-quality photos.**

TAKE HIGH-' UALITY PHOTOGRAPHS of your clothes. Use bright, consistent lighting and an uncluttered background.

YOU SHOULD ALSO take pictures from multiple angles, so customers know exactly what they'll be getting.

- **Set a realistic price.**

IF YOU'RE responsible for setting your own price, consider the "one-third rule." When you sell clothes for cash, you typically set the price at about one-third of the original retail price.

IF YOU'RE SELLING a pre-worn North Face jacket that you bought at $150, then you should set the price around $50. If the jacket is like new, you could try selling it for more, perhaps $75 to $100.

- **Label the brand, color, and size.**

FINALLY, make sure that shoppers can find your item. If you're putting a label on it, write down the brand, color, size, and other important information.

. . .

By GETTING straight to the point, you ensure your item appears in search results. For instance, "Blue North Face Jacket, Size 4 in Great Condition" is nice and clear.

ONLINE CONSIGNMENT SHOPS connect you with a huge market, but they're not the only option if you want to sell clothes for cash. You could also take your outfits to a brick-and-mortar store.

SECONDHAND STORES to Sell Used Clothes

IF YOU'D rather take your clothes to a brick-and-mortar shop, you can hand-deliver them to one of these secondhand stores. **These are four of the top secondhand clothing stores with locations across the U.S:**

- **Clothes Mentor.**

CLOTHES MENTOR HAS 127 stores across the country, so you can likely find one near you. You don't need an appointment, but instead can walk in and get cash on the spot.

- **Buffalo Exchange.**

BUFFALO EXCHANGE SELLS pre-worn men's and women's stores in 17 states and the District of Columbia. All the locations normally accept walk-ins, or you can send clothes through its "sell by mail" program.

- **Uptown Cheapskate.**

UPTOWN CHEAPSKATE HAS OVER 80 locations. They accept walk-ins and donate spare clothes to charity.

TIPS FOR SELLING Used Clothes to Secondhand Stores

MOST SECONDHAND clothing stores have high standards for quality. The clothes should be fashionable, cared for, and appropriate for the upcoming season.

SECONDHAND STORES typically price items at one-third of the original cost. As for your profit, they'll give you one-third of that.

FOR THAT $150 North Face jacket, you may only get $16. The payout won't knock your socks off, but it does exceed the zero dollars you'd get from the jacket sitting in a closet.

WHAT ABOUT those clothes that are a little too pre-worn for you to sell? Can you get any financial advantage from those?

3. Shoe Resale.

This is similar to clothing resale but is more niche, and if you find the right pairs, you can make some serious cash. Start with pairs in your closet but after those have sold, you can also find some at thrift stores and garage sales. Sell for a profit on StockX, Poshmark, and Mercari.

The Shoe Reselling Industry

FORBES ESTIMATES that the resale market for sneakers is estimated to be over $1 billion annually.

By carefully and expertly exciting each new product launch, the manufacturers cater to loyal fans and strategically never make enough to satisfy the demand fully. It's that constant shortfall on the supply side that fuels the resale market.

This is also a trend that doesn't appear to be slowing anytime soon. That same Forbes article notes that the international sneaker market is up 40% since 2004.

Even though only an estimated 4% of sneakers are purchased for immediate resale, the market has attracted side hustlers and entrepreneurs. Some resellers are moving more than $2 million in inventory a year at the top of the heap.

WHAT SHOES TO BUY?

. . .

ONE OF THE most common questions I get is how do I know which shoes to buy? Which brands and models will be profitable? To get an idea of what is hot in streetwear, follow sneaker and fashion publishers like Hypebeast or High Snobiety.

Immerse yourself in your local sneaker communities by attending a sneaker convention and getting an idea of what people are wearing and what people are talking about.

Learn about the Jordan brand. Begin to follow Instagram accounts that have to do with sneakers and sneaker news, so you'll automatically be doing research every time you're killing time on the 'gram. Combine all of the above with checking aftermarket prices on sites like eBay and calculating your estimated profit.

Notes: In the advanced search, you can check the box just to see completed listings to see the items' price.

I suggest starting small with one or two pairs, so you don't have huge risk.

WHERE DO You Buy These Shoes to Resell?

I LIKE to buy older models either through eBay or Facebook groups and sneaker conventions. For new shoes, you'll go directly to the brand's website (adidas.com, nike.com, etc.) and either press your luck right on the release time, or you can utilize a sneaker bot to greatly increase your chances of securing a pair at retail price.

There are also authorized retailers that stock desired shoes, like FootLocker or Eastbay, but it's best to go with lesser-known sites like Mr. Porter and END to increase your odds of getting the shoes at retail.

. . . .

How to Sell Sneakers on eBay

EBAY IS one of the top e-commerce marketplaces in the world, next to Amazon. Selling on eBay is rather simple. The seller first creates a listing that typically includes photos, descriptions, pricing, and general details. The buyer can then bid on that item in an auction or 'buy it now' and pay a fixed price. The process is the same for flipping sneakers on eBay.

But why sell on eBay in the first place instead of other marketplaces? With eBay, you have the advantage of finding rare gems in the sneaker-sphere. As a seller, that means you could bank a nice profit for shoes that do well through an auction as people bid higher and higher to "win" the prize.

The learning curve for how to sell sneakers on eBay is rather easy. But you'll need all of your spidey senses and judgment in order not to get ripped off (which does happen, so be careful).

WHERE CAN I Sell My Shoes Fast?

IF YOU SIMPLY want to sell your shoes fast, there's no need to build a business empire. You could simply turn to sites like your local Craigslist. Facebook even has its own seller's marketplace that will show consumers in the area near you.

Here are a few places where you **can sell shoes fast**:

- Craigslist, Facebook
- Local consignment shops
- StockX (not to analyze the market but for fast transactions)
- LetGo (app marketplace to buy and sell locally)

- Oodle

Anyone who wants to get a side hustle going but doesn't know where to start, selling shoes is one of the best ways to learn valuable entrepreneurial skills in real life, like customer service, profitably managing inventory, and learning to set and achieve goals.

4. Sell Textbooks.

Resell old textbooks from your classes, resell your classmates or find textbooks on the cheap on college Facebook groups or at local thrift stores. You can resell them through Chegg.com or Facebook marketplace.

How To Sell Used Books Online

WHILE A FULL BOOKSHELF of interesting hardbacks can make for beautiful interior decorating, it doesn't put crisp bills into your wallet. It can be frustrating to buy books that you only use once, and their cost isn't much of an investment if you can't sell them after the fact. Luckily, you can sell them to get back the buying cost or even make a profit. **Here's a list of sites you can use to sell your books and make money in the process:**

- **BookScouter.com** allows you to sell your books for the best price. Listing your books to receive the best price is a bit of a game as you can watch the average price for your ISBN fluctuate. When competitor books are at high prices, you can undercut them to get the sale and still make the profit you're looking for.
- **Powells.com** is housed in Portland, Oregon, and is one of the world's biggest independent book stores. Part of their charm is found in the sprawling 'city of books' that mixes new and used inventory. They now have warehouses across the United States ready to purchase and house your used books.
- **Amazon** has been a major player in the used book industry because it's amazingly easy to set up a seller account. The one thing you need to watch out for is the percentage that Amazon takes of every transaction. Be certain that you sell the book for enough money that you can afford the shipping and Amazon cut without owing money in the end.

SELLING BOOKS ON AMAZON, eBay, and AbeBooks.

AMAZON, AbeBooks and eBay are popular websites for selling second-hand and used books. Anyone can list books for sale on them and name their asking price. However, if you want to make regular sales, don't be greedy; price realistically. You can scan the book by using a book pricing app and a portable Bluetooth scanner to make finding and pricing stock much easier than it used to be. This scanner and phone app combo has saved me hours of time.

IF YOU FIND you enjoy selling books online and are making a profit, you'll need to find more stock. Thrift stores and charity shops sell cheap second-hand books. However, the internet makes possible prices visible to everyone, making it more difficult to find hidden gems in these stores.

WHETHER YOU ARE planning to sell textbooks and books that you've already purchased or are planning to go to scout garage sales for hidden treasures, there are lots of online sites you can take advantage of to earn a profit.

5 KEY STEPS to Successful Book-Selling

- Be professional when dealing with customers. Good customer service brings repeat purchases.
- Describe the goods clearly in your ads. State condition, year of publication, publisher, and ISBN.
- Price the books fairly. Research competitor websites and specialist book auctions.
- Ensure your books are in the best condition they can be. They should be clean and have no pages missing.
- State shipping costs in your advert. Mail them promptly once they're sold, and use a trackable delivery service.

How Do You Know if a Book Has Significant Monetary Value?

RARE AND ANTI' UE books are a specialist market within the general antiques and collectibles trade. Their price is determined not just by a book's condition but also by how other investment markets are doing. There are always investors with cash to splash even in a recession. When interest rates are low, cash moves into other investment classes. The value of antiQues and other "collectibles," including books, may rise as a result.

IF YOU HAVE any books you think may have special value, I recommend you take photos of the covers and a few of the books' inside pages. Then after phoning first, email the pictures to some auction houses or specialist book traders. Other traders can be generous with their knowledge and time. Even if you don't have a hidden gem on your bookshelf, you may learn a little more about collectible books.

5. Logo Design.

Are you a graphic designer, or do you have some artistic talents that you know others are looking for? Why not make some extra money for your bottom line by designing logos or other graphics for people's websites, newsletters, or other print applications?

ESSENTIAL TOOLS FOR Your Logo Design Hustle

YEP, it's a business. Think of it as a real business, and you'll make more money and have more success than if you always consider it a hobby or a supplementary income source. So what kind of software do you need to get your graphic design business off the ground? Luckily, many different free and premium software products and apps offer high-quality tools that designers could only dream of 10 years ago. The power of online web design and graphic design tools for freelance graphic design hustlers is comparable to the most high-end products a decade ago.

- Crello

Crello is a slick tool for quickly putting together social posts, blog headers, images for content marketing, general marketing materials for any business, ads, and video content.

- **Stencil**

Stencil is definitely one of the easiest tools for getting started with. That doesn't mean it's not powerful. It's one of the primary tools I use in my marketing agency (and other properties) for creating graphics.

- **RelayThat**

If you want an easy way to produce images that have consistent branding and are simple to edit, RelayThat is a great choice. The software focuses on making it simple to create on-brand images in different formats.

- **Canva**

This list wouldn't be complete without mentioning the company that helped bring easy-to-use design tools to the masses.

- **Pixlr**

Pixlr is one of the newest tools on the market. It has been available online for a while as a completely free product. There are now paid options, but the free tool is still available. It's a competent graphics tool that many people compare to Adobe Photoshop.

- **Offeo**

Offeo is a fairly new online video platform (started in 2017 and gaining a lot of traction in 2020) but one that has turned heads thanks to a sharp set of tools and templates.

TIPS FOR BEING Successful as a Graphic Designer

TO BE A SUCCESSFUL GRAPHIC DESIGNER, there are a few guidelines that you should hold yourself to.

- **Be realistic**

The first essential thing is being realistic about what you can accomplish and holding yourself accountable to any deadlines and agreements. Don't give yourself deadlines that you don't think you can easily make, and always communicate with your client if something comes up.

- **Create contracts**

If you find that you're working outside of a platform like Upwork and you've managed to snag a client of your own, always make sure that you create a contract for legal reasons.

SOME OF THE best websites for storing and creating these include And.Co and Honeybook. PayPal Business is also a viable option.

- **Stay on top of industry trends**

With any creative service-based business, you must stay on top of what's currently popular. You don't want to create something for your client that isn't going to appeal to today's audience unless it's genuinely what your client wants.

- **Set your own guidelines**

As a freelancer, you get to set your own guidelines, which is something to keep in mind.

YOU DECIDE how much work to have at a given time, you help set deadlines with your client, and you create your own work hours. If you find that some part of the puzzle isn't quite working out, then change it!

WHERE TO FIND Freelance Graphic Design Jobs

LUCKILY, it's easier than ever to find jobs using online resources. Below are a few of the best places to search if you're wondering where to find a graphic design job.

- **Upwork**

When I was first wondering how to become a freelance graphic designer, this is where I looked.

UPWORK PROVIDES an easy-to-use interface where you can create your own profile, set your rates, and connect with clients from around the world. Plus, contracts are all made for you, and you can always guarantee that you'll get paid under Upwork's protection policy.

- Fiverr

Similar to Upwork, Fiverr is another popular online freelancing platform that works the opposite way.

ON FIVERR, the freelancer creates pre-made packages for services with a set price, usually starting at $5 and having tiered prices going up after that. There are tons of graphic design packages that you could make on this website.

- Flexjobs

Flexjobs is one of the best websites out there to find remote work-from-home positions. There are usually around 1,000 graphic design positions on this website at a time, ranging between a whole bunch of different industries, so you can choose what you're most interested in.

- LinkedIn

This social media platform is often overlooked as a great spot to find freelance jobs, but their jobs posting board has a fair amount of freelance gigs.

LINKEDIN IS ALSO a great place to connect with other small business owners who may require your services in the future.

How Much Money Do Graphic Designers Make?

. . .

THE AVERAGE GRAPHIC designer will make approximately $45,000 per year, but that's if they work full-time hours. This equates to about $22 per hour, but this can quite obviously change depending on a designer's skill level, specializations, education, and more.

Customer Service Is Key

NOW THAT YOU'VE DECIDED to do logo design as your side hustle, word of mouth does the best job of bringing in new work. When you're doing your design work for your customers (or other services), remember that customer service is key. Make sure to maintain good communication, keep your turnaround times as short as possible, and remember that the customer is always right. If you do those things, you'll be on your way towards having a nice secondary source of income.

6. Sell Print On Demand Items.

If you know how to design, you can sell items with those designs using print on demand sites like TeeSpring and Etsy. You don't need to hold any inventory, and things are created as they are purchased in your online store. If you don't know how to design, you can pay someone to create a design using a site like Fiverr.

. . .

CAN YOU MAKE Money from Print on Demand?

YOU most definitely can make money from the print on demand model, but there are some things that you need to take into consideration.

IF YOU HAVE some great looking graphics or catchy quotes and know how to market your business well or have a great following, you can start to generate a good income.

TRENDY SLOGANS, attractive graphics, and having your branded products seen by the right audience is very important. Many print-on-demand services actually start out on platforms like Instagram before branching out and creating their ecommerce sites.

CREATING PRINT ON demand products is a great way to start earning a passive income. You only have to design your graphics/slogans once. Whichever printing platform you choose, your customers can purchase your well-designed products repeatedly without you having to do any of the heavy liftings.

WHAT TYPE OF Products can be Sold with Print on Demand?

. . .

NORMALLY WHEN YOU think about print on demand, you think mainly about T-shirts. Still, there are so many other products that you can choose to add your designs to, such as pens, mugs, caps, bags, coasters, mousepads, phone cases, shower curtains, towels, cushions, doormats, flip flops, sneakers, hoodies, jackets, water bottles, wall art. The list is endless.

IF YOU HAVE an eye for a design using any of the convenient apps such as Picmonkey, Canva, iPiccy, Photoshop, InDesign, or if you're a dab hand at using Procreate on your iPad, then you can start selling your artistic designs by adding them and selling them via print on demand.

BEST PRINT-ON-DEMAND Companies to Start Making Money

HERE'S A GREAT LIST of companies that offer the best print-on-demand services.

- **Printify**

Printify is one of the leading print-on-demand ecommerce markets related to large print networks like t-shirts. They cater to designing, sourcing, and fulfillment, plus shipping of products.

PRINTIFY ALLOWS you to get the best prices for custom-made products. The company allows integration with other popular ecommerce platforms like WooCommerce and Etsy. This allows you to choose a platform that matches your interests to start selling your products.

- **Society 6**

Society 6 focuses on the artistic prints niche. This ecommerce marketplace is easy to set up and use. It allows you to sell a range of products that include pillowcases, mobile phone cases, and t-shirts.

ANOTHER BENEFIT OF using Society 6 is that it allows you to retain copyrights to the designs as a seller. The website also runs different marketing campaigns that can boost your sales.

- **Printful**

Printful is a site that works well for entrepreneurs. You can print clothes for all ages, accessories, pillow covers, towels, and wall art. Printful enables you to advertise with other ecommerce platforms.

WHEN AN ORDER IS RECEIVED, Printful communicates with you and then delivers the products to the customers.

PRINTFUL GUARANTEES HIGH-QUALITY products and dropshipping. This allows you as a seller to focus on creating and improving your products. The company also takes care of stocks, printing, and all the production.

- **Spreadshirt**

Spreadshirt is a great option for new sellers looking to set up a print on demand shop. The platform allows you to generate income, and it is easy to use.

. . .

WHEN YOU PUT your products on Spreadshirt, everyone on the platform can sell your designs. In the process, you earn a commission on each sale made.

IF YOU DESIRE to have control over your designs, you can open your Spread shop. All your designs' sales are now made on your site, and you can make regular profits.

- **Redbubble**

Redbubble is a viable print-on-demand platform for sellers looking for a big consumer base. A diverse creative community submits their artwork on a platform that you can easily join.

SOME OF the products that you can print on Redbubble include notebooks, t-shirts, hoodies, postcards, duvet covers, stickers, among other products.

THE PLATFORM HAS A USER-FRIENDLY INTERFACE, a free to join setup, and a fast uploading process. It also allows you to set your pricing margins for each product.

- **Teespring**

Teespring is a competitive print on demand company. They have several categories of products that can be browsed based on hobbies, interests, age, animals, location, and sports.

. . .

TEESPRING HAS AN interface option where customers can remarket their products and designs. You can print products like mugs, gifts, home decor, t-shirts, and hoodies.

TEESPRING ALSO ALLOWS you to set different prices for different products and offers dropshipping of products to consumers.

- Zazzle

Zazzle is an online business that assists creatives and designers in making products using their art. You can upload your designs, set your margin rates, and earn referrals on any sale. Zazzle offers you a straight forward platform with no listings.

YOUR DESIGNS ARE listed within the main site, and you can share them on your social media to drive more sales. The site also offers you tips and tutorials on ways of improving your products and designs.

- Teelaunch

Teelaunch is a great option to get started in print on demand online business. It integrates with Shopify. Teelaunch print-on-demand pricing structure allows designers and artists to start their stores with no investment. The website is easy-to-use and offers the best solution for quality customized products.

THERE ARE many prints-on-demand options to choose from based on your needs and interests, and if you're looking for a way to start earning from home without having to hold stock and still use your creativity, then print on demand may just be for you.

USING PRINT ON demand companies offers you the opportunity to create designs that are highly in demand. A great way to check for this is to look at Google Trends or whatever is trending on the popular social platforms; you can quickly scale up your production and sell to a global market. You can also customize quality products and offer more value to your customers for very little outlay to yourself.

7. Dropshipping

If you like the automated aspects of print-on-demand but are more interested in marketing and operations over creating custom designs, consider starting a dropshipping business. Dropshipping is another online business model where a third party manufactures and ships existing products for you. All you have to do is set up your store, price your products, and market the business.

DROPSHIPPING IS ALSO a low-risk opportunity because products are only being shipped when they're purchased, which leaves plenty of room for profit so long as your marketing expenses are reasonable. With a third party in charge of manufacturing and shipping, dropshipping also frees up a lot of time. You can also dropship on marketplaces like Amazon and eBay to reach more customers.

IF YOU DON'T want to deal with designs, there are tons of items to dropship. You can create a store on a platform like Shopify and integrate it with dropshipping suppliers like Oberlo or AliExpress.

THE time you save dropshipping can be spent finding a niche to sell to, marketing your products, reaching new buyers, or helping your customers. With product development and design being noticeably absent from this equation, dropshipping is definitely a side hustle for those who want to flex their marketing muscles.

WHAT TO CONSIDER Before You Get Started

THIS IS why it always pays to do your research before you jump into any side hustle only to find out you bought some phony course that drained your bank account.

ADVANTAGES

- **Cheap to get started.**

It's incredibly cheap to get started with drop shipping. All you need is a product to sell, a website, and a little advertising, and you'll be up and running.

OKAY, maybe I made that sound a little easier than it really is, so let me break it down for you a little more.

- **The website** – I prefer Shopify since it's built for those who what to start an eCommerce business. More on this later. Total cost: $29 a month.
- **The product** – As a dropshipper, you only need to buy a product when someone buys it from you.
- **Advertising** – The final piece of the puzzle is advertising your products online. The great part about this is that you can usually get your first $100 of ad spend from Google for free.

IN THE END, your initial cost is very low, but as you grow your business, you'll spend more, but as you spend more, you should hopefully be earning more.

- **Shopify platform**

Starting your own eCommerce business years ago was extremely hard. You needed a good website, which required you to hire a web designer. The site also needed to be very secure to prevent hackers from breaking into it.

IN THE END, you likely had to piece together two or three programs to get your business up and running.

. . .

TODAY, starting an eCommerce business is much easier because of one simple tool, Shopify. Shopify is a full-on eCommerce solution that does all the hard work to focus on your business's more important things.

HERE ARE a few of the things you get when you sign up with Shopify.

- Unlimited bandwidth hosting that will handle as many visitors as you can throw at it.
- Done for You Payment Processing that allows you to accept credit card payments on your site.
- Fully Customizable Website that lets you design your website exactly how you want with no coding.

SHOPIFY IS the go-to platform for starting your dropshipping business when it comes down to it.

- 1 to 2 weeks before your first sale.

Another big benefit is that once you have your Shopify site setup, found your suppliers, and have a few ads running, you can expect to start receiving your first sales in a week or two typically.

. . .

WHEN YOU LOOK at other ways to earn a buck online, dropshipping can get up and earning income faster if you're starting from scratch.

- **You don't have to buy a bunch of products.**

The final benefit of dropshipping is that you don't have to stock many products you hope to sell. This is because you don't have to buy the product until your customer does.

THIS IS the real benefit of drop shipping. It allows you to take no risk investing in a product that doesn't sell and make you money. The worst thing that can happen with drop shipping if something doesn't sell is to move on to a new product.

Disadvantages

- **You only earn 20% to 30% of total sales.**

One negative that held me back from pulling the trigger on starting a drop shipping business is that you only earn between 20% to 30% of the entire sale.

THIS IS a hard pill to swallow when you can make nearly the same amount of money doing something like affiliate marketing and not have to deal with half the issues that drop shipping has.

FOR EXAMPLE, if you own a dropshipping store and someone orders a product from your online store, you can order that product from your wholesaler. On top of that, if they return the product, you'll be in charge of processing that as well.

ON THE OTHER HAND, if you are selling a product as an affiliate and someone buys a product from you, they are responsible for shipping the product, processing any returns, and paying you the commission.

WHEN IT comes down to it, most affiliate programs pay anywhere from 4% to 50%. If you can earn that much of the sale and do less work, why not just become an affiliate instead.

- **No control over products in stock.**

WHEN IT COMES TO DROPSHIPPING, you don't have control of the product. If someone comes to your site and orders a product from you, there is a chance that it could be out of stock.

THIS CAN BE BECAUSE the product is in high demand or is going out of stock. So how do you deal with this issue?

- **You work with multiple suppliers.**

WHEN YOU WORK with several suppliers that all sell the same product, you run less of a chance that you'll run out of product to sell. This can mean more work but the last thing you want to do is let a customer down. After all, trust is the most important currency on the web.

- **You need to find the right suppliers.**

ONE OF THE toughest parts of starting a drop shipping business is finding the right suppliers to deal with. Having the right suppliers can mean the difference between success and failure.

THE THING IS, you just can't go with any supplier. You need the right supplier that meets a few criteria to work with them.

SO HERE ARE A FEW TIPS TO CONSIDER.

- **MAP policies** – First off, a good supplier will enforce something known as Minimum Advertising Price policies (MAP). This means that the wholesaler has set the lowest price they will accept to sell their product, thus eliminating the cut throat pricing wars.
- **Subscription wholesalers** – Second, you'll want to stay away from subscription wholesalers who are basically middlemen. A good example of this is Doba. The problem with services like this is that they overeat your profit margin, and you should never have to pay a fee to work with a wholesaler. Instead, you'll want to work directly with the wholesalers themselves.
- **Contact them in person** – To have the best chance of getting a wholesaler to work with you, you'll want to contact them in person over the phone. I know many people today like to email people, which can work, but if you want the best chance, you'll want to contact them over the phone.
- **Set your site up** – Finally, the last tip is to set your

dropshipping site up before contacting your wholesalers. The reason for this is because your wholesalers like to see what your site looks like before they decide to work with you.

Is DropShipping Worth It?

So is it worth getting into dropshipping? If you're someone who doesn't mind rolling up their sleeves and putting in a little hard work up front, this can be a great way to get an online side hustle going.

8. Social Media Influencer.

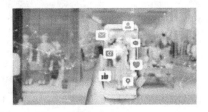

You can create an online profile on sites like YouTube, Instagram, or Tik Tok. Make ad revenue from sites like YouTube. Sell paid product placements on sites like Instagram or Tik Tok. You can also sell your own products whether they're print on demand or drop-shipped to your audience. Don't have a "social media personality"? Create an Instagram account using user-generated content. Find a niche like fashion, or makeup or sports, or comedy. Follow other accounts in that niche and repost their content using an app like Repost for Instagram. Once you start gaining a following, monetize it by selling print on demand or drop shipping products that resonate with that audience.

How to Make Money as a Social Media Influencer

WHETHER YOU'RE STARTING OUT in business, building a side hustle, or expanding an already successful business, you can leverage the power of social media.

BECOMING AN INFLUENCER in your own right isn't difficult. You can build a strong presence and use "influencer marketing" strategies to cash in on the ever-growing number of people spending more and more time (and money) on social media.

How can you establish your value as an influencer?

GETTING THESE BASICS right can help you gain more credibility and win the trust of potential partners. Some of the basics will also make it easier for you to get into the radar of brands looking for influencers.

HERE ARE SOME of the ways to make money as a social media influencer:

- **Produce high-quality content.**

THE ' UALITY of your content can determine the kind of impression you'll make on potential partners. And of course, high-quality content is crucial if you want to make a good first impression.

WHEN BRANDS look for potential social media influencers to work with, they'll look at the influencer's relevance, reach, and engagement rate. But they'll also go through the influencer's content to see how good of a content creator they are.

SO WHAT DOES THIS MEAN?

WHATEVER CONTENT YOU post on social media should be of high quality if you want to make money on social media. Invest in a decent camera if possible so you can produce better images.

- **Engage your audience.**

BRANDS also look for engagement rate when searching for influencers to work with. That's why you must build an engaged and loyal audience if you want to make money on social media.

INSTEAD OF SIMPLY creating content about yourself, you need to engage your followers in a two-sided conversation.

. . .

For example: Even if you post a photo of a certain product that you really like, you could ask questions such as:

- Have you used it before?
- What do you think about it?

Or you could encourage them to create content in tune with what you've created and ask them to tag you in it.

- **Join an influencer network.**

Whether you're just starting out as an influencer or you want to monetize your influence further, joining an influencer network can be a great way to find brands to work with.

It's especially beneficial for micro-influencers who haven't yet received many proposals from brands and marketers.

These influencer networks match you with brands that are in search of influencers fitting your characteristics. This is one of the best things to do if you want to make money on social media and make your mark as an influencer.

In some cases, brands and marketers may also use the network to search for influencers in a certain niche. Some networks may even let you choose brands that you wish to promote.

. . .

ALL OF these options will prove to be beneficial for both influencers and brands. And there are plenty of networks and platforms to choose from.

I RECOMMEND USING FOURSTARZZ MEDIA. This platform is specially geared towards micro-and nano-influencers, so there's a good chance that you'll be able to get connected with a brand with ease.

- Social media sponsored posts.

SPONSORED social media posts are among the most popular ways for influencers to make money on social media. It's when brands or marketers pay you to promote a certain brand or product in a social media post.

WHAT CAN YOU POST ABOUT?

THE POST CAN either be entirely about the product or feature several products at a time. You could create review posts, informational posts, or simply feature and tag the products.

INSTAGRAM INFLUENCERS CAN charge between $124 and $1,405 per sponsored post. But the cost can vary according to several factors, such as the number of followers you have and the industry in which you specialize.

. . .

THE REPORT found that influencers who have fewer than 2000 followers may charge around $124 per post, and those with 2000 to 5000 followers charge an average of $137 per post.

THE COST for one sponsored post increases, and by the time you have more than a million followers, you could charge around $1,405 for a single Instagram post.

So, what's the drill?

SIMPLE, the more followers you have, the more likely you will make money on social media as an influencer.

WHAT DOES this mean for you?

IT MEANS THAT you need to try to further increase your following by creating engaging content regularly and hosting giveaway contests that require participants to follow you.

- **Become a brand representative/ambassador.**

YOU CAN ALSO make money on social media by becoming a brand representative or brand ambassador.

WHAT'S so good about this form of partnership?

. . .

THIS WOULD NORMALLY be an extended contract lasting for at least a couple of months instead of just a one-off partnership. In some cases, the contract may last for several years as well.

WHEN YOU'RE a brand representative or a brand ambassador, you'll get free products from the brand. In exchange, you'll have to promote these products on social media.

SOME BRANDS MAY pay an additional fee for every piece of content their ambassadors create. Or there may also be a compensation clause in which you earn a percentage or a fixed sum for every conversion you drive.

YOU CAN LOOK for top brands that offer a brand ambassador program and see if those brands would be suitable for you.

WHAT ELSE?

YOU CAN even check out whether or not some of your favorite brands have an ambassador program you could sign up for.

9. Social Media Marketing Services.

Are you a social media pro? Use your skills by helping local business owners manage their social media marketing. You can find work on sites like Craigslist and Thumbtack.

Paid Marketing & Media Side Hustles

These marketing skills involve paid media, where a potential client would need to pay you and have funds allocated for running media.

These side hustles are great for media planners, media buyers, campaign managers, ad operations professionals, and digital marketing specialists.

- **Paid search (adwords) setup and management.**

If you've worked at a marketing agency in your past on the digital side, you may have had clients run paid search campaigns through platforms like Google AdWords.

. . .

FORTUNATELY, optimizing paid ad campaigns is a lucrative marketing skill you can apply to help other businesses if you need some side income.

For one, you can take your AdWords skills that you used in your previous work and leverage them to help small businesses in your area show up on Google searches. It's as simple as telling a business owner you can place them at the top of search results and only pay when somebody clicks the ad.

THAT MAKES IT EASIER to sell through (for you) because, unlike other forms of advertising, you're only paying for clicks and not just for impressions (having your ads show up).

- **Social media advertising management.**

SUPPOSE YOU'RE able to create unique targeted audiences and have a knack for social media advertising. In that case, you can find clients on the side and charge them monthly fees to manage paid social media campaigns on networks like Facebook, Instagram, LinkedIn, and Twitter for them.

IT'D BE hugely beneficial to offer the actual creation of the social media ads, use their existing branding assets, or team up with a graphic designer and split the profits. Social media advertising can be incredibly profitable for businesses, but they don't necessarily know how to do it effectively without wasting marketing dollars.

- **Display advertising (online banner ads).**

DISPLAY ADVERTISING CAN BE COMPLICATED. You know that if you've worked for an agency and built this marketing skill in the past. If you can simplify the world of display advertising for a client and tell them you can get millions of ad impressions, they will be very interested in working with you.

THESE SKILLS OFTEN become second nature in full-time media roles. Just don't forget you can leverage them to sell your own services to other businesses. Companies might not know the first thing about digital display or the questions to ask vendors. Hiring a freelance digital display resource could help them avoid getting bad deals.

- Traditional media planning and buying.

BEING ABLE to negotiate media and know when something is a good deal... is a powerful marketing skill.

CLIENTS will potentially pay you on a freelance basis to manage and negotiate the media planning and buying process. On a local level, if you know some of the best magazines, newspapers, billboard locations, signage locations in the mall, etc., you can leverage that knowledge to sell your skills to clients who need a local media presence on an ongoing basis.

DIGITAL IS HUGE, but traditional is not dead. Clients just get ripped off because much of traditional media is overpriced compared to what you can achieve with Facebook or search engine advertising.

- **Native advertising.**

THERE ARE websites out there that allow businesses to post sponsored content that looks native to the site itself. This is called native advertising. It's a way to post content sponsored that looks organic and less like an advertisement.

SUPPOSE YOU'VE learned how to find, evaluate, and run these types of advertising campaigns. In that case, there are businesses you can reach out to who would be very interested in putting your marketing skills to good use with booking native campaigns. On top of that, if you're actually producing the native ad spot's content, that's even more money you can make from this marketing skill.

- **Paid influencer outreach, coordination, and management.**

ANOTHER MARKETING SKILL you can use to turn into a side hustle is finding influencers who are good fits for brands. Maybe you are a brand whose target audience is very active and into athletics. You might know the best ways to reach out to fitness bloggers, and fitness Instagram accounts with huge potential for promotion.

NOT EVERYBODY IS great at finding these sorts of niche influencers. If you are, you can use that to manage influencer programs. Influencer programs take a lot of work, and you can charge a monthly fee to take this off of somebody's plate. If they see good results, they will keep using your expertise in the future.

- **Email marketing management.**

IF YOU KNOW how to run email marketing campaigns, what are you waiting for? Companies everywhere need people with the marketing skills that can help them capture email addresses, build an email list from scratch, and follow up with that list to create more paying customers.

IF YOU HAVE expertise in capturing email addresses and designing/sending emails, this can be a special marketing skill as a side hustle.

- **Content promotion.**

IF YOU WANT to go the extra mile, write articles and then use your content promotion marketing skills to help them promote each post (and see actual results). There are a couple of ways to do this.

YOU COULD START your OWN site in a certain blog niche, work for a few months to get it somewhat popular, then start writing for others and use your following to blast your clients' content out to bigger audiences. That way, it doesn't end with the writing—you focus on content promotion for them as well, which will inevitably lead to higher-paying contracts with these clients.

. . .

ALTERNATIVELY, you could create content for them, then help them strategically find ways to promote it. One example of this would offer a package deal where you write articles and advertise those articles on LinkedIn and Facebook. Then, you just charge a service fee for that entire bundle of services.

- **Infographics.**

COMPANIES LOVE INFOGRAPHICS, just like our brains do. They explain things in a visually appealing manner and are very shareable online.

IF YOU'VE GOT the marketing skills and design chops to make infographics, this can definitely fit into a content marketing strategy because of the high shareability of infographics. With a high potential to be seen by many people, you can easily make $300-$500 (or much, much more based on experience) for the right infographic idea that aligns well with a brand—depending on the client's budget.

AS YOU CAN SEE, no matter which marketing skills you've been exposed to in previous roles, you can take so many of those marketing skills and leverage those strengths to work for yourself on the side (and full-time eventually).

10. Multi-Level Marketing.

While these might have gotten a bad reputation once ago, they are still a very viable way of making extra money. Either direct sell products or do network marketing where you build a team and make money from others' efforts. Mary Kay and Legalshield are a few of the larger ones.

Multi-level marketing, otherwise known as pyramid selling, is a business model in which a company distributes products through a network of distributors—often known as representatives—who earn income from retail sales and recruitment.

MLMs have always been around. You might recognize names like Tupperware, Herbalife, Avon, Mary Kay, and Amway. It's quite possible that your mother threw an MLM party while you were crawling around in diapers. They have been around forever.

Sounds innocent enough, right? The tricky part is this. Typically, to become a representative for an MLM or pyramid scheme, you need to buy the products outright. If you cannot sell the products and expand the business, whether through hosting at-home parties or by recruiting your friends and family on Facebook, you're out of luck, and you're out of money.

Aside from this initial buy-in, representatives are typically required to buy a certain product every month to maintain their status. Partially due to expectations like these, the longevity of an MLM representative is... not that long.

. . .

How Do I Recognize an MLM Scheme?

IT CAN be difficult to differentiate an MLM from a legitimate opportunity. Like we touched on earlier, many MLMs and pyramid schemes adopt the "entrepreneurship" language. I looked through a few "iffy" MLMs, and this is the kind of language we found:

- Opportunity
- Showcase yourself
- Be confident
- Empowering
- Ambitious
- Your business
- Your paycheck
- Invest in you
- Empower women
- Support your family
- Reach your dreams

Sounds familiar, right? Aside from the language used, it is very clear that these marketing websites are geared towards women trying to initiate a tide change in their own lives. They use a combination of fancy fonts, delicate pastels, inspirational testimonials from sellers, and encouraging promises of (almost) instant prosperity.

Making Money in MLM

CAN YOU MAKE money in an MLM company? The short answer is yes, but in reality, only a tiny percentage of representatives actually realize the high earnings advertised in MLM promotional materials and at meetings. Some people don't make any money at all, and some people actually lose money.

The AARP Foundation found that only about 25% of those surveyed made a profit with MLM, 27% broke even, and about half of them lost money. Of the quarter that made a profit:

- 14% made less than $5,000
- 6% made between $5,000 and $9,999
- 3% made between $10,000 and $24,999
- 3% made $25,000 or more
- .05% made $100,000 or more

How Does One Typically Get Paid?

THE BASIC PREMISE IS THIS – **the sales distributor is compensated in two ways:**

- On their own sales of the product/service to customers, and
- On the sales of the recruited team (this is where residual or passive income comes into play, as the team grows).

However, the specifics can vary widely among different MLM companies. This is where you want to do your due diligence. If a compensation plan doesn't seem fair (only the early adopters are making money) or you have a tough time understanding it (it's super convoluted), this may be a reason for pause.

Are Multi-Level Marketing Products Inferior?

. . .

THIS ONE is hard to answer because every company and product/service is different. However, just like with any other product, do your research. Read reviews, look at customer satisfaction, and take note of their return policies and rates. A good company will stand behind its product and have a generous return policy and low return rates.

11. Babysit/Petsitting/Dog Walking.

You can use local social networks like Nextdoor or specific online networks like UrbanSitter.com or Rover.com.

There are over fifty million dogs in the United States. One in four homes has a dog. Many dogs sit home all day while their doggie parents work. A lot live in Condominiums and apartments, which means they don't get to be outside during the day at all. Dog walking has become a necessity. If you love dogs, this is your chance to cash in on a fantastic career and start your own dog walking service.

Do you like dogs? Then a dog walking service may be the perfect home business for you. A dog walking business can be a fun and profitable way of making money from home. A professional dog walker takes clients' dogs for regular walks, either one dog at a time or a few dogs together. There is a growing demand for these services as so many families have busy schedules and are away from home all day unable to exercise their dogs themselves. Exercise is an essential component of correct pet care, and many people look to dog walkers to help them out.

The Advantages of Becoming a Dog Walker

There are many advantages to starting a dog walking service. The only real skills you need are a genuine affection for dogs and the physical stamina to walk the dogs. Commitment to your dog walk routine and reliability are essential. Many information about dog care and dog behavior can be found in books in your local library or relevant internet sites.

Once you build up your client base, being a dog-walker can be a fantastic side hustle.

- **It is extremely flexible** – Since you're your own boss, you can decide and work out times for your dog walking that suit you. Dogs can be walked during the mornings or the evenings, so if you have a flexible schedule, this can help you.
- **You get some exercise** – This job is great as you'll provide a beneficial service to someone and get some light exercise along the way.
- **Minimum startups costs** – There are arguably no startup costs at all when it comes to dog walking. You may need to bring your own leash, but if any friends or family members who are dog-owners have a spare going, simply just ask to borrow it, and you are good to go. Chances are, your client will let you use their own leashes most of the time too.

How to Get Started as a Dog Walker

THE FIRST STEP TO getting started is the hardest, and that is finding your clients. You can find these clients in many ways, and if you try all these, I guarantee you'll get someone interested.

- **Ask friends and family** – Chances are, you know at least ONE person who owns a dog. And the chances are that person will know SOMEONE else who owns a dog. Simply just put the word out that you're planning on starting a part-time dog-walking business and if they would be interested or if they could pass on the word to anyone else they know. Hopefully, someone will get back to you, and then you'll have your first client.
- **Advertise locally** – If no-one you immediately ask is interested, then don't worry! Your next step will be to do some local advertising. This can be as simple as visiting local community areas in your town/city and posting flyers advertising your services. If you're feeling brave, you also could do cold-calling on doors in your local neighborhood, or if you're feeling extra brave, striking up conversations with local dog walkers. This doesn't have to be a sales pitch either! Just compliment the dog and start up a conversation. Casually bring up the fact you're starting a dog-walking service and see if the person would be interested. If they are, given them your details (Printing out some business cards can help with this!) and arrange the first walk. Another option is also advertising on social media such as local Facebook Groups or Instagram. Join groups of

dog lovers, and you'll have a huge list of potential clients ready for you to contact.

How to Earn Money from Being a Dog Walker

ONCE YOU'VE GOT your first client, next, you need to arrange payment. Figure out what rates you'll be charging. I would recommend a flat fee for the amount of time it will take you, for example, $15 per hour. You can then arrange to collect your payment either electronically or with good old fashioned cash.

Your start-up costs are low. You may have to purchase a few good leashes, pooper scoopers and bags. Buying liability insurance is always advisable. Your business expenses are limited, and there is good profit potential with a dog walking service. Also, you can stay healthy and fit while making money!

Before starting this home business, you need to plan a few things. You need to work out your daily walks and routes. Find out where you can best walk the dogs and work out some good thirty-minute routes. You need to set your fees. Research other dog walking businesses in your area and see what the competition is charging. Decide on the type of dog walks you will offer - private or group walks, the number of walks per week and so on. If you are just starting out, you can get some relevant experience by volunteering to walk dogs at local animal shelters and dog rescue centers. This will provide you with good experience in handling several different dogs and give you the confidence and credibility to find paying dog walking jobs.

Finding dog walking jobs can be done on a small marketing and advertising budget. Cost-effective ways to advertise your pet services include designing and printing eye-catching and informative flyers. Post these flyers around your neighborhood, targeting potential clients. People likely to use a dog walker include busy professionals and older adults so post flyers in office blocks and retirement communities. Pet owners going on vacation will often need a dog walker. Post your flyers on local community boards. Another good place to post your flyers is veterinarian offices, pet grooming services and pet supply stores. Once you have your first clients, you will be amazed at the number of referrals you get if you provide a good and reliable service.

Walking dogs is a good way to earn income from home. It is fun, rewarding and keeps you fit and healthy!

12. Photography/Videography.

Take senior photos, photos for bar events, headshots for small business owners, etc. Photography is a creative art form. A good photographer should have aesthetic sense and technical expertise. With the latest digital photography, it has become more popular. Photography plays a vital role in media, like print and electronic media. Photography needs more than just training; it requires inherent talent.

Photography is a very good side hustle to pursue. With persistence, it may afford you both money and fame. Sometimes an important message may be conveyed through a photo. These choose a subject and present it interestingly. One can become a photographer by becoming an assistant to a senior photographer and learn the techniques. There are more training institutions and different fields to get employment for people who want to become a good photographer. There is a lot of competition in photography in the fields of fashion, journalism, advertising, wildlife photography etc.

- **Feature photography** usually tells a story through a photo. A few photographers work with magazines; their main task is to illustrate what is written in the magazine or any article. Other commercial photographers work for advertising agencies. These people are professionals; they take pictures of different products or different companies offering services. They take pictures of indoor or outdoor and make the products look astounding.
- **Wildlife photographers** and sports photographers may work as freelancers or work within the media. Nature and wildlife photography is an interesting subject. Photographers take pictures of different animals, birds, nature, beautiful scenery, flowers, mountains, snow, sunset, trees, waterfalls, sea, lake, greeneries and all other beautiful things on this earth. It can take a long time to get the perfect image, but that image can be worth a fortune.
- **Forensic photography** is a very useful form of photography which is used at crime scenes. For this kind of photography, the photographer should have an eye for detail. These photographers can find employment with the police service.
- **Fashion photography** is booming. It is a very creative and also a well-paid profession. Portrait photography is used to take pictures at celebrations like weddings. Art photography is where a photographer sells his photos as fine artwork.

10 Ways to Make Money With Photography

There are literally hundreds of ways to make money with photography. Some methods only require a digital camera and a connection to the internet. With other techniques, you'll need to travel and go on special assignment to capture the shot. **Here are ten of the top money-making photography tactics:**

1. **Upload your images to stock photography websites** - These stock photo websites pay you every time someone downloads one of your images. On average, you make a 30-50% commission each time a purchase is made.

2. **Set up a photo blog** - Hosting your images on your own website is a great way to make extra income and showcase your work. You can make money from adverting, selling photography services, or selling photos online.

3. **Create custom products** - Many people love to see their loved ones on a favorite mug, blanket, pillow, or t-shirt. Offering these custom products is easy using free online tools.

4. **Offer your photography services** - Many offline businesses need photographers to take pictures of their products or storefronts for use online. You can make a high income just by focusing on providing these services to needy businesses.

5. **Take images for people to sell items on consignment** - There are tons of people helping others list their items for auction or sale on popular classified websites. Craigslist and eBay are two effective websites to help facilitate this method.

6. **Work as a freelance photographer on outsourcing websites** - There are thousands of people actively searching for a professional to do photo and design

work on outsourcing websites and forums right now. By accepting these photo jobs, you can make a part-time or full-time income.

7. **Photo touch-ups and restoring** - As more and more people move to digital photography, there is a huge demand to digitize old photos to help preserve them.

8. **Working as a photojournalist** - Many publications need images to go with their stories. These photo jobs can be erratic and fast-paced. However, they often provide a variety of job assignments and excitement.

9. **Take pictures of local events** - Many schools, non-profit organizations, and companies need pictures taken of their local events. Try networking at local group meetings to meet connections and find these opportunities.

10. **Sell public domain images on eBay** - Many people love old reproductions of images in the public domain. Often these images can be found online at a very low cost and resold for a high income.

How to Sell Your Photos Online to Make More Money

MANY PEOPLE BELIEVE that a professional camera is necessary to start making money with photography. The truth is that you can earn an income from photography with almost any camera if it provides a good enough resolution. One of the easiest ways to do so is to sell photos online.

You may be surprised to know that many of these stock photo sites accept images from any camera which have a resolution of 6 megapixels or high. Sure, not just anyone can sign up and start making money taking pictures of the family dog.

But with some research and practice, you could eventually start selling your pictures at some of these sites.

So what does it take to become a good photographer and earn money through photography? It requires dedication, a decent camera, and a good eye. You can even learn basic photography with your simple point and shoot camera.

Once you have developed your photographic skills, it is important to understand some criteria to sell photos best online. **Here are a few things to consider:**

- **Choose a Subject** - There are wildlife, landscape, urban, industrial, fashion photography, and many more categories. Pick an area of interest at first as you gain expertise.
- **Learn Composition** - You can find hundreds of online tutorials on composing images to bring out the best results. If you learn one composition technique per day, you will be taking perfect pictures within a couple of weeks.
- **Choose a Stock Photo Site** - Every stock photography site is different, so familiarize yourself with places you can sell your pictures and read up on each site's terms. Since you are a beginner, you will want a less rigid site as far as requirements.

As you start submitting photos to stock sites for sale, pay attention to your fellow submitters, especially the veterans. Things like proper titling and tagging can be important when you sell photos online as you compete against a large pool of people.

Photography is clearly a career pursuit that has many facets. Once one has realized where one's strength as a photographer lies, one can specialize in this regard.

. . .

13. Ridesharing.

Do you have a car? You can make extra money while driving for Uber or Lyft.

Many people prefer rideshare companies because of how good they are at saving transport costs. Essentially, they connect drivers and passengers within a given locality, making it possible for them to share rides to matching destinations, thus cutting on transport costs. Most of these companies work through mobile applications to make it easy for the passengers and drivers to hook up for the rides.

If you wish to become a rideshare driver, but you do not have your car, you can still make a living through some financing. The fact is that some of these companies work as rental companies as well and hence you can lease a car from them to become a driver at reasonable rates. Such financing offers a straightforward way to start making your money as a rideshare driver without much-starting capital.

RIDESHARE SIDE-HUSTLE: Tips to Prepare Your Car

Looking to earn some extra cash? A rideshare side-hustle with a company like Uber or Lyft could be very lucrative. But there's a lot you need to know. If you're thinking about becoming a rideshare driver, start by visiting experts like "The Rideshare Guy," where you can learn the business's ins-and-outs, including what's required for insurance and what to do if you get in an accident. Next, prepare your car to pick up and deliver passengers to their destination without any unexpected events. Remember, you want to provide a safe, comforting and efficient experience for passengers while ensuring a headache-free time for yourself. **Here are a few tips to prepare your car for rideshare side-hustle:**

- **Give your ride a complete once-over.**

Start by checking your tires. Ensure the air pressure is right, the tire tread is healthy, and your spare is in good working order. Check oil and coolant levels and ensure all lights (taillights and running lights) are working properly. If the Check Engine light is on (or any other light signaling that your vehicle needs maintenance), make an appointment with an automotive professional.

- **Registration and inspection.**

Make sure that your registration and inspection are valid before you start your rideshare side-hustle. You should have a copy of the registration in your car. If you can't find it, get a new copy from your local Department of Motor Vehicles and store it securely in your vehicle. Look at your inspection sticker and make sure it's not about to expire. If it is, get the inspection done as soon as possible. You won't have time once you start your side-hustle.

- **Rideshare technology.**

Keeping track of your mileage is important at tax time (the federal tax deduction is 54.5 cents per mile of business travel driven). Track miles manually or use a mileage tracker apps. HyreCar has put together a list of 14 to choose from. Should there be an incident, dash cams will show exactly what happened. Dashcams range in size, price, and features. Features can include night vision, external and internal facing cameras, and rearview mirror functionality.

Get these rideshare necessities.

- **Toll Pass or Toll Tag:** Get a toll pass or toll tag and automate toll paying. If you're operating on the east coast, many toll booths are automated, so you must obtain an E-ZPass. E-ZPasses are accepted in 17 states.
- **Uber/Lyft Sticker:** Stickers (also known as trade dress) not only help passengers identify your car, they're required.
- **Provide snacks and water:** Having water and snacks, on-hand will delight your customers and may lead to a higher rating. Provide them free-of-charge or earn extra money by selling them via a company such as Cargo.
- **Phone mount:** Use a phone mount when driving. Holding your phone is inconvenient and dangerous, not to mention illegal in some states. There are many mounts to choose from, ranging in size, price, and how they attach to the vehicle.
- **Jumper cables:** Keep a pair of jumper cables handy if the battery dies and be sure you know how to jumpstart your car.
- **Sickness bags and cleaning supplies:** Prevent your car from needing a deep-clean by keeping bags like these on hand. Sanitizing wipes are great for cleaning up spills and wiping down surfaces touched most often by passengers.
- **Charging accessories:** You'll always have a ride-hailing app engaged on your device. Make sure you

have everything you need to keep the device powered and your side-hustle running. Passengers will also appreciate it if you have a cord they can use to charge up if needed.

How Does The Payment Systems Work With Rideshare Companies and How Much Can You Make?

THE BEST PART about rideshare is that it's entirely cashless. You can accept tips in cash, but it's not recommended. Most companies actually offer free credit for new users ($25 with Lyft and $10 with Uber), but after that, the prices vary depending on your city.

The prices are on average 25-50% lower than a comparable taxi, and the rides are generally much more enjoyable.

As a driver, your payment will vary depending on what times you drive. Uber employs surge pricing, which means that the cost of a fare will go up during busy times, thus increasing your earnings potential.

Lyft uses a similar strategy, but they cap it at double the price of the fare; there is no cap with Uber. I'd estimate you can make up to $30/hr on average and all the way up to $50 or even $60/hr during hectic times or when you get long rides.

14. Scooter Charging.

Do you have a truck? You can make extra money as well charging scooters for companies like Bird, Razor, and Lime.

For those who live in urban areas, charging electric scooters can be a great way to earn some money with minimal impact on your current life.

Electric scooter rentals through companies like Bird and Lime have become very popular in many cities, leading to a great side hustle opportunity. These companies will pay you to charge their scooters and get them back on the streets to be rented again.

What Do Lime and Bird Do?

LIME AND BIRD are both companies offering electric scooters for a low-cost rental by the public for use in cities. Lime also offers Electric-Assist Bikes and Smart Pedal Bikes. Using their individual apps, you can find a scooter (or bike) available near you, unlock it, and use it to help you get around town.

What Can You Do for Lime and Bird?

WITH SO many electric scooters flooding into cities across the States, Lime and Bird both need people on the ground willing to help them keep their scooters charged and distributed across the area. In true gig economy form, they're offering this opportunity to anyone who applies and is approved.

Things to Keep in Mind

. . .

MAXIMIZING your charge ability may come with an investment – you're only given a few chargers to get you started, and you may be charged for them. Determine how many scooters you can reliably charge a night, then decide whether the expense of investing in enough charging cables is worth it.

You'll also be paying for the electricity to charge these scooters. You'll need to review your electricity statement to determine the actual cost and decide whether the money you're making is worth the time and energy investment as well.

Since users of these Lime or Bird scooters aren't always required to return the scooters to a specific dock when they're finished using them, the scooters can be left in out-of-the-way or difficult-to-access places. This can make it very inconvenient to pick some of these scooters up for charging – so be sure to consider whether picking up a particular scooter in the first place is worth it. Also, as this side gig becomes more popular, you may find yourself facing competition to be the first to get to those scooters that require charging.

THE OPPORTUNITY

SIGNING UP TO be a Lime Juicer, Skip Ranger, or Bird Charger is as easy as filling in a simple form on the company's website. They'll ask for your name, email address, and phone number, along with your zip code. You'll also be consenting to each company's Terms and Conditions and Privacy Policy. Each company also specifies that you'll get paid right away – Bird goes on to explain that you'll be paid each morning for the charging you did the previous night. Each company will provide you with a certain number of chargers so that you can plug the scooters in at home and charge them up. General requirements include having a smartphone to access the app, a vehicle large enough to carry the scooters to your home for charging, and access to electrical outlets to do the charging.

Finding scooters to charge is a simple matter of opening up either the Lime or Bird app, accessing the locations of scooters in need of charging, then picking them up, charging them, and returning them to locations specified by Lime or Bird once you're done. The app will walk you through the process of picking them up, which may involve scanning the scooter to unlock it so that you can take it home.

It looks like it can take anywhere between four to seven hours to charge a scooter, depending on the scooter and how much charge it still has left.

Since these scooters are meant to be used in high-traffic areas during high-traffic times – early in the morning up to rush hour as everyone heads to after-work errands or home – you can expect to be required to drop off the scooters in the early AM. Reportedly, you may even be paid less if you deliver the charged scooters after 7 AM. You also can't pick up scooters with some companies until after 9 PM (unless they are almost out of charge). To really excel at this side hustle, make sure you're both somewhat of a night owl and an early riser.

Payment information for charging is not publicly posted on their site at this time, but I've seen ads that Bird will pay between $5 to $20 for each scooter charged, and Lime is reported to offer around the same. The amount you're paid may depend on where you're located and what time of day you're charging.

15. Teach A Skill.

Know how to play an instrument, a foreign language, or a unique skill? Teach lessons for a fee. You can use sites like Cohere.live for a platform to do it all virtually and you can market around campus, or by using local sites like NextDoor, or Craigslist.

If you possess a valuable set of skills from your experience on a past job, there's certainly an audience online who'd be willing to pay to help accelerate their learning curve and achieve their own career goals. There are now many online course marketplaces, like CreativeLive, Skillshare, and Udemy, with various audience demographics, features, and payout structures. You could earn a substantial passive income of several hundred to even thousands per month from your library of online courses.

Once you've established an audience, you can even host courses on your own website to retain a larger share of the revenue by using course platforms like Teachable, Thinkific, and Zippy Courses. While it may seem like a far reach and you shouldn't start with this high of a goal for your side hustle, one of the most experienced online educators in the business, Ramit Sethi, lays out a detailed blueprint for how he generated more than $5 Million in just one week from sales of his online courses.

16. Moving Service.

You can make money helping students more in/out of their dorm rooms, in/out of apartments, or make money helping people locally move into houses. Rent a Uhaul for a low fee, pay a friend a little of the cash to help, and make some good money for a day's work.

A Side Business That Keeps Things Moving... Literally

When the economy is booming, Americans trade-up: Bigger homes, bigger offices, better furniture, and more expensive equipment. And what happens when the market's down, and money's tight? They move again!

Individuals relocate to smaller homes; businesses downsize, families sell furniture. The Declaration of Independence states that every US citizen has the right to pursue happiness, and more often than not: Happiness is on the move.

If you have strength, stamina, and organizational skills, you might be able to earn money immediately...

The good news? Competent movers rarely lack work. Larger economic cycles pass by like seasons—movers provide an essential service. Even during a recession, when families and business tighten their belts, most people still find it necessary to pay a professional to move oversize or fragile items.

This year, approximately 40 million Americans, including

thousands of small business owners, will relocate. Technology has enabled a mobile class of young professionals, individuals in their twenties and thirties who pull up stakes every two or three years.

We are a country of wanderers, and freelance movers turn our natural restlessness into a business opportunity.

If you have strength, stamina, and keen organizational skills, then you might be able to earn money immediately as a freelance mover. If you're able to market your services effectively, you might even be able to turn your moving gig into a full-time business.

GETTING STARTED: **The Truck and Beyond**

ANYBODY WITH A TRUCK or van can supplement their income by starting a small moving business on the side. However, if you plan to advertise your services to the general public, you should probably purchase insurance to protect yourself against defamation or lawsuits.

Contact an insurance agent to learn more about commercial insurance for your vehicle and liability insurance for your business.

So how does a mover get started? It's easy! People need help schlepping their belongings from one place to another; you assist them with the task for a fee. Begin by letting your friends and family know that you are setting up shop as a mover. Monitor your social media networks to find out if someone you know is planning to relocate—people often announce a move months or weeks in advance on Facebook or Twitter.

Additionally, you can advertise your business on community websites such as Craigslist. Gradually, you will build a network that extends beyond your friends and loved ones.

As a mover, your direct expenses will be insurance and fuel. Before you reach out to potential customers, you will need to develop a pricing structure for your services—be sure to include the cost of gasoline and insurance; otherwise, they can eat away at your bottom line.

Getting Into Second Gear

As you build your moving business, you are likely to encounter a few bumps in the road. Relying on your friends and family for business will quickly bring you to a dead end. To build buzz and grow your network, get a website up and running as soon as possible.

Be sure to include pictures of your equipment, as well as testimonials. Provide potential customers with a moving check-list—anything you can do to convince a would-be customer that you are knowledgeable and reliable is a plus.

Freelancers and solopreneurs need to focus on providing a quality experience for their customers. As a mover, this means being punctual, polite, and careful. The things you are being paid to move are precious (even if they look like junk to you), and you should strive to treat each object as if it were your own prized possession.

Is a moving business a practical, cost-effective option for earning money part-time or full-time? Absolutely. Build your business slowly, focus on quality, and the pieces will fall into place.

Different Ways That You Can Get Started.

- Dolly.com

Dolly.com is a website/app that lets you hire (or hire out as) moving help.

- Lugg.com

Lugg.com is another site very similar to Dolly, where you can get paid to help people move things. They say that you can earn up to $2,500 per week if you have a truck capable of helping people with their move!

The qualifications to work on Lugg are not so different from the qualifications on Dolly.

You need...

- To be able to lift at least 100 pounds
- A vehicle that is 2001 or newer if you plan to use a vehicle to help move people's things
- A recent smartphone, running either iOS or Android
- To be at least 21 years of age to be a driver and at least 18 years old to be a helper

Lugg.com seems to be about the same as Dolly, with some minor differences... but it could be a great way to leverage your vehicle (and your muscles) to make some extra money!

Who Isn't This Side Hustle Good For?

IF YOU HAVE A BAD BACK, bad knees, or are otherwise physically impaired in pretty much any way, this will definitely not be the right type of side-hustle for you.

. . .

17. Yardwork/Day Laborer.

    This is the original youth hustle. Make money cutting grass, pulling weeds, cutting shrubs, or whatever might be needed. It's not the most glamorous side hustle globally, but the fact is nearly every yard in the country requires some maintenance. But this is something that more and more homeowners have started outsourcing, which means there's a big business opportunity. You can also rent tools for cheap from Home Depot if you don't have any.

Making Money Mowing Lawns

WE ALL KNOW that lawn mowing services are a necessary part of modern civilization. Every home and business with any grass on the property needs to ensure that it gets taken care of.

    Some homeowners take care of this themselves, and some businesses just pay their employees to take care of it. But what about the rest? Are there any businesses or homeowners out there willing to pay a small-time lawn care service to take care of their yard?

. . .

How Much Can You Make Every Month?

Obviously, this varies based on how much effort you are able/willing to put into it. If you only mow one lawn per month, you may only make $20-$50.

Suppose you're someone that can mow five or six lawns in a single day! Even if you only had this many lawns to mow every weekend, you are still looking at $800 or so extra per month!

As you can see, there is a pretty wide chasm between these two figures—so if you do manage to land some lawn care jobs, how much you make will mostly depend on your geographic location, how much you charge, how far they are from your own home, what kind of equipment you are hauling, etc.

How Do You Get Business Mowing Lawns?

The first and most obvious way to promote your business would be online. You could use several different sites, including:

- Craigslist
- Facebook (paid ads and groups)
- Instagram (paid ads)
- Your own website, combined with SEO marketing and a blog (I would absolutely recommend starting your own website if you choose to be serious about finding side-hustle work for a mowing business)

But this is only one element of self-promotion that could work to bring in some lawn-mowing business for your side hustle.

You could also go door to door and find customers that way. To do this, you would have to pump up your sales skills.

You could start by introducing yourself and handing them a card. Ask them if they have a lawn-care service already. If they say yes, ask them how much they are paying.

18. Create And Sell Your Own Handmade Goods.

Something is satisfying about hobbies that make money. It's no surprise that many Shopify merchants start successful small businesses out of a hobby they did in their spare time. If you enjoy doing the work, it doesn't feel like work. Think of something you enjoy doing, even when no one's paying you. Whether it's carpentry, knitting, painting, or crafting—these hobbies can serve as the foundation for many unique side hustles.

Almost everyone has a hobby or creative outlet that they're passionate about. You're in a perfect position if yours involves making something with your hands. Although creating hand-made products requires plenty of time spent learning a craft, it's one of the best ways to stand out in a sea of commodity products. You can also sell handmade items on Etsy alongside your Shopify store to connect with more potential customers.

On top of this, sourcing raw materials put you in a unique position to ensure your manufacturing process aligns with your brand values. Many business owners use their values to create products containing recyclable materials as part of their sales pitch. Take Dick Moby, a retailer that makes sunglasses using only oil-free acetate, an eco-friendly plastic substitute.

From bags made of old car seats to broken radios refashioned as Bluetooth speakers, using recyclable materials can be a great way to maintain your product's environmental sustainability while keeping costs low. If you love taking old materials and turning them into something new, this may be the side hustle for you.

How to Sell Handmade Items and Make a Profit

YOU PROBABLY HAVE IMAGINED what it would be like to live exclusively from your creations, be your own boss, and profit from your own business. However, how do you start? How do you organize your products, find customers, and sell? Most businesses don't grow overnight, and to start a project of this sort, you will need to dedicate your time and efforts to it, even if just a little bit every day. Small steps can put you on the right track with time.

RESEARCH YOUR NICHE and Target Audience

HANDMADE PRODUCTS ARE unique and have their specific market segments. You will have better success if you understand from the beginning which niche your products belong to and who is the target audience. As an entrepreneur, you need to develop varied tasks to launch a product, and this is the time for you to wear the researcher "hat."

Research your competitors, what customers are looking for,

and what they can't find in the current market. Once you find the gap, start planning your product line.

Tips for Keeping Your Costs Down

- **Negotiate!** When buying your supplies, always negotiate for wholesale prices or look for materials on sale. If you purchase raw materials at their retail prices, you will never be competitive enough within your market.
- **Don't multitask.** You should always optimize your creative process to do the most within the least time possible. When working from home, it is common to fall into the trap of multitasking. Doing several things simultaneously is highly counterproductive as you can't give your full attention to what you are crafting. If you have to stop and restart several times, this will lead to a low rate per hour. Create a routine for work, have a particular room just for crafting, and keep yourself away from distractions, like TV, for example.

Price Your Products Correctly

CONSIDER ALL YOUR COSTS, including supplies and your time. Yes, time is money! When you sell your product, every hour you spend crafting should be paid, as well as every material you use.

After you optimize your costs and time, it is time to set your price! The price should cover your expense and still give you some profit so that you can invest this profit back into your business and personal life. Remember to set apart your "salary" from your business profit. Don't mix them both, or you might lose track of what your profits are being invested on.

Before setting your price, also check for your competitor's retailing practices. Try to place yourself within the price range your competitors are selling, so you can be sure you will not be overpricing your item, and people will still be drawn to buy. Also, don't place your price too low, even if you are getting your supplies for free, for example. Always aim to increase what you're earning and avoid undercutting your fellow makers.

CREATE Your Brand

EVERY BUSINESS NEEDS A BRAND, and so does yours! Branding will identify your products and company; it includes your logo, mission, and values. You will incorporate a signature into packages, labels, shops, exhibition booth blogs, and business cards. If marketing and branding are new for you, we would suggest you educate yourself in the field. You can find several articles on the web, giving details and tips as a starter. It is okay to start small and learn as you evolve.

Label Your Handmade Products

A LABEL IS one thing that will set your product apart from your competitors; it adds a signature to your work and makes people remember your brand. It also shows how seriously you take your business. You can easily design and produce your own labels online, just adding your brand's logo or name. Depending on your product, you might also need to add additional tags with size, care instructions, and fabric content.

. . .

How to Sell Your Products

AFTER SETTING THE basics of your business, it is time to market and advertise it! You can follow; you just need to identify which one is the best for achieving your goals.

- **Sell at craft fairs and shows.**

If you are a beginner, it might feel scary to show your creations to a bigger audience for the first time. However, this is precisely what you need. People need to know you, your brand, and your products. Local craft fairs are perfect; you can look into competitors, check if the target audience likes your products, and if your price is indeed within the expectations.

- **Sell locally, where, and how?**

If you don't own a shop, you can sell your products to a boutique retailer, flea markets, pop-up stores, charity events, cafes, or art galleries. These are great options to grow your local customer base; you will just need to find the right place to do it. The proper venue will depend on the type of product you're selling, your niche market, and the audience. Maybe your craft is somehow related to coffee? Or is it something pet owners would love to buy?

After deciding what's the best place to display your products, it is time to pitch the spot with the venue owner. Some might charge you a fee for displaying the products; others might buy from you, re-sell, or even agree on a consignment contract. Check what is best for your business and close the deal!

- **Sell on marketplaces.**

Some fantastic marketplaces can help you show your products to a global audience. Etsy, eBay, and Amazon Handmade are just a few of the best-known ones. Each platform will charge you specific rates for selling your product, and you should consider their pros and cons before committing.

- **Share on social media.**

Handmade products are visual, and you should look for social media platforms that help you show this aspect. Pinterest and Instagram are the most popular choices since they are explicitly intended for sharing images and have an incredibly visual approach. Long texts here are not the right approach, but you can use hashtags.

If planning a paid campaign, remember to segment your audience to maximize your investment's return. Instagram and Facebook ads allow you to define your target and how much you want to spend on a determined campaign.

- **Sell on your own website.**

Having your own website might require a little bit more investment, but it is a great way to sell your products online without paying fees to marketplaces. Several e-commerce platforms offer basic starter plans for an affordable price, such as Wix, BigCommerce, and Shopify.

19. Baking.

Do people love your desserts? Maybe you could provide cake, cookies, or cupcakes to some corporate event in town.

Baking side hustles can help you earn some extra cash doing what you love. You may think the only side job for bakers is, well, baking! But there many other things that are food-related money makers that you can do at home or in your community for minimal start-up costs. First off, make sure it's legal in your state to sell home-baked goods. The regulations surrounding this industry are called cottage food laws, and they vary by state. Abide by any required regulations; you may have to apply for a permit or license.

How to Make Money Selling Baked Goods From Your Home

Do you enjoy baking? Are you the go-to person for the school or local non-profit organizations' cookie-sale fundraiser? Do you binge-watch baking competitions on TV, wishing you could compete to earn the grand prize to open your own bakery? Then you might want to consider profiting from your ability to bake yummy treats.

Baked goods businesses have grown in popularity over the last few years, but actually, they've been around for a while. Mrs. Fields started selling her decadent cookies in the 1970s. More recently, many entrepreneurs have started selling their cakes, cupcakes, and cookies from home and have grown into regular retail bakeries and even franchises.

When it comes to home baking, there are many different treats you can make, **including:**

- Cakes and cupcakes
- Cookies
- Brownies and bars
- Pies
- Muffins
- Breads
- Pastries
- Biscotti
- Dog treats

Starting a home-based bakery might sound fun and easy to do – after all, you're already baking. But there are a few cons to running a home-based baking business that you'll need to consider before baking your first batch of goodies.

Benefits of a Home-Based Baking Business

THERE ARE SEVERAL great reasons to start selling your baked goods from home, **including:**

- Do what you love, assuming you love baking.
- Creative expression. Perhaps you put a unique twist on your baked goods.
- Easy to start. You already have a kitchen and knowledge of cooking.
- There's always a market for yummy baked goods.

- Can sell locally and/or online, depending on your baked good's ability to be delivered or shipped.

What You Need to Start a Home-Based Baking Business

YOU SHOULD KNOW HOW to bake and that your concoctions are delicious. There are several other things to know or obtain when starting a baking business, **including:**

- Sufficient skill and knowledge of safe food preparation and potential dietary issues. For example, you'll want to disclose if you have peanuts in your kitchen to warn consumers who are allergic to the nut.
- A retail or food-service background would be helpful.
- A supply of ingredients plus room to store them, a regular shopping regimen, and good suppliers. Remember, you may need to store your equipment and ingredients separately from your personal ones.
- Any licenses or inspections required by your state, county, and/or city. A health inspector may visit your home.
- An understanding of your competition and how your baked goods will stand out in the crowd.

How Much to Charge for Home-Baked Goods

WHEN YOU START selling baked goods, figuring out how much to charge will be one of your biggest hurdles.

The first step is to assess your target market. How much are other bakers charging? And for what types of products? Next, look at your skillset. How much experience do you have? How quickly will you be able to complete the work?

As for how much you can earn, it depends on how much work you put into both the baking and the marketing. If you're just taking special orders, the bakers estimated you could earn between $200 and $400 per month; if you're working 20 hours per week, $800 to $1,200; and if you start baking lots of wedding cakes, much, much more.

20. *Being A TaskRabbit.*

Task Rabbit is an on-demand errand-running service that enlists regular people to help out. You can earn money in your spare time completing real-world tasks on their unique platform.

How Does TaskRabbit Work?

When you become a Tasker, you download the TaskRabbit app. The company will send you notifications about gigs in your area, and you can select which ones you want to complete. Once you do so, you can confirm details, such as your arrival time, with the client. When the project is complete, you'll submit your invoice and get paid through the app.

There are literally hundreds of tasks you can complete as a

Tasker. If you don't mind manual labor, you can earn money moving furniture, doing home repairs, or doing yard work. But you can also make money doing things like planning birthday parties, wrapping gifts, or even waiting in line for concert tickets.

WHO CAN USE TASKRABBIT?

TaskRabbit could be a decent side gig, but it won't replace a full-time salary. If your goal is to earn $10,000 per month (or more), TaskRabbit probably won't be enough to get you there.

Instead, becoming a Tasker may be a good idea if you want to earn supplemental income during your spare time, such as during the evenings or on weekends. This can help you pay down your credit card or student loan debt.

Unlike most part-time jobs, you can complete tasks whenever it's convenient for you, and you can scale the work to meet your needs. For example, if you're saving money for a new car, you can take on more tasks until you get the cash you need, then take a break.

To be a Tasker in the United States, **you must meet the following requirements:**

- Have a valid Social Security number
- Be at least 18 years old
- Be able to work in one of TaskRabbit's active cities
- Provide information, like a copy of your driver's license so that you can undergo a background check
- Have an active checking account
- Have a valid credit card
- Own a smartphone

Be aware that signing up to become a Tasker requires a

one-time, non-refundable $25 registration fee paid via credit card.

How Much Can You Earn With TaskRabbit?

How much you can earn with TaskRabbit is dependent on your skill set, location, and the type of jobs available.

For example, cleaners in the Orlando, FL area charge $21 to $40 per hour, while painters can charge $104 to $200 per hour to paint one bedroom.

In Las Vegas, you could wait in line at an event's ticket booth for $18 per hour. Or you could organize someone's closet and earn between $18 and $30 per hour.

Over time, that can really add up. If you worked 10 hours a week and charged $20 per hour, you'd earn $800 per month.

However, keep in mind that TaskRabbit charges a 15% service fee, which is deducted from the total amount you earn. For example, if a gig paid $50, TaskRabbit would take $7.50, and you'd get the remaining $42.50.

You can earn even more by providing excellent service. TaskRabbit allows clients to tip Taskers up to 30% of the total bill. And you get to keep 100% of any tips you receive.

Once you complete a task, you submit an invoice through the TaskRabbit app. Taskers are paid through direct deposit using either Braintree or Stripe, depending on where you live.

Maximizing Your Earnings With Taskrabbit

To make as much money with TaskRabbit as possible, use these tips:

- **Create a standout profile:** Your profile is your opportunity to sell yourself. Post a clear profile picture, and use the profile to highlight your experience and work ethic. If you have a professional website, include a link to it, too. If you need help, check out the profiles of TaskRabbit's Elite; they're Taskers with positive ratings of 98% or higher who complete many tasks each month.

- **Take on a range of tasks:** Don't be afraid to undertake many different types of tasks. By diversifying the gigs you're willing to complete, you can increase your chances of earning money.
- **Learn skills:** Skilled positions typically pay more than other gigs. If possible, learn specialized skills, like painting, assembling furniture, or handyman services.
- **Raise your rates:** When you're just starting out, you'll likely have to charge low rates to land your first gigs. But once you've completed a few tasks and have gotten good reviews, continually raise your rates after every job.

How to Get Good Reviews on TaskRabbit

Good reviews are essential to your success as a Tasker. To ensure you get the best reviews, **follow these steps:**

- **Be professional:** When you communicate with the client, whether it's through the app or in person, be professional. Be friendly and polite, and when you show up at their home, dress neatly.
- **Show up on time:** If possible, try to be a few minutes early so you can start work right on time. Being punctual is a big factor in your reviews.
- **Do the best work possible:** Even though it's a side gig, treat each task like it's an assignment at your full-time job. Do the best work you can do to meet or exceed your client's expectations.

How to Stay Safe as a Tasker

TaskRabbit has been around for a while, but you should still exercise caution as a Tasker. The job means going into strangers' homes, so it's important to be careful.

Let a friend or relative know where you're going beforehand, and text them when you arrive and leave so they know you're safe. If at any point you feel uncomfortable at a client's location, leave immediately and contact TaskRabbit's Tasker Support team.

TaskRabbit offers a Happiness Pledge for clients, which gives them insurance in case of property damage, bodily injury, or theft. However, it may be a good idea to get your insurance to ensure you're covered in case of an emergency.

21. Teach An Online Course.

LEARNING A NEW TRADE, skill, or subject is challenging. It requires research, time, and a genuine interest in the subject matter. But chances are there are topics and talents you're already well-versed in, especially compared to the general public. Why not teach them?

Teaching is one of the most rewarding opportunities. With online platforms like Udemy and Coursera, it's become easy for experienced teachers to side hustle across the world and connect with enthusiastic students.

The beauty of teaching online is that your course's subject is limited only by your own knowledge and imagination. Are you an expert on the history of the Roman Empire? Teach that! Have experience in graphic design? Share what you know! As long as there are people who want to learn from your experience and are willing to pay to have the information packaged and presented in an accessible way, you can make a course about nearly anything.

22. Start A Blog.

BLOGGING IS ONE of the most popular side hustles because it can be done from just about anywhere. With just a laptop and a WiFi connection, any location can be turned into your publishing den.

It may not be profitable right away, but for bloggers looking to build up a personal brand, audience, and portfolio, a blog goes a long way in advancing your career. One of the most interesting things about blogging is the roundabout way it may benefit your current career—sharing your work can show employers and hiring managers how you think about problems and what projects you've worked on. Getting this knowledge down can help you get discovered or stand out from a barrage of resumes if you decide to apply to a new role.

Like teaching, blogging can be about anything so long as some kind of audience is keen to learn, which means there's a lot of space to take a deep dive into a subject you're passionate about. One challenge with this side hustle is learning how to start a blog that makes money.

Pageviews don't pay the bills, so you'll likely need to do some adjacent work, like referring readers to products, offering sponsored posts or advertisements, or even providing a connecting service for blogging to be profitable in the long run. The upside? You'll have done the hard work of creating an audience already.

23. Start A Podcast.

. . .

LISTENERSHIP FOR PODCASTS HAS been growing steadily every year. A podcast used to be a must-have for comedians. Then it became a must-have for writers and journalists. Now, podcasting has morphed into a must-have for almost anyone looking to build an online audience for their brand and turn a side gig from home into a profitable business.

There have been concerns that podcasts' oversaturation could kill podcasting, but data shows the appetite for podcasts hasn't slowed down. Like social media and blogging, podcasting has become a staple of the broader world of online content.

Podcasting is comparatively cheap, too. A decent USB microphone (many of which are sold specifically for podcasting) can be purchased for less than $100, and recording platforms like Audacity is free and easy to use. When you want to upgrade your tools to an XLR microphone, mixer, or other accessories to improve quality, you can still produce professional-sounding audio for a few hundred dollars.

24. Become An Affiliate Marketer.

AFFILIATE MARKETING IS one of those side hustle ideas that can either make you a lot of money or nothing. It's not just about finding the right product to sell but also finding the right brand to partner with. If you chose to be an affiliate marketer for eCommerce stores, your commission would likely be a lot lower than if you were just to dropship them yourself. However, tech companies will pay a hefty price tag to affiliates who bring them new customers.

How much money can this side hustle make? It depends on

what product you're selling and what affiliate network you use. For example, if you were an affiliate marketer for a tech company like Shopify, you could potentially make an extra $2,000 for every merchant you refer. Sweet!

Tip: Ask the affiliate program or content creator for assets you can use to help you market their product. For example, there may be a lead magnet or free tool you can use to incentivize people to purchase the product. Often, a piece of content can help ease a potential customer from a cold lead into a warm one, giving you a better chance of succeeding with this side hustle.

25. Selling On eBay.

EBAY CAN BE A TOUGH, low-margin, competitive environment, but that's not to say there aren't many opportunities left to earn extra cash on the world's largest marketplace.

Are you thinking about selling on eBay? Possibly you have heard that you can make money on eBay and now you hope to understand how you can begin to sell on eBay.

Do you believe that with all of the promises of riches that you should simply jump right in and start selling on eBay as quickly as possible? Well, I would advise you to take a step back before you jump right in and because you need to take the time to learn how to sell on eBay the right way.

Do you realize that eBay now has over 100 million members? If you take the time to understand this, you will see that your customer base can be just as big. Think about 100 million people who are shopping on eBay and they will be just waiting for you to begin to sell so that they can buy products from you, but... how will they find your auction site? How will they even know that you are there? After all, 100 million people are many people, and they just won't ever reach your page if you don't take the time to do things correctly.

The fact is that no matter how great your product is or how well you do on eBay, you simply won't be able to reach all 100 million eBay buyers.

Many people selling on eBay actually started out as customers, and you might want to consider starting out that way as well. You can think about this as part of your consumer research so that you will appreciate exactly how the method actually works. When you start out as a buyer, you can get more of a feel for how things work from a buyers opinion.

Although you might not think that this is necessary, starting out as a buyer on eBay will ultimately make you a much better seller right from the start.

As a buyer, you will need to consider the type of customer service you receive from the seller. Be aware of how you want to be treated and pay attention to whether you got the service you feel you deserved.

By taking the time to network with other sellers, you will start to appreciate the best way to interact with your customers when you start to sell on eBay. Pay attention to the hot items that are selling, and at this time, you might even choose to take notes since they will come in handy at some time in the future.

Keep in mind that selling on eBay is a business and you will want to appreciate what it is that people want to buy before you can begin to build a successful business as an eBay seller. Find out what sells by watching other seller's auctions and when you really know what things sell well on eBay, you can start to find resources for where to purchase these items at wholesale prices so that you can sell them on eBay for a profit.

Another thing you may want to consider before jumping in as a seller is to attend what is called the eBay university where you can get more information and training on how to become successful as an eBay seller.

eBay provides a lot of information on their site. While it will make you an instant success by no means by reading and taking advantage of eBay's free training, you will raise your chances of becoming a success and making money selling on eBay.

Taking the time to learn how to sell on eBay the right way will help you avoid making some of the most common mistakes that many new eBay sellers have made in the past. Take advantage of eBay's resources, especially since they are offered for free, and you can be successful when it comes to selling on eBay.

26. Selling On Amazon.

ONE OF THE most popular sides hustles lately has been Amazon's FBA program, in which you find bargain deals locally, and ship them off to sell on Amazon.

Amazon is among the largest and most popular online shopping sites. Millions of online shoppers use the site each day to purchase various items. Almost anything is readily available on the site, and buyers can buy virtually anything, and some good examples are mobile phones, television sets, laptop computers and many more. Many people currently sell their products on Amazon since they enjoy the benefit of reaching lots of prospective customers.

The initial step you need to take if you wish to make money selling items on Amazon is to create an account. Also, you can read online guides and instructions that make the process simpler. By creating your own seller account, you are also expected to list down the items you would like to sell. You should bear in mind, however, that certain products cannot be sold on Amazon. To find out more about the restrictions, visit the page that dwells on facts and information. This is important for people wondering how to make money selling on Amazon.

Fees are clearly indicated for sellers during the initial sign up, and sellers can choose between two account types. One is best suited for people who intend to sell plenty of items while the other package is meant for sellers who plan on selling only a few items. However, fees charged vary depending on the account type selected.

In case you are wondering how to make money selling on Amazon, you will be glad to learn that the site offers a unique opportunity for people who plan to transform this into a business idea. Sellers are expected to take pictures of products they would like to sell after listing them on the site. Despite this, sellers are required to ship their merchandise to Amazon. Upon completing the procedures, Amazon will ship the sold products to consumers who make purchases, thereby allowing sellers to keep track of their products' inventory easily.

There is also an alternative of selling items on your own if you wish to know how to make money selling on Amazon. You would have to take pictures of your product and list it in the most suitable category. Remember to make a clear description of your product to make it easier for buyers to know what they are purchasing. Clear descriptions and good pictures reduce instances where buyers return items. Moreover, pricing must be done right because other sellers will also price their products competitively.

Yet another important point to remember regarding how to make money selling on Amazon faster is quick shipping. Items sold should ideally be shipped to the buyers within two days. Remember to promptly reply to buyers' emails, which will prevent them from making purchases from other sellers.

. . .

27. *Join The Gig Economy.*

GOT a skill set you can make money online with legitimately? Consider becoming a part of the gig economy. The gig economy is a free market system where companies work with independent contractors or freelancers rather than hire full-time staff. The Bureau of Labor Statistics reported in 2017 that 55 million people in the United States were "gig workers," making up 34% of the economy. That number is expected to breach 43% by the end of 2021.

Freelancing has become one of the best side hustle ideas for millennials because of efficiency—it's now easier than ever for experienced (and up-and-coming) writers, programmers, designers, and other specialists to connect with clients and provide their services from anywhere in the world. You can start by finding jobs on Fiverr, Craigslist, or Upwork and building your skills and portfolio there.

If you're looking for a side gig from home that provides a lot of room for growth and comparatively quick returns, free-lancing might be for you. While freelancing does require you to trade time for money directly, the path to revenue is more straightforward than waiting for a product to pick up traction.

Freelancing is an especially great online side hustle for soon-to-be or recent graduates from high school or college who find themselves getting crowded out of full-time jobs by more experienced peers. For some professionals, working on a project-by-project basis allows them to earn extra cash while building a valuable portfolio and strengthening their resumes with a list of satisfied clients.

Some young entrepreneurs even start freelancing while in school. Services like tutoring and exam prep are so popular in universities among student freelancers that the test-prep market is worth $24 billion. Some students even sell their own study material and lecture notes or teach English.

When you consider that any university sees a guaranteed batch of new customers year after year, it's not hard to understand why young freelancers have jumped at the opportunity.

Remember that your network is everything when starting an online side hustle, whether you want to get into freelance writing or become a virtual assistant. Get on Twitter to have conversations with people in your industry or get involved in Slack groups and private communities to share tips and tricks. This will help you build a sustainable business from your side gig that you can depend on for income.

28. Becoming An Adjunct Professor.

YOU MAY NEED a graduate degree for this one, but it can be a fun way to share your knowledge with the next generation of students and earn some good money on the side -- especially if you can teach online or with prerecorded lectures.

29. Postmates Delivery.

RIDE, drive or walk to make local deliveries in your town with the Postmates app and earn up to $25 an hour doing so.

Another option for earning a side income is to deliver for PostMates. Similar to working for Uber and Lyft, you can work whenever you want. While the pay might not be enormous, you do have the ability to earn tips. If you're in a highly-trafficked area such as Los Angeles or New York City, this is a great way to earn some cash, and you don't even need a car.

30. Selling On Etsy.

ETSY IS THE world's largest marketplace for unique handcrafted goods. What can you make?

Are you a crafter who has wondered how to sell on Etsy? Most people in the crafting world have heard of Etsy, but not everyone knows how to sell on an online marketplace like Etsy. Selling successfully on Etsy takes a little practice and know-how. A common mistake that almost every "newbie" makes is to think that just because you set up a shop on Etsy, the customers will come flocking! That is far from the case. Learning how to sell on Etsy takes some trial and error and a good understanding of how internet marketplaces for crafts and artwork.

Etsy has been online since June 2005 and now helps more than 100,000 sellers worldwide sell their handmade goods. If you sell handmade goods from candles to jewelry, pet products to food and even digital products, Etsy is a great way to expand your audience and boost profits. Etsy has become the premier website for buying and selling all things homemade. It's growing rapidly and doesn't show signs of stopping. If you sell homemade goods or are considering selling homemade goods, take advantage of Etsy to reach a large and targeted audience and grow your business.

31. Selling On Teespring.

. . .

TEESPRING IS A PRINT-ON-DEMAND T-SHIRT PLATFORM, where you can custom-design your own shirts and sell them through the site.

Starting a t-shirt line was a difficult proposition for entrepreneurs. Thanks to the Internet, it's now easier than ever to create a t-shirt line and rake in the dough. One of the best ways to profit from custom t-shirts is with Teespring, a hot new startup that's making major waves in the fashion industry. All you have to do to sell shirts with Teespring is come up with a catchy design that sells to your target market. Teespring produces the t-shirts and ships them to customers for you.

32. Web Design.

Do you have skills in programming and/or web design? Many companies are willing to pay people to design or edit web pages for them. This is a freelance job, meaning you could get paid by multiple companies. This is also a flexible job that you could do on nights or weekends when you aren't working. You can also do this kind of work from your own home.

33. Rental Properties.

REAL ESTATE investing is one of the oldest and most popular side hustles in the books. New platforms like Roofstock make it easy to shop for and buy income-generating properties with tenants and property management already in place.

34. Alterations.

. . .

HANDY WITH A SEWING MACHINE? I believe the market for clothing alteration is ripe for disruption because of a lack of transparency in pricing. I've had some suits altered from a couple of different places with dramatically different rates.

Tip: Post flyers at the gym or other places where people may have lost a lot of weight and need their clothes altered.

35. Pool Cleaning Service.

IF YOU live in a warm climate with many pools, this could be a fun, and interesting side hustles to enjoy the summer outdoors.

For the aspiring freelancer who wants to be his/her own boss, a pool cleaning business is a perfect way to earn some extra income or a full-time livelihood. The entry barrier in this field isn't nearly as high as you'd think, and a pool cleaning business can be started for roughly $2,000 or less. With a solid game plan in place, anyone can become a pool cleaner and make a decent living at it regardless of experience or location.

36. Building Niche Websites.

BUILDING niche sites is a popular side hustle because they can be a relatively hands-off income source after some initial research and time investment. These types of sites generally cover a particular topic and earn money through advertising, affiliate relationships, or digital products.

. . .

37. *Virtual Assistant Service.*

VIRTUAL ASSISTANTS PROVIDE administrative support to clients from their home office and generally charge $15-40 an hour if that sounds like a fun side hustle you can set up shop on your own or jump on board with an established VA company.

Are you interested in making extra money on the side from home? Then you may consider starting a virtual assistant side hustle. If you have excellent computer and communication skills, are organized and reliable, then working from home as a virtual assistant, or "VA" for short, can be a great side hustle for you.

The amount of money virtual assistants make each month depends on their skills, experience, and who they work for. A beginner virtual assistant can earn anywhere from $10-$25 per hour. An experienced VA can make anywhere from $50 and $100 per hour or way more.

If you work for a VA company, they will dictate your own hourly rate. Most VA companies pay $10-$20 per hour, depending on the company. Some of them require you to have some experience and certain skills to join them. But if you work as a freelance VA or start your own virtual assistant business, you have full control over how much you charge for your services.

If you are just starting out as a VA, you may not earn as much money as an experienced VA who has been in business for a while already. But if you specialize in a particular area such as graphic design, SEO, or WordPress services, you can charge much more for your services even if you are just starting out.   ·

38. *Food Or Grocery Delivery Service.*

. . .

WITH SERVICES LIKE INSTACART, DoorDash, and Postmates you can earn money (generally $10-25 an hour) on your own schedule delivering groceries and take-out orders in your town. And you don't have to worry about keeping your car spotless for passengers!

Everyone needs to eat, but not everyone likes to shop. In a world where the time crunch is constantly crunching harder, plenty of people happily pay to have someone else get their groceries. Like when starting any business, you'll need to do market research, advertise and research local business-licensing laws. But if you have a reliable vehicle and the time to drive, the service can be a money-maker.

39. Rent Your Spare Room On Airbnb.

AIRBNB OFFERS a great resource for people that are willing to rent out a spare room or even their entire home. If you're in a bind for some fast cash, AirBnB offers you an avenue for creating an income. You'll get paid 24 hours after a guest checks in, which is to avoid any problems or potential scams that might arrive. Some people earn their primary income just by renting out rooms or homes on Airbnb.

40. Answer Questions On JustAnswer.

WEBSITES LIKE JUSTANSWER pay you to answer professional questions. Suppose you have a high-level skill such, as experience in law, medicine or information technology. In that case, you could get paid to help others navigate certain topics or areas of contention that they might be faced with in life.

41. Do Micro-Jobs On Mechanical Turk.

AMAZON'S MECHANICAL TURK platform is one way you can earn money, though it won't make you rich by any measure. However, if you're looking to take on micro-jobs that can be done in a few minutes each, by stringing them together, you could earn some cash that might help you out if you're in a bind.

42. Tutor Over Skype.

YOU CAN TUTOR people over Skype, no matter where you might live. This is great, especially if you're a digital nomad and you're looking to earn more money than the local job market can potentially provide. Tutor people from the U.S. or U.K. if you're traveling through Asia or another low-cost-of-living country worldwide.

43. Build A Sales Funnel With ClickFunnels.

AS AN ONLINE MARKETER MYSELF, I am obsessed with sales funnels. However, many people struggle with creating the proper funnel that converts. It takes a high degree of technical and marketing knowledge. However, ClickFunnels, a SaaS business with over 40,000 customers, which Russell Brunson started, takes all the guesswork out of that. Build a sales funnel and automate your selling with a platform like this.

44. Produce An Audiobook.

USE A PLATFORM LIKE ACX to create and sell audiobooks on Audible and iTunes platforms. Suppose you have a great idea for a non-fiction audiobook where you can teach a difficult skill like stock trading, foreign currency investing, accounting, online marketing or others. In that case, you can easily create a five-figure monthly income with the right volume of audiobooks.

45. Become A Personal Chef.

ARE YOU A GOOD COOK? You could become a personal chef and prepare meals for other people. You could easily market your services on social media or even go all out and build yourself a website. There are also plenty of websites you can use to market your services such as HireAChef.

46. Do Mystery Shopping.

COMPANIES OF ALL kinds are looking for mystery shoppers. Mystery shoppers buy in secret, documenting their experiences with the retailer. This can be done at a physical store or an online store. If you do a simple search on becoming a mystery shopper, you can likely locate several services to assist you. Or, you can simply contact companies directly to pitch your mystery shopping services to them.

47. Clean Houses.

HOUSEKEEPING IS ALWAYS AN OPTION. There are loads of private families and homeowners that are renting out their homes on a short-term basis that need housekeeping or house cleaning services. You can list your services on a site like HouseKeeper.com and many others to promote yourself.

48. Create YouTube Tutorials.

ALTHOUGH THIS ISN'T the quickest way you can make money with a side income, creating YouTube tutorials can help you earn a respectable amount of income as long as what you deliver is engaging and keeps people interested for long enough. You could also use free tutorials to upsell viewers on the products and services you might be offering.

49. Design Logos On 99Designs.

IF YOU'RE graphically inclined and get programs like Photoshop and Illustrator, you could potentially compete for design work on 99Designs. However, you won't get paid unless your design is chosen as the winning design, meaning you need to be a very good designer to make an income that's worthwhile here.

. . .

50. Be An Extra In Movies.

IF YOU'RE LOOKING to make a few extra bucks without a major investment of yours, try your hand at being an extra in a movie. There's a lot of sitting around and waiting, but the pay is good if you're in a production city like Los Angeles, New York, London or Vancouver.

51. Start A GoFundMe Page.

TRY raising some personal funds using GoFundMe. You can advertise your page to your network through social media, and if you can create a compelling enough story, you might just have enough takers that decide to help you out.

52. Sell Your Hair.

DO YOU HAVE LONG HAIR? Looking good is good business. If you are confused about what sort of business to invest in this may just be for you. Why not sell it to make a few extra bucks? Advertise your hair for sale on a site like HairSellOn or any number of others that are out there.

Of course, it is better if you are interested in hair that is if you are a user of hair extensions yourself. You should be your own brand ambassador that is the fastest way to sell.

53. Teach Driving Lessons To Students.

.   .   .

ARE YOU A GREAT DRIVER? Why not get licensed as a driving instructor? You can advertise your services both online and offline or use a site like Indeed.com to search for part-time driving instructor jobs.

Everybody drives. Plain and simple, almost everybody will need to learn how to operate an automobile at some point in their life safely. While it is true that you can receive a license to drive in most states without driver's education training, driving schools are still in high demand.

Car insurance bills usually drop substantially if you can show a graduation certificate from a certified driver's education school. And in most states, anyone under the age of 18 will need driver's education to obtain a learner's permit. For these reasons, starting your own driving school can be a lucrative career opportunity.

54. Become A Local Tour Guide.

IF YOU live in a vacation destination, consider becoming a local tour guide. You could even offer your services for free and then ask for a tip at the end, drawing more people into touring with you.

Set your own hours and earn some money on the side by working as a local tour guide! Read on to discover how to become one and how much they make.

Do you love bragging about your hometown? Are you an extrovert that gets energized at the thought of being around people every day? If so, then being a local tour guide might be the perfect job for you!

If you want the flexibility of working from home and setting your own schedule, but you don't actually like to stay at home, then you perhaps should consider a job as a local tour guide of your hometown.

Depending on where you live, you could earn a nice income just by giving tours. There are so many different kinds of tour guides – from adventure guides to the ones that give historical or ghost tours to culinary guides. You can do some market research around the area to see what works best.

55. Do Interior Decorating.

IF YOU HAVE an eye for design, consider doing interior decorating for clients. Use a site like Houzz to advertise your services to the masses.

You can do interior decorating/styling/staging as a side hustle. Interior designers get into more architectural stuff which deals with building codes and a more in-depth understanding of building systems.

56. Party Planning.

ARE YOU KNOWN among your friends as being a great party planner? Are you organized, with an eye for detail? Consider offering your services as a party planner. You can help plan anything from a child's birthday party to a Bar Mitzvah to a wedding. If you are not interested in the planning aspect of events, you might consider playing another role at parties based on your skills. Consider starting a small catering service, or (if you are musically inclined) offering your services as a DJ. If you are a good baker, offer to sell baked goods (such as cakes or cupcakes) for parties and events.

· · ·

57. Writing And Editing.

ARE YOU A GOOD WRITER? Many side hustles allow you to put your writing skills to good use. You might edit college essays for students, or do freelance writing or editing for a website. Many companies list their freelance editing jobs online. If there is a topic you are particularly passionate about, consider starting a blog based on the topic. It might take a while, but there are ways to generate income from a blog.

58. Invest With LendingClub.

LENDINGCLUB IS a peer-to-peer lending service that you can invest in. If you have some extra cash and you're looking to put it to use, you can leverage this platform to invest in businesses from a wide range of industries. Risk is calculated for you using algorithms, and the more risk in an investment, the more potential for reward.

59. Create A Smartphone App.

IF YOU HAVE some app development skills and you're proficient at Swift or Android-based development platforms, you could try your hand at creating a smartphone app. This isn't a quick or easy way to make money but could pay off big with the right idea.

· · ·

60. *Painting Service.*

PAINTING SERVICES ARE another common side hustle for college students. If you have time on weekends and during the summer, you can paint houses or join a painting company. It's not easy, but it can pay well in the right neighborhoods.

If you don't know where to start, check out online classified ads. There are always painters looking for laborers to help with their existing projects and clients.

61. *Shoveling Snow.*

IN THE WINTER, shoveling snow can be a lucrative side hustle, depending on where you live. If you're non-disabled, have a truck, shovel, and/or snow blower - you could earn a nice side income.

While you used to go door to door and see if your neighbors wanted to pay for your services, there's now an app that can help you find work and get paid.

62. *Donate Plasma.*

THIS IS ONE of the more interesting ways to make money. You go to your local blood bank or plasma donation center, and they will pay you a small fee for your blood plasma.

It doesn't sound amazing, but if you need extra money, this could be a great way to earn it. You can expect to be paid anywhere from $20 to $50 per donation.

. . .

63. Employee Referral Program.

AGAIN, not a true side hustle but a great way to earn extra money. Many companies offer referral programs where you can earn anywhere from $25 to $1,000 per employee you refer. That could go a long way.

If you know someone who would be a great fit for your company, refer them and see if you can get a bonus for the effort.

64. Catering.

DO YOU WANT to side hustle just on Friday and Saturday nights? Well, you should team up with a catering company, as they often need servers and wait staff just for the events they host on the weekend. Many companies are "call-in," which means you can work when you choose to.

If you don't know where to start, head to the Craigslist Gigs section, where jobs like catering help will be posted. You can earn a nice flat fee per event.

65. Loan Signing Agent And Notary.

BEING A LOAN SIGNING AGENT is a great side hustle because you can make $75 to $200 per hour-long appointment working for yourself on your own schedule. Retired people, working professionals, and students can be signing agents and earn extra cash when they want. The best part is you need nothing more than a notary commission (which can often be attained by simply filling out an application)!

You can automatically get loan signing jobs by simply putting your name in a database, and they'll call you when there's a pre-set appointment in your area. Once you get a loan signing job, you just need to know how to walk a homeowner through a set of loan paperwork.

Can you say..."sign here, date there!?"

If you want to make $75 to $200 per hour-long appointment working for yourself on your own schedule, be sure to get the proper training. One of the top-rated courses we found that is really impacting how people make money is Loan Signing System.

66. Website User Testing.

DID you know that you could get paid to try out a new website and give feedback?

Sites like UserTesting.com are always looking for users to rate and give feedback about websites. Website owners post gigs to the site, and you simply login and give feedback and usability ratings on different websites and online apps. You can earn up to $10 for each test you participate in.

67. Just Search The Internet.

DO YOU SEARCH THE INTERNET? Want to get paid for it? Swagbucks is a site that rewards you for doing various online tasks like taking surveys, watching videos, and using their search engine. When using their search engine, you get reward points after several searches, usually in the amount of 10-15 points. You can start cashing out rewards at the 500 points mark.

If you Swagbucks, you can earn a $5 bonus!

Another option is InboxDollars. Similar to Swagbucks, they offer cash bonuses for searching the web or shopping online.

68. Deliver For DoorDash.

DOORDASH IS a delivery service that has been growing nation-wide. It's an alternative to not having people in your car but still getting paid to deliver. The great thing with DoorDash is that you get to keep 100% of the delivery fees! DoorDash makes money by charging the restaurants, not you!

More and more restaurants are signing up, so you can likely find gigs in your area.

69. Human Billboard.

IF YOU'RE NOT afraid of embarrassing yourself on a street corner, there are always businesses looking to hire sign-spinners or people in costume to attract attention.

70. Ironing/Mobile Laundry Service.

MANY PEOPLE HATE IRONING! I'm certain a decent chunk of the population is with me on this one and would be willing to pay to make that problem go away.

. . .

71. *Mobile Oil Change Service.*

SAVE people time by bringing the shop and supplies to them. If you're comfortable fixing cars, you might actually check out YourMechanic.com, which helps match you with customers in need of car repairs.

72. *Organize a Bundle Sale.*

AN ONLINE BUNDLE sale brings together a bunch of digital products for a limited time. Each contributor earns a cut on every bundle they sell, and you take a percentage as the organizer.

73. *Rec Sports Officiating.*

RECREATIONAL SPORTS leagues are often in need of referees and umpires, and this can be a fun way to spend your evenings and earn a little extra cash.

74. *Teaching Yoga.*

A CERTAIN LEVEL of expertise and certification may be required, but becoming a yoga instructor could be a fun and healthy part-time business.

. . .

75. *Travel Agent Service.*

ARE YOU A SEASONED TRAVELER? Do you always know where to get the best deals and the best experiences? It might be surprising that despite widespread access to travel information, there is still a healthy demand both for insider travel knowledge and the hands-off experience of letting an expert handle the booking. Plus, you can put your travel-hacking skills to the test and earn money at the same time with services like FlightFox.

76. *Voiceover Acting.*

COMPANIES ARE ALWAYS on the look for professional voiceover talent. Once you start listening to it, you'll hear voiceover work everywhere.

77. *Cover Letter and Resume Service.*

ESPECIALLY IF YOU have HR experience, there is a massive opportunity to help job seekers with their resumes and cover letters. Since the payoff of landing a job is so high, it can be worthwhile for applicants to seek some professional assistance on their documents.

It would be interesting to see this sold on a pay-for-performance model, where you only get paid if the applicant gets the interview.

. . .

78. Car Wash and Detailing.

A MOBILE DETAILING service would be a super-low cost startup, and you could get clients in bunches at office parks, shopping malls, schools, sporting events, and other places where cars like to gather.

79. Carpet Cleaning.

CARPET CLEANING WOULD be a relatively low-cost and straight-forward business to start. You could get clients on an annual or semi-annual recurring schedule like the dentist.

80. Book Flipping.

USE THE FREE Bookscouter app to scan barcodes and see what old books are worth. You can do this both for the ones collecting dust on your shelf and for the ones at garage sales or the library book store.

81. Become A Bridesmaid Or Groomsman For Hire.

TAKE ADVANTAGE OF all of those hours spent delivering the perfect toast and holding your friend's train out of the dirt by offering up your services as a professional bridesmaid or groomsman on Craigslist.org.

. . .

82. Make Money Planning High-End Retreats.

IF YOU ENJOY EVENT PLANNING, try reaching out to friends and family you think would be interested in upscale retreats. Many people would love to create these unique experiences for themselves, but they lack time to put them together. See if you can create them yourself and charge a service fee for putting it all together.

83. Capitalize On Unique Fitness Trends.

STICKING WITH A CARDIO routine and schedule can be challenging to do, and many people get bored with more traditional cardio methods over time. Offering an interesting and fun alternative to your everyday cardio workout can put you on the fast track to success! Many studios do not operate at full capacity every day, and that's time that you could be using to teach your unique cardio class. Once you have an idea, reach out to local fitness studios to see if they'd be open to letting you rent out one of their vacant spaces.

84. Make And Sell Healthy, Natural Pet Food.

FOR MANY, pets are as much a part of the family as their children. If you'd like to help furry and feathered friends get on a more well-balanced diet, check out the guidelines for starting your own pet food or treat business!

. . .

85. Start Your Own Karaoke League!

WHO DOESN'T LOVE to belt out their favorite tunes over beers with friends? If you're part of the karaoke community in your city, get some people together and launch your very own karaoke league where you can create teams and battle it out on stage!

Tip: reach out to local businesses to see if they'd like to join the league as part of a team-building exercise and increase morale.

86. Bee A Beekeeping Advocate.

IT'S NEVER BEEN more important to save the bees, and you can help! Learn more about bees and beekeeping and help to provide your local community with a healthy, sustainable habitat for honeybees. This buzzworthy mission can promote urban beekeeping and education, all while bringing you some sweet cash.

87. Learn How To Make And Sell Candles.

IF YOU'RE HAVING a difficult time discovering a skill you already have, consider picking up an easy-to-learn skill like candle making. Not only are there plenty of free, online tutorials on sites like CandleScience, learning the basics can take as little as an hour, and the candle business has long-term appeal independent of trends.

. . .

88. Become An Online Storyteller.

IF YOU love to write and are a natural storyteller, share your stories online in the form of a digital magazine. Not only are startup costs low, but there are also sponsorship services out there like Patreon that allow you to fund your writing through readers and allow you to focus on what you do the best writing!

89. Jump On The Meal Prepping Bandwagon!

YOU CAN'T visit Reddit or Instagram without coming across a multitude of meal prepping pictures, and if you love to cook and plan out recipes, this may just be the side hustle for you. Spend some time researching with Keyword Planner to see what words associated with meal prepping pop up the most in search engines and use those to streamline your SEO(Search Engine Optimization). If meal prepping isn't your thing, use Google Trends to find the next big thing!

90. Snuggle For Dollars (It's Not What You Think).

SINCE the rise of the technological era, it's never been easier to connect with others at the touch of a button. Despite the advantages this provides, an increase in texting and socializing on social media may result in less substantial relationships, leaving users feeling isolated and disconnected. Snuggling services offer a new way to fill this void and respond to a growing need without judgment.

. . .

91. Turn A Hobby Into Cold, Hard Cash.

MORE THAN ANYTHING, side hustles should be fun and something you look forward to doing! The sky is the limit, so don't settle for something that you don't truly enjoy doing. Here, a social worker uses her jewelry-making hobby to make extra money on the side and even lands her work in several major tv shows with The Artisan Group's help.

Note: if you're not sure that your hobby would be profitable, test it on a starter site first!

92. Launch A Subscription Box Service.

SUBSCRIPTION BOXES ARE very trendy right now, and the types of boxes are almost as numerous as the number of people who subscribe to them! If you're not sure how to get started, here's a handy guide from an e-commerce site called Cratejoy that essentially serves as a platform for all kinds of different boxes and makes it easy to sell your subscription box no matter where you are in the process.

Tip: whatever you decide to focus your box on, make sure that it's as niche as possible. In a world full of subscription boxes, you want yours to stand out from the rest!

93. Create A Service That Rents Out Homes For Events.

IS THERE an event in your city that happens frequently or maybe even every year? Create your own Airbnb style home rental service! Research the habits of others, what people are willing to pay for, and what side-bar business you might be able to create. Tens of thousands of people attend the Super Bowl every year, and more often than not, they spend lots of money having a good time, eating, drinking, and renting cars and hotel rooms. Since they're in the habit of doing that anyway, why not jump in front of that wave and get paid?

94. Create A Fun Novelty Item.

SOME OF THE MOST AWESOME IDEAS CAN COME TO YOU OVER DRINKS WITH FRIENDS, and—in some cases—those ideas have the potential to lead to a new source of income. Is there something that you've been sitting on that just maybe crazy enough to work? Here, a group of friends decides to upgrade the small pockets on t-shirts to double as puppy carriers and mobile drink coolers.

95. Start Your Own Private Wine Label (It's Easier Than You Think!).

HAVE you dreamed of launching your own wine label but never thought you could without having to manage your own full-fledged vineyard? Think again! The days of growing, fermenting, and even bottling your own wine are long gone, and several innovative private wine label companies have popped up. Some of these offer certain varietals bottled and ready to go, and some like Terravant will even go as far as helping you design your label and build your brand for you!

. . .

96. Put Your Art of iPhone Cases; Get Paid When People Buy It

IF YOU'RE AN ARTIST, you might be surprised to learn that people might want your work on their phone cases. Use Society6 to upload images—they'll do the rest. The service is free, and whenever customers purchase, you'll receive a commission.

97. Caregiving.

SOME PEOPLE HAVE a knack for taking care of others. If that is your case, consider offering babysitting or daycare services in your area. There are also many opportunities to take care of elderly or disabled people who need help during the day. Finally, if you are better with animals than people, you might help take care of someone's pet. You can offer dog walking or dog grooming services. You can offer these services through word of mouth or take advantage of the many caregiving websites and apps. For example, Care.com allows you to offer your nannying services to others, and Rover.com allows you to find people looking for dog sitters and dog walkers.

98. Online Freelancing.

THERE IS a lot of freelance work online. You can sign up for sites like UpWork, Fiverr, Guru, Freelancer, PeoplePerHour, etc., or you can even become your own online freelancer, as I did. I've made over $10,000 on the side by online freelancing.
   One of the more popular ways to make money freelancing

right now is by doing SEO consulting. If you're a little savvy and analytical, you can make \$75/hr or more.

You could also do something like proofreading or transcription work. Many bloggers and authors need proofreaders to make sure their writing is on point.

99. EBOOK PUBLISHING.

DO YOU HAVE a story you want to tell? Maybe you should write an eBook and sell them on Amazon or Barnes and Noble.

I've met several authors you've never heard of that sell ton of eBooks on Amazon every year. One author has almost 100 different books he's selling on Amazon.

If you don't want to put together a blog, you could go this route of selling your content online.

100. Online Surveys.

IF YOU HAVE some time to spare online, you could spend it filling out online surveys. Some sites will pay you to do so, and it's very easy. All you have to do is register, and these companies will contact you when they have a survey that fits your profile. Typically these are online market research surveys for big brands.

Bonus: Instead of doing surveys, what if you just installed an app on your phone? That's what Nielson offers. Install the Nielson app and earn money.

Some of the most popular **online survey sites include:**

- Survey Junkie - Earn cash and rewards for sharing your thoughts and opinions. Click here.
- Swagbucks Surveys - Swagbucks now has a dedicated survey section, and you can get $5 just for signing up.
- MyPoints - Earn a $5 gift card for signing up, verifying your email, and for every 5 surveys you complete.
- Opinion Outpost - Earn cash for filling out surveys. Lots of options. Click here.
- Fetch Rewards - An app that pays you for filling out surveys and doing other tasks.
- Branded Surveys - Fill out surveys and get cash and gift cards.

Special offer for 18-24-year-olds: PineCone offers unique high paying surveys for just your age group.

101. Recycle.

RECYCLING CAN BE a great way to earn some extra money. I'm not talking about becoming a bum at the park rummaging for cans (although you can do that) - I'm talking about encouraging your friends and neighbors to leave their cans and bottles aside for you.

If you want to take it up a notch, look for recycling metal and scrap to get even more money. This is even easier if you have a truck and are willing to haul for others.

Income Potential: $150 per month

102. Modeling.

. . .

THIS IS the side hustle for the good looking people of the world. You can go to school or work and still take modeling jobs at night and on the weekends.

There isn't always a steady stream of work for many models, but if you succeed at a few gigs, this could become very lucrative.

103. Be Someone's Friend.

DID you know that you could actually be paid to be someone's friend for some time? I am talking strictly platonic stuff here (although we've heard that being a sugar baby can be extremely lucrative).

Maybe someone wants to see a movie, but they have a phobia of going alone. You could be that friend for them!

Check out RentAFriend and see if you can find a friend that will pay for your time.

CONCLUSION

An underappreciated benefit of side hustles is that they can act as a sandbox where you learn how to make money from home legitimately. Making money is a distinct skill, and since most of us rely on traditional careers to pay the bills, it doesn't always feel intuitive. Side hustles offer you a way to test business ideas and practice in public.

And side hustles aren't just a tool for making side income. Starting a side hustle is a way to teach yourself valuable skills and help yourself grow as a professional and as an entrepreneur. For writers, actors, painters, musicians, and artists of all types, a side hustle can provide artistic independence, professional growth, and, eventually, a profitable way to turn your passion into your career.

A side hustle can help you reach financial independence more quickly only if you are willing to put in the time and effort required to build a successful side hustle. If you are up for the challenge, it can be an exciting way to completely revolutionize your life.

Your side hustle can help you make some extra money each month. But it can also help you develop new skills, build your brand or portfolio, and achieve more freedom. So, have fun with it! Take a risk by starting a business or pursue a new hobby you've always been curious about. A side hustle is your best opportunity to live life on your own terms. And with some more money in your pocket, nothing is stopping you from making your dreams come true.